INTERPRETING A CONTINENT

INTERPRETING A CONTINENT
Voices from Colonial America

Edited by
Kathleen DuVal
and
John DuVal

ROWMAN & LITTLEFIELD PUBLISHERS, INC.
Lanham • Boulder • New York • Toronto • Plymouth, UK

ROWMAN & LITTLEFIELD PUBLISHERS, INC.

Published in the United States of America
by Rowman & Littlefield Publishers, Inc.
A wholly owned subsidary of The Rowman & Littlefield Publishing Group, Inc.
4501 Forbes Boulevard, Suite 200, Lanham, Maryland 20706
www.rowmanlittlefield.com

Estover Road
Plymouth PL6 7PY
United Kingdom

British Library Cataloguing in Publication Information Available

Library of Congress Cataloging-in-Publication Data:

Interpreting a continent: voices from colonial America / edited by Kathleen DuVal and
John DuVal.
     p. cm.
   Includes bibliographical references and index.
   ISBN-13: 978-0-7425-5182-4 (cloth : alk. paper)
   ISBN-10: 0-7425-5182-2 (cloth : alk. paper)
   ISBN-13: 978-0-7425-5183-1 (paper : alk. paper)
   ISBN-10: 0-7425-5183-0 (paper : alk. paper)
   eISBN-13: 978-0-7425-6464-0
   eISBN-10: 0-7425-6464-9
   1. United States—History—Colonial period, ca. 1600–1775—Sources. 2. North
America—History—Colonial period, ca. 1600–1775—Sources. 3. Europeans—United
States—History—Sources. 4. Indians of North America—History—Colonial period, ca.
1600–1775—Sources. 5. Africans—United States—History—Sources. 6. United States—
Race relations—History—17th century—Sources. 7. United States—Race relations—
History—18th century—Sources. 8. Acculturation—United States—History—17th
century—Sources. 9. Acculturation—United States—History—18th century—Sources.
I. DuVal, Kathleen. II. DuVal, John, 1940–
   E187.I58 2009
   973.2—dc22   2008040518

Printed in the United States of America

⊗™ The paper used in this publication meets the minimum requirements of American
National Standard for Information Sciences—Permanence of Paper for Printed Library
Materials, ANSI/NISO Z39.48-1992.

To the DuVal-Quigley-Smith-Wong clan

Contents

Acknowledgments

THE AUTHORS PARTICULARLY THANK Tiffany Griffith, Sabine Schmidt, and Natalia Shchegoleva for their translations. For helping us find documents and illustrations, we thank Birte Pfleger and Greg Waselkov, as well as Anne Pritchard of the University of Arkansas Special Collections, Jessica Lemieux of the Bancroft Library, and the staffs of the University of North Carolina's (UNC) Wilson Library, Duke's Special Collections, and Interlibrary Loan at the University of Arkansas and UNC. Thanks to the many people who read portions of the manuscript for us, answered questions in their areas of expertise, or tried the documents out in their classrooms: Dirk Bonker, Holly Brewer, Kathryn Burns, Kay DuVal, Elizabeth Fenn, David Griffiths, Jonathan Hancock, George Jarrett, Jocelyn Olcott, Kay Pritchett, Luis Fernando Restrepo, Seth Rockman, Jon Sensbach, Pete Sigal, Katy Smith, Marty Smith, Christina Snyder, Jennifer Spear, John Wood Sweet, David Weber, and Peter Wood. Thanks to the students of UNC's fall 2007 colonial American history class, who found several mistakes and made helpful suggestions. We dedicate the book to our family, especially to Kay, wife of one and mother of the other.

Maps

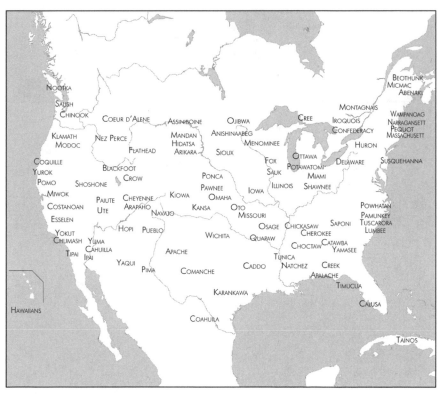

MAP 1
Approximate Locations of American Indian Groups During the Colonial Period

Maps

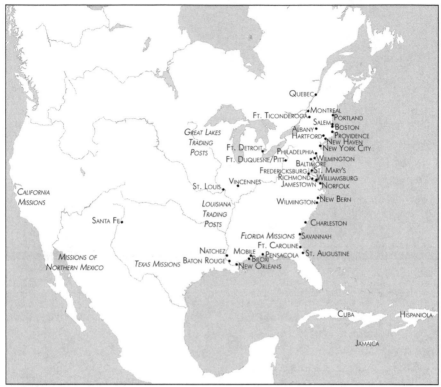

MAP 2
European Settlements During the Colonial Period

Introduction

IN 1607, CHIEF POWHATAN HEARD NEWS OF HUNGRY STRANGERS trespassing on his lands and demanding corn from his people. The strangers were Englishmen, and their brand-new colony was Jamestown, Virginia. We know that Virginia became a permanent colony, that tobacco and slaves made many of its settlers wealthy, and that they eventually crowded the Powhatan Indians from their lands to make room for more tobacco plantations. Because we know that future, we might assume that, in 1607, Chief Powhatan felt desperate and helpless when confronted by these powerful Europeans. But when we learn a bit more about the Powhatans and their history, we see that the situation was the opposite—Powhatan believed that these newcomers would be fairly easy to subordinate. He assumed he would dominate them.

The English had stumbled onto one of the most powerful Indian nations in North America. Fifteen to twenty years earlier, Chief Powhatan had inherited the Powhatan chiefdom (and adopted its name as his name). At the time he took power, the Powhatans dominated several other chiefdoms. Using force and persuasion, the new chief conquered more than twenty additional chiefdoms in the Chesapeake Bay region. He was accustomed to having more power than his rivals, not less. Also, unbeknownst to the English, Powhatan's people had known Europeans for nearly a century before 1607. Spanish ships had often stopped to trade or raid and, in 1561, a Powhatan boy had traveled to Mexico City and to Spain, where he met King Felipe II. In 1570, the boy, whom the Spanish christened Luis de Velasco, led several Jesuit priests back to the Powhatan homeland, where they founded a mission. During Velasco's absence, many Powhatans had died from a severe famine and possibly from disease spread by the Spanish. Velasco and his fellow Powhatans came to the conclusion that the Spanish were dangerous and should be expelled. In February 1571, the Powhatans attacked the new Jesuit mission and killed the priests. In the summer of 1572, Spaniards who had heard news of the attack landed in Chesapeake Bay and killed and captured several Powhatans, but Velasco and his people succeeded in preventing the Spanish from establishing a colony in their homeland.

When the English arrived several decades later, Chief Powhatan used his past experiences with other Indians and Europeans to decide what to do about them. (In fact, some scholars have hypothesized that Powhatan himself was Luis de Velasco or one of his brothers.) Powhatan had to decide whether to destroy Jamestown, as his people had destroyed the Spanish settlement, or to use threats, small-scale force, and persuasion to subordinate them, as he had with other Indian chiefdoms. In the document by John Smith in this volume, you can see Powhatan's choice.

We cannot understand the history of Jamestown without knowing about the Powhatans' previous relations with the Spanish and other American Indians—so why does U.S. history usually start with Jamestown? Why do American schoolchildren know the story of Pocahontas and Captain John Smith but not of Luis de Velasco and the Jesuits? There is a reason. In the late 1700s, settlers in Virginia and twelve other English colonies successfully rebelled against their empire and created the United States, a country that later expanded across the west, seized control of the formerly French, Spanish, and American Indian lands, and eventually established political, economic, and linguistic dominance over most of North America. Jamestown was the first successful English settlement in a country that would become heavily influenced by the English in the succeeding decades.

The problem with this reasoning, however, is that it is circular. We study Virginia and the other English colonies that lasted and grew *because* they lasted and grew. Of course, Virginia's and New England's longevity and success make them important subjects of study, but focusing on them alone gives the false impression that all European colonies lasted and grew. In fact, most colonies failed, including the Jesuits' mission to the Powhatans and the English colony of Roanoke.

The documents in this collection transport us to situations that no longer exist. Here we see American Indians before they were displaced and marginalized, in a time when most people in North America were Indians. We see Europeans not only before they were dominant but before anyone knew that Europeans would come to dominate the continent or which Europeans would dominate the others. The readings reflect the diversity of

Europeans who came to North America and their reasons for coming. And we see the diversity of people held in bondage during the colonial period. Millions of people from different societies in Africa were enslaved and brought to the Americas. In smaller numbers, Indians and Europeans too were captured and forced to work for others. Most slaves in the colonial period did not work on plantations, and many achieved at least some degree of freedom.

Examining a multitude of interactions among diverse peoples reveals that there were other kinds of power relations besides European dominance. In some places, no group was able to establish dominance and instead had to compromise. In many parts of North America, Indians dominated Europeans. The Spaniard Alvar Núñez Cabeza de Vaca and the African slave Esteban wandered around the American South for several years in the 1520s and 1530s until they finally stumbled back into Mexico. Their rambling was hardly a step forward for European dominance of the continent. During the colonial period, an important difference emerged between English and non-English relations with Indians because most European immigrants went to England's colonies. By the 1770s, people of European descent were in the majority in the rebellious thirteen British colonies. In contrast, the vast majority of people living on the rest of the land that would become the United States were American Indians. Partly as a result, Spanish and French settlers were more likely to intertwine their lives with Indians, through marriage, trade, and diplomacy.

Indian power and differences among Europeans also led to conditions of slavery different from the chattel slavery that developed in English colonies. The opportunities for freedom were greater where European slaveholders were a comparatively weak minority, as in Florida. There, former slaves from the Carolinas were able to pressure the Spanish to give them their freedom. In Louisiana, fear of a joint Indian-African war dissuaded the French from establishing plantations like those in the English colonies.

The History

This book focuses on the land that became the United States, making connections along the way to Mexico, Canada, the Caribbean, and across the Atlantic and Pacific. Long before Europeans and Africans arrived, for thousands and thousands of years, Indians spread across the Americas, developed agriculture, and established elaborate trade networks. By the 1400s, in North America alone, at least five million American Indians lived in thousands of independent societies and spoke more than 300 languages. In most societies, men hunted and women farmed corn, beans, and squash. They had developed long-distance trading networks, through which they exchanged such goods as seashells from the Gulf of Mexico, copper from the Great Lakes, and war captives from enemy societies. Most believed that the spirit world was part of everyday life, and they sought spiritual power as well as trade goods through contact with outsiders.

American Indians did not see themselves as one kind of people, distinct from all Europeans and all Africans, much less as a biological "race." The terms *Indian, American Indian, Native American*, and *Native* all impose a false unity on Chickasaws, Mohawks, Querechos, and hundreds of other peoples who had no common identity. These terms have other problems too. *Indians* results from Columbus's faulty geography. He thought he had found the Indies (present-day Indonesia, India, China, and Japan), not a new continent. *American Indians* or *Native Americans* names them after Florentine explorer Amerigo Vespucci simply because a European mapmaker put Amerigo's name on an early map. The term *Native* is generic and can be confusing, as generations of other peoples were born in North America and came to call themselves native. Nevertheless, this book uses these terms because we need to be able to discuss Indians' general importance in history, as well as the particular stories of Powhatans, Micmacs, and others.

Africans who came to the Americas were no more monolithic than Indians. Like Native Americans, Africans did not think of themselves as belonging to an entire continent or a single race. West Africans belonged to a variety of societies and ethnic groups, including Igbo, Wolof, and Yoruba. They spoke dozens of different languages and had diverse political, social, and religious practices. The descendants of slaves who came from Africa had even more complicated identities, often combining their parents' beliefs and practices with those of their fellow slaves and their new home.

Similarly, Europeans were hardly unified. Some of the bloodiest conflicts of the colonial period were fought between rival European groups. The nations of Great Britain and Spain did not exist at the beginning of the colonial period. Isabella of Castile and Ferdinand of Aragon combined their kingdoms by marriage in 1469, and their union only slowly grew into the nation we know as Spain. England did not unite with Scotland as "Great Britain" until 1707.

Various European groups were fighting Islamic empires, in addition to one another. Europeans knew that trade with the Indies in the Far East contributed to their Islamic rivals' wealth. These Europeans longed for a way to bypass Islamic merchants, trade with the Indies, and use the profits to fund their religious wars. Portuguese sailors made the first attempts, sailing around Africa to avoid the Middle East. A sailor from the Italian state of Genoa, Christopher Columbus, had a different idea. With funding from Isabella and

Ferdinand of Spain, Columbus sailed west, across the Atlantic, hoping to reach the Indies from the other side. Of course, Columbus found the Americas instead. Despite Columbus's failure to discover an easy route to the Indies, opportunities for profits in the Caribbean stimulated European interest in these new lands and their peoples, which came to be called the "West Indies" and "Indians."

It was the mainland, not the islands where Columbus landed, that would become the heart of the Spanish empire. In 1519, Hernán Cortés sailed from the Spanish settlements in the West Indies to the eastern coast of Mexico, intending to establish a trading post and conduct slave raids. Cortés formed a more ambitious plan when Indians who lived on the coast told him about the wealthy Mexica (Aztec) empire, with its great city of Tenochtitlán. Aided by indigenous allies, European diseases, horses, and steel weapons, Cortés and his men took Tenochtitlán in August 1521 and built Mexico City on its ruins. Spanish explorers and their European rivals spent the rest of the sixteenth century looking for more Tenochtitláns. In the Andes, Francisco Pizarro found the gold-rich Incan empire, but the explorers who came north—including Hernando de Soto and Francisco Vázquez de Coronado—found nothing they considered riches.

In their earliest contacts, these newcomers and the American Indians they met were disappointed with one another. There were large Indian civilizations north of Mexico. For instance, Mississippian chiefdoms built cities housing tens of thousands of people on impressive mounds, which rose above their river valleys and could be seen for miles around. The residents of Pecos and other communities along the Rio Grande River in New Mexico farmed in the desert using terracing and irrigation and lived in large apartment-like buildings on the sides of cliffs, which the Spanish called Pueblos. But, as impressive as Mississippian and Pueblo societies were, they did not have the gold and silver that sixteenth-century Spaniards sought.

While the Mexicas' enemies viewed Cortés as a useful ally, most Indians north of Mexico disdained European explorers' demands for goods and food if they brought nothing to offer in exchange. For example, in the 1560s and 1570s, following Velasco's attack on the Jesuit mission in Chesapeake Bay, Indians across the Southeast destroyed the Spanish missions and posts and forced the Spanish to abandon all but one, St. Augustine. Indian opposition and the lack of gold and silver decreased Spanish interest in the lands north of Mexico.

Unlike the sixteenth century, seventeenth- and eighteenth-century America experienced more determined colonization and sustained clashes among the European powers. In most of their settlements north of Mexico, the Spanish responded to Indian violence by lowering their ambitions and scaling back their demands. The only mission that the Spanish preserved in the attacks of the 1560s and 1570s, St. Augustine, lasted and is the oldest permanent European settlement in the United States. Similarly, when the Spanish founded Santa Fe, New Mexico, in 1598, priests there became too demanding, and the people of the Pueblos eventually cast them out. Returning in the early 1690s, the Spanish were less strict in their demands for labor and conversion to Catholicism. By the mid-1700s, Spaniards were exploring and spreading Christianity into Texas and California, but the lack of gold and silver and the power of northern Indians made few Spaniards interested in settling there.

The French faced similar difficulties attracting settlers. Beginning in the early 1600s, French traders and priests established New France (Canada). Their desires for furs fit well with Indian trading practices, and the Jesuit priests soon realized that learning Indian languages and trying slowly to change Indian beliefs worked better than forcing Indians to convert. Starting in the mid-1600s, French fur traders began to travel down the Mississippi River, and France founded the colony of Louisiana, a region that spread across both sides of the Mississippi River, from Canada to the Gulf of Mexico. As French colonization expanded, they and their Indian allies increasingly clashed with the growing British settlements on the east coast, culminating in the Seven Years' War of 1756–1763 (called the French and Indian War in British North America).

Although the European population increased over the centuries, even in the mid-1700s Indians still occupied most of the continent. Europeans controlled their core settlements in Santa Fe, St. Augustine, the English eastern seaboard, Quebec, and New Orleans, but their claims to lands beyond their population centers held little force. Chickasaws ruled their country along the Tennessee River. Osage Indians were expanding their territories west of the Mississippi River, driving out other Indians and Europeans who got in their way. On the Great Plains, Comanches, Kiowas, Apaches, Cheyennes, and Lakotas created a new way of life based on hunting buffalo and making war on horseback. Even as the American Revolution ended, Anglo-American domination of the continent was not assured.

Historiography

The readings in the book reflect historians' shift away from seeing the colonial history of the United States as the inevitable settlement and expansion of English colonies. When colonial history considered only the English colonies, it began with 1607 and the founding of Jamestown and ended with 1776 when thirteen colonies declared their independence from Great Britain. The new view of colonial history encompasses centuries of interactions and rivalries among Europeans, Indians, and Africans, and among specific groups within those larger categories. This new history includes fifteenth-century Spanish exploration and even eleventh-century Viking voyages, while recognizing the relevance of Indian history before the arrival of Europeans. Because most of the continent did not become part of the United States in the 1770s, colonial history cannot neatly end there either.

Three recent historiographic trends work together toward this new vision. The oldest of these is ethnohistory, the combining of historical, anthropological, and archaeological methods to study peoples who did not leave written records. In the mid-twentieth century, historians and anthropologists who studied American Indians began to borrow each other's tools to learn more about the peoples who had arrived first and occupied the Americas for the longest time. Particularly, they sought to understand societies of the past as ethnographers study present-day cultures, using a holistic approach to uncover worldviews, societal relations, political structures, and other basic tenets of a culture. Ethnohistorians, as these scholars came to call themselves, compile all types of evidence they can about a particular people from the past—written documents, archaeology, oral traditions, and later ethnographic studies. They acknowledge the biases and limitations of all their sources but seek to combine and carefully analyze information from all of the sources to understand people's lives, beliefs, and motivations. Seeking a fuller understanding of colonial American cultures, ethnohistorians have applied their methods to Europeans and Africans as well, allowing for a truly multi-perspectival history.

The second trend in how historians analyze the past is Atlantic world history, a way of seeing the colonial past that focuses on the whole of the Atlantic and the lands bordering it and the connections and interactions of the peoples who lived there. Atlantic history first gained popularity as a way to connect British history and early American history, in order to provide context for the thirteen mainland colonies. Historians have broadened Atlantic world history to include the entire Atlantic, finding links and comparisons with Africa, Latin America, and the non-British parts of North America and Europe to give a fuller view of this interconnected world's imperial conflicts, cross-cultural interactions, and long-distance trade, including the Atlantic slave trade.

The third historiographic trend is to see colonial American history as a continental narrative. This approach views early America as the whole continental United States rather than what has been presumed to be the nascent United States in the thirteen English colonies. By extending study to those places west of the English colonies, we see that power relations were diverse and colonization was precarious. The continent's history is a series of conflicts and alliances between Indian groups, between various Indians and Europeans, and between Europeans. Because Africans were brought as slaves, they seldom had the power of Europeans or Indians; however, they too played important roles in these conflicts and alliances. For example, in the violent struggle between the French and the Natchez Indians in 1729, both sides tried to secure the loyalty of African slaves. Examining the entire region that became the United States also reminds us that today's immigrants to Texas, California, New Mexico, and the South are not those regions' first Spanish-speakers.

Scholars have long studied the lands beyond the English colonies. In the early twentieth century, Herbert Eugene Bolton pioneered the study of "Spanish borderlands," the northern reaches of Spain's empire. In 1975, Elizabeth A. H. John wrote *Storms Brewed in Other Men's Worlds: The Confrontation of Indians, Spanish, and French in the Southwest, 1540–1795*, a sweeping history of how western Indians interacted with Europeans in the centuries before 1800. John's work was path-breaking because she used ethnohistorical methods to accomplish what most historians thought was impossible—writing a colonial history whose central characters were American Indians. In more recent years, scholars have incorporated Bolton's and John's interests into the larger narrative of U.S. history. They argue that colonial history is incomplete and distorted if it does not include Spaniards, Indians, and other non-English groups.

Encountering the Documents

John and other historians faced a challenge that you will confront in these readings—how do we learn about colonial-era Indians or Africans using sources written by Europeans? In this time period, most Indians and Africans used oral history to remember past events. In part because their histories were so disrupted by Europeans, little oral history describing this period survives. This book includes some relatively direct accounts from Africans and Indians, including Venture Smith's autobiography and Iroquois laws. However, for the most part, we must derive our knowledge of colonial-era North American Indians and Africans from documents written by Europeans.

For example, French explorer Jacques Cartier described Micmac Indians who waved animal furs at the ends of sticks. At the time of Cartier's explorations in the 1530s, the Micmacs and the French did not have a common language, so Cartier had to infer the Micmacs' meaning. Adding to the complications, his own reasons for exploration surely affected both how he interpreted the Micmacs' actions and what he chose to report in his journal. Luckily, we do not have to rely solely on Cartier. We know from archaeological sources that trade was important to these Indians before Europeans arrived, and we know from other accounts that the news of Europeans spread through Indian trading networks. We must also use our powers of deduction. Given that the Micmacs had an active trading culture and probably knew that

Europeans had valuable trade goods to offer in exchange for furs, it is a reasonable hypothesis that the Micmacs showed animal furs to Cartier to signal that they wanted to trade them for French goods.

Ethnohistorical methods help us to combine archaeological and other non-written evidence with careful readings of European documents to dig out the actions and possible motives of people who did not leave their own documents. We have to read these documents against the grain, looking for the writers' biases and areas of ignorance and trying to see what messages the subjects were sending, even if the writer missed them. For example, the discussion questions following the Columbus letter ask you to hypothesize what the Taino Indians may have thought about Columbus and his men, based on the actions that Columbus reports. It's okay to use your imagination, when you do it carefully and based on the evidence you have. Interpretation is what historians do.

The history and perspectives of the Micmacs, Tainos, and other North American peoples are so important that we must try to understand them. But we must be careful. We must recognize that, for example, an explorer's account may give us more information about his assumptions and motivations than about whatever he was exploring. Laws written by slaveholders may reflect their incorrect assumptions about their slaves. And, as with all history, we should remember that we will never know the whole story. Still, careful use of available sources, written and otherwise, can help us to contextualize colonizers and see power dynamics as they changed over time.

Most of the documents in this volume are new English translations of colonial-era documents, originally written in Icelandic, Spanish, French, Dutch, Russian, or German. Selected documents from English colonies will help you draw comparisons and fill out the picture of colonial America. Obviously, one book must omit countless important documents. We have tried to choose sources that are important and interesting in themselves while reflecting themes that cross colonies. For example, you can explore how women in places as diverse as Quebec, New England, and the Illinois country viewed colonization and their roles within it. In the English documents, we have modernized spelling and capitalization, edited punctuation for clarity, and spelled out abbreviations. In a shaded box at the beginning of each section, we have included a short excerpt of one document in its original language, also with modernized spelling, to allow those of you who know some French or Spanish to read the words as they were written. The full text of many of the non-English documents can be found by consulting Rowman & Littlefield's website.

Kathleen DuVal
Chapel Hill, North Carolina
June 2008

I

EXPLORATION

THIS FIRST SECTION OF DOCUMENTS CONTAINS ACCOUNTS of exploration. We begin with an Icelandic saga, which tells of the first recorded European visit to the Americas. Throughout the section, pay particular attention to what explorers were looking for, what they found, and how the people whom they met received them.

Cristóbal Colón a Luis de Santángel

Excerpt

SEÑOR, *PORQUE SÉ QUE HABRÉIS PLACER DE LA GRAN VICTORIA QUE NUESTRO Señor me ha dado en mi viaje, vos escribo esta por la cual sabréys cómo en veinte días pasé a las Indias con la armada que los illustríssimos Rey e Reyna nuestros señores me dieron, donde yo fallé muy muchas Islas pobladas con gente sin número. Y d'ellas todas he tomado posesión por sus Altezas con pregón y bandera real extendida y non me fue contradicho.*

A la primera que yo fallé puse nonbre San Salvador a conmemoración de su alta Magestat el cual maravillosamente todo esto an dado (los Indios la llaman Guanahani); a la segunda puse nonbre la isla de Santa María de Concepción; a la tercera, Fernandina; a la quarta, la Isla Bella; a la quinta la Isla Juana; e así a cada una, nonbre nuevo. *

*From facsimiles of Columbus's original letter, in John Boyd Thatcher, *Christopher Columbus: His Life, His Work, His Remains* (New York, 1903), 2: 17–20, 33–40. Translation begins on p. 18.

Greenlanders' Saga, c. 1000

*T*HIS TALE OF NORSE EXPLORATION, THE GREENLANDERS' SAGA, *was written down in about 1200, after being passed down as oral history for two hundred years after the events took place. In the 980s, Eirík the Red founded a settlement on the optimistically named Greenland. According to the Greenlanders' Saga, another Viking sailor, Bjarni Herjólfsson, was blown off course in about 1000 on his way from Norway to the settlement at Greenland and returned with tales of a fruitful and promising land that he had discovered but not explored.*

There was now much talk of exploration. Leif, son of Eirík the Red of Brattahlíd, went to see Bjarni Herjólfsson and bought a ship from him and gathered a crew of thirty-five men. Leif asked his father, Eirík, if he would lead the expedition once more. Eirík said that he would rather not, declaring himself too old and much less hardy than he used to be. Leif said that he still had the best luck of any of his kinsmen. Eirík conceded to Leif and rode from home as soon as they were ready. A short distance from the ships, the horse Eirík was riding stumbled, and he fell from his horse and injured his leg. "It seems I'm not fated to find more land than the one we now inhabit," Eirík said. "We'll no longer travel together." Eirík went home to Brattahlíd, and Leif and his crew of thirty-five rode to the ship. There was one southerner on the journey who was called Tyrkir.

They prepared the ship and sailed out to sea. The first land that they found was the one that Bjarni and his crew had found last. They sailed up to the land, cast anchor, launched a small boat, and went ashore, but they saw no grass. The inland part of the country was covered by great glaciers, and as far as the eye could see the land looked like one flat stone. The land seemed barren. Then Leif said, "We aren't as bad off as Bjarni who never made it ashore. I shall give this land a name and call it Helluland."[1] . . .

[They come upon another land they call Markland (Forest Land).]

Now they sailed out to sea with a northeast wind and were out at sea two days before they saw land. They sailed toward the land and came to an island which lay to the north of the mainland. They went to have a look around and found good weather and dew on the grass, and the first thing they did was scoop the dew up in their hands and bring it to their mouths; they had never tasted anything so sweet. Afterwards, they returned to their ship and sailed into the strait which lay between the island and the headland jutting north out of the land, turning west around the cape. There was a great shallows near the fjord, and their ship ran aground on the sea floor; and the sea couldn't be seen for a long way around the ship. Their curiosity to get ashore was so great that they couldn't bear to wait for the tide to rise under the ship, and they ran ashore where a river flowed out of a lake. As soon as the sea rose up under the ship again, they rowed the boat back to the ship and steered it up the river to the lake, dropped the anchor, and unloaded leather hammocks and built temporary dwellings.[2]

They decided to camp there for the winter and built great houses.[3] Neither the river nor the lake was lacking in salmon, and they had never seen bigger salmon. The country's resources were so good that it didn't seem to them that they would need fodder for the cattle that winter; there was no frost, and the grass hardly wilted at all. The days and nights were more of equal length than in Greenland or Iceland; the sun was up by breakfast time and was still up late into the afternoon, even on the short winter days. When they finished building the houses, Leif said to his crew, "Now I'll divide our company into two groups, and we will search the land. Half of the crew shall stay at the compound and the other half must search the land but not be gone so long that they can't be home by evening, and they should not part company."

So that's what they did. Leif took turns going out with the men and staying at the compound. Leif was a great, strong man, magnificent to behold as well as a wise and just man in all respects.

One evening it came to pass that a man was missing, and it was Tyrkir the Southerner. Leif was very unhappy because Tyrkir had been with both him and his father a long time and had been very fond of Leif in his childhood. Leif lashed out at his companions, and he together with twelve men went out to search. They had gone only a short distance from the hall when Tyrkir came walking toward them, and he was greeted joyfully. Leif soon noticed that his foster father was in good spirits. . . .

Then Leif asked him, "Why were you so late, Foster Father, and separated from your companions?" Tyrkir spoke then a long time, at first in German, rolling his eyes all over and making faces, but they couldn't understand what he said. After a while, he said in the Norse tongue, "I didn't go much farther than you, but I have some news about what I saw. I found grapevines and grapes."

"Can that be true, Foster Father?" asked Leif.

"Certainly it's true," he said. "We didn't lack for grapevines or grapes where I was born."

They slept through the night, and in the morning Leif spoke with his crew: "Now we shall have two kinds of work. On alternating days we will gather grapes and hew grapevines and fell the forest to make cargo for my ship." So that's what they did, and it is said that they towed a small boat filled with grapes behind their ship. A full cargo of timber was cut for the ship, and when spring came, they prepared to go. Leif gave the land a name based upon the good things they found there and called it Vínland.[4]

They sailed out to sea with a favourable wind until they saw Greenland under its mountain of glaciers. Then one man took to talking and spoke with Leif, "Why do you steer the ship so close to the wind?"

Leif answered, "I am keeping my eye on my steering but also on something more. Don't you see anything unusual?" They said they didn't see anything out of place. "I can't tell," said Leif, "whether I see a ship or a skerry."[5]

Now they saw it and said it was a skerry, but Leif could see better than they did and saw men on the rock. "Now I will sail near the wind," said Leif, "so that we can see if these men need help, and if they do, we must help them. If they are not men of peace, all of the advantage is on our side rather than theirs." So they drew near the rock, lowered the sail, cast anchor, and got out another little boat they had with them. Then Tyrkir asked who their leader was. The leader said he was called Thorir and was Norwegian by birth and asked, "And what is your name?"

Leif told him.

"Are you the son of Eirík the Red of Brattahlíd?" he asked.

Leif said that he was. "Now," said Leif, "I invite you all onto my ship and as many of your possessions as the ship can hold." They accepted this offer and sailed afterwards to Eríksfjard with their load. Then they came to Brattahlíd where they unloaded the cargo. Leif bade Thorir and his wife Gudrid and three other men to lodge with him and procured lodging for the other crewmen, both Thorir's crew and his own. Leif pulled fifteen men from the rock and was thereafter called Leif the Lucky. Leif grew in wealth and in honor.

That winter, a terrible illness befell Thorir's crew, and Thorir and many of his people died. That winter, Eirík the Red also died.

Now there was much discussion about Leif's Vínland voyage, and Thorvald, his brother, thought that the land had been explored too carelessly. Then Leif

spoke with Thorvald, "You shall go with my ship, brother, if you will, to Vínland, but first I will go in that ship and get the timber that Thorir left on the
rock."

And so it was done.

Now Thorvald, with much discussion with his brother Leif, prepared for his
voyage along with thirty men. After they prepared their ship and went to sea,
nothing is told of their journey until they arrived at Leifsbud in Vínland,[6]
where they laid up their ship and settled in for the winter, catching fish for
their provisions. In the spring, Thorvald said that they should prepare the ship
and that some of the crew should take the small boat and travel west along the
coast and explore there that summer.

They saw beautiful land and forests, and the woods were only a short distance from the shining white sand. There were many islands and much shallow water. Nowhere did they find men's lodging nor animals, but on a west-
erly isle they did find a wooden cornstack. They found no other work by
human hands and returned to Leifsbud in the autumn.

The next summer, Thorvald went out to the east with his merchant ship
and sailed north along the coast . . . and into the mouth of a fjord, next to the
headland, which jutted out and was all overgrown with woods. They anchored
the ship, shot out the gangway, and Thorvald went ashore and all his crew with
him.

He said then, "Here it is fair, and here I want to build my home."

Then they headed back to the ship and spotted three mounds in the sand
along the headland and went toward them and discovered three skin-covered
canoes with three men under each.[7] Thorvald and his crew split up and seized
them all, except one who escaped in his canoe. They killed the other eight and
went back to the headland and looked around and saw several mounds along
the fjord and guessed that they were dwellings.

After that, such a great drowsiness struck them that they could not stay
awake, and they all fell asleep. Then a call came and woke them all; the call
said, "Wake up, Thorvald, and all your company, if you wish to save your life,
and go to your ship, you and all your men, and leave this land as fast as you
can." Then a fleet of skin-boats came at them down the fjord.

Thorvald said, "We must raise the barricades on the gunwales of the ship
and defend ourselves as best we can, but attack them little."

They did this, and the Skrælings[8] shot at them for a while and then fled as
fast as they could. Then Thorvald spoke to his men and asked if anyone was
wounded, and they reported that there was not one wound.

"I have a wound in my armpit," said Thorvald. "An arrow flew between the
gunwales and the shield and under my arm, and here it is. It will lead to my
death. I order that you prepare to leave as soon as possible. You will bring me

to that headland that I thought to make my home; it occurs to me that I shall dwell there for a while after all. There shall you bury me and lay a cross at my head and at my feet, and call that place Krossanes[9] ever after."

Greenland was Christianized by then, even though Eirík the Red died before the coming of Christianity.

Now Thorvald breathed his last, and they did all according to what he had said and went afterward to meet with their companions and exchanged such tidings as they knew. They settled there that winter and gathered grapes and grapevines to put in the ship. They prepared to return to Greenland in the spring, at which time the ship sailed into Eiríksfjord with much news for Leif.

Translated by Tiffany Griffith from *The Vinland Sagas*, ed. Halldór Hermannsson (Ithaca, 1944), 49–54.

Discussion Questions

1. Why were Leif Eiriksson and his brother Thorvald eager to explore? Why were Eirík and Bjarni less interested?

2. What were they looking for? Why were Leif and his men excited to find grapevines?

3. Why do you think this story was remembered and passed down for two hundred years? What might listeners have found important, interesting, or instructive?

4. What happened when Thorvald and his men found people living in Vínland? Was this the first European-Indian encounter? What does it forebode, if anything?

Notes

1. Flatstone Land.

2. The literal translation here is "booth." A booth is a temporary dwelling not unlike a tent except that it is covered with tree boughs.

3. Archaeologists have found this site on the coast of Newfoundland, Canada, at a place called L'Anse aux Meadows.

4. Wine Land.

5. A skerry is a rocky island.

6. Leif's booths, or houses—the place Leif had wintered.

7. These were probably an Algonquian people, perhaps Beothuks.

8. The Vikings' word for the natives.

9. Place of the cross.

Christopher Columbus to Luis de Santángel, Official Notary for King Ferdinand and Queen Isabella of Spain, 1493

CHRISTOPHER COLUMBUS WROTE THIS LETTER on his way home from his first voyage to the Caribbean, believing that he had landed in the Indies. Soon, Europeans would realize that he had found an entire continent that they had not known existed. Columbus's letters had a significant effect on how Europeans thought about and dealt with the peoples of the Americas. Most obviously, the name "Indians," based on Columbus's misunderstanding of geography, stuck. The people that Columbus writes about meeting, the Tainos (sometimes called Arawaks), did not leave written records, so we must use Columbus's version to imagine what tales they told about him, his ships, his men, and the goods that they brought.

Sir: Because I know you will take pleasure in the great victory which Our Lord has given me in my voyage, I write you this, so that you may know how in twenty days[1] with the armada which our lords the most famous King and Queen gave me I reached the Indies, where I found many, many islands inhabited by countless people. Of all of them I took possession on behalf of their Highnesses with oral proclamation and the royal banner flying, and nobody contradicted.

The first one that I found, I named *San Salvador* in honor of his glorious Majesty, who has marvelously given all this (the Indians call it Guanahani). The second, I named the island of *Santa María de Concepción*. The third, *Fernandina*. The fourth, *Isla Bella*. The fifth, *Juana* island.[2] And so a new name for each.

When I reached Juana, I followed its coastline westward and discovered it to be so large that I thought it must be the mainland of the province of

Cathay.[3] And since I didn't find any towns or villages along the coast, except for little clusters of people[4] that we didn't get a chance to speak with because they all ran away, I kept sailing along the same route, thinking that way I wouldn't miss any large cities or towns. And after many leagues, there was nothing new and the coast was taking me to the north, which was not where I wanted to go because it was still winter and I meant to sail south. Besides, the wind was against me. I decided not to wait any longer and turned back as far as a certain harbor, from which I sent two men inland to find out if there was a king or any large cities. They traveled for three days and found an infinite number of little villages and countless people, but no political organization, so they returned.

I kept hearing from some Indians whom we had taken that this land was one island after another, so I followed the coastline eastward a hundred and seven leagues to where it ended, from which point I saw another island to the east, ten or eight leagues off, which I named Española,[5] and I went to it and continued along the northern side for a hundred seventy-eight great leagues straight east, as with Juana. This island is magnificent, as are all the others, but this one excessively so. Here there are many harbors along the seacoast with nothing that I know of in Christendom to compare them with, and plenty of rivers that are marvelously large and good. Both islands rise well above sea level, with many mountain ranges and high mountain peaks—nothing on the island of Centrefrei[6] comparable to them—all beautiful, with a thousand different formations, all accessible and full of trees of a thousand species that are tall and seem to reach to heaven. And I have been told they never lose their leaves, which I can believe, because I saw them as green and beautiful as trees in May in Spain. Some have flowers; some, fruit; others, in other stages according to their nature. And the nightingale was singing and so were other birds of a thousand species in the month of November wherever I went.

There are palm trees of six or eight species, and it's amazing to behold their beautiful variety, which is greater than among the other trees and fruit trees and plants. There are all manner of pine groves, and vast meadows, and there's honey, and many kinds of birds and various fruits. There are mines in the earth and countless people. Española is a wonder: the mountains and mountain ranges, the plains and meadows and fields so beautiful and rich for planting and sowing, and for raising all kinds of livestock, and for buildings and towns and villages.

The harbors—here in Spain you would never believe without seeing them! And the rivers—very big, with good water, most of which have gold in them. The trees and fruits and plants are very different from those on Juana. On this one there are many spices, and large mines for gold and other metals that I have discovered and heard about.

All of the people, men and women, go naked as the day they were born, although some women do cover themselves in a certain place with the leaf of a plant or some cotton material that they make for that purpose. They have neither iron nor steel, nor any arms, nor are they warlike, not because they aren't well built and beautifully proportioned, but because they are wondrously timid.

They carry no weapon except that when they are planting they attach a pointed stick to the end of a cane, and they don't even dare to use it, because many times I have put two or three of my men ashore at some town to speak with them, and countless of the inhabitants have come out, and, at the sight of my men approaching, run away, not one father waiting for his son, and not because anybody has done any harm to them, because at every point where I have landed and had occasion to speak with them, I have given to them of everything I had—fabric and many other things without getting anything in return—but because they are hopelessly timid. The truth is, though, after we reassured them and they lost their fears, they were so artless and so generous with what they owned, you wouldn't believe it without seeing. Anything they own, all you have to do is ask for it and they never say no, but give themselves with it and show so much love that they would give their hearts, and whether they are wanting something valuable or of little value, they are satisfied with any little thing you give them in exchange.

I forbade my men to give them anything so trashy as pieces of broken bowls or broken glass or bits of needles, although when they did get them, they held them like the finest jewels in the world, and there was one sailor who for a needle got gold weighing two and a half castellanos,[7] and there were other sailors who, for other, less valuable things, got much more. In exchange for new pennies they gave whatever they had, even if it were two or three castellanos of gold or twenty-five to fifty pounds[8] of spun cotton. They were even taking pieces of broken barrel hoops and giving back whatever they had like dumb beasts, which seemed wrong to me, and I forbade it. And I was gratefully giving them a thousand good things that I had brought to win their love. And so they will become Christian, because they are well disposed to the love and service of their Highnesses and all the land of Castille and they try to be close with us and give us things that we need and that they have in abundance.

They have no acquaintance with religious sects or idolatry, but they all believe that power and goodness is in the heavens. They firmly believed that I came down with these people and these ships from the sky, and at every point they receive me with that kind of respect as soon as they lose their fears. And this is not because they are ignorant—indeed, they have very subtle minds and navigate these seas so well that it's wonderful how good an account they give of them—but because they never saw people wearing clothes before or ships like ours.

As soon as I arrived in the Indies, on the first island I came upon I seized some of them to get them to tell me about the region, and they did, because they understood us and we them by words and signs, which have much improved since then. I am bringing them to you now, and they still believe that I come from the sky, in spite of all the conversations I've had with them. These were the first to proclaim it when I arrived, and others ran from house to house and to the nearby towns crying out, "Come! Come see the people from the sky!" So everybody, men and women, as soon as they were reassured of us, came, not leaving a child or a grownup behind, all of them bringing things to eat and drink, which they gave with wonderful love.

On all the islands they have many canoes, somewhat like galley boats, some larger, some smaller, and some—many—are larger than an eighteen-bench galley boat, only not so wide because they are carved from one tree. One of our galley boats wouldn't be able to catch one of theirs, because they move in ways you wouldn't believe. With them they navigate all those countless islands, bringing their merchandise with them. I have seen some of these canoes with seventy or eighty men, each with his oar. . . .

I have already mentioned how I had gone a hundred seven leagues along the coast of Juana in a straight line from west to east. From having taken this route, I can say that the island is larger than England and Scotland together, because eastward beyond those hundred seven leagues lie two provinces that I didn't reach, one of which is called Avan, where the people are born with tails, and these provinces cannot extend for less than fifty or sixty leagues, according to what I hear from the Indians I have, who know all these islands.

The other island, Española, is larger in its circumference than all of Spain. . . . Española [is] the most convenient place and best region for gold mines and for trade with both the continent of Europe and the land of the Great Khan, with whom there will be great trade and profit. I have taken possession of a large town which I have named Villa de Navidad, where I have established a force and a fortress which by this time should be completely finished. And I have left people there with enough arms and artillery and provisions for a year as well as a boat and a master shipbuilder with all the skills to build more boats and in great friendship with the King of that land, so great that he was proud to call me and hold me as a brother. And even if they did change their minds and attacked, these people—neither he nor his subjects—know nothing of weapons and they go naked, as I have already mentioned. They are the timidest people in the world. So only the men who remained behind are capable of destroying the whole land, and it is an island without danger for those who know how to govern it.

It seems to me that all the men on all the islands are content with one wife, and to the chief or King they give as many as twenty. It also seems to me that the women work harder than the men, nor have I been able to ascertain whether they own private property, because I think I observed that whatever one person owned, everybody shared, especially food supplies.

Up until now I have not discovered on these islands any men that are monsters, as many people expected; rather, they are all lovely people. Nor are they black, as in Guinea, except for their flowing hair. They aren't reared where the rays of the sun would burn them, although the sun there is very strong, since it is twenty-six degrees from the equator. On the islands where there are high mountains, the cold was harsh this winter, but they bear it by force of habit and with the help of their foods, which they eat with many extremely hot spices.

Anyway, I haven't found any evidence of monsters, except that one of the islands, the second after entering the Indies, is inhabited by people whom the other islanders consider extremely ferocious, and who eat human flesh. . . . They are ferocious with the other people, who are great cowards, but they are no more of a concern for me than the others are. These are the ones who barter for wives in marriage with the Indian women on the first island we discovered after leaving Spain, an island with no men on it. Those women don't engage in womanly activities. Instead they arm themselves with bows and arrows like those canes I mentioned, and they cover themselves with plates of copper, which they have plenty of.

They tell me there is another island larger than Española where the people have no hair on their heads and there is gold beyond measure, and I am bringing Indians with me bearing witness of those and other islands.

In conclusion, speaking only of this one voyage, which was just a rapid run, their Highnesses can see that I will give them however much gold they need with what little aid they give me now: spices and cotton as much as they call for, and as much as they order to be shipped to them of mastic[9] . . . and aloe as much as they order to be shipped, and slaves as many as they order to be shipped (from among those who worship idols), and I think I have found rhubarb and cinnamon, and I will find a thousand other significant things. . . . Even though other people had spoken about these lands, it was all conjecture and nothing seen. Rather than understanding, as long as people were hearing about them, most people were listening and making up their minds according to fable more than anything else.[10]

Therefore, since our Redeemer has given this victory to our illustrious King and Queen and to their famously successful reigns, all Christians should rejoice, hold grand celebrations, and with solemn prayers give thanks to the Holy Trinity for the exaltation of turning so many peoples to our Holy Faith, and secondly for the temporal benefits from which not only Spain but all Christendom will have comfort and profit.

This is a very brief account of what was done. Written on board the caravel at the Canary Islands, February 15, 1493.

Translated by John DuVal from facsimile copies of Columbus's original letter, in John Boyd Thatcher, *Christopher Columbus: His Life, His Work, His Remains* (New York, 1903), 2: 17–20, 33–40.

Discussion Questions

1. What was Columbus looking for? How did his goals compare to those of the Vikings?

2. Who was Columbus's audience? Did that audience influence how he wrote? Does any of his information seem suspect? Did he get the geography right?

3. How might the Tainos have described their visitors to their neighbors who did not meet them?

4. How pleased do you think Ferdinand and Isabella were to learn that the "king of the land" was proud to call Columbus brother and that Columbus believed that many of the natives thought he was a god?

5. If you didn't know what happened later, what might you predict for European-Indian relations?

Notes

1. It was actually thirty-three days, as Columbus makes clear in a postscript to this letter and in a separate letter to Ferdinand and Isabella.

2. San Salvador, Santa María de Concepción, Fernandina (Exuma Grande), and Isabella (Larga) are islands in the Bahamas. Juana is Cuba. Columbus puns Isabella and Isla Bella, "beautiful island."

3. Cathay is the name by which Marco Polo in the twelfth century referred to the empire of Kubla Khan and which came to be generally associated with China. Fifteenth-century Europeans employed measurements of latitude but did not have a system of longitude, so estimating east-west distances was difficult.

4. All of the people whom Columbus saw on this voyage were Tainos. They lived in communities across most of the West Indies.

5. Hispaniola, where present-day Haiti and the Dominican Republic are situated.

6. Tenerife, Canary Islands.

7. A *castellano* is about a fourth of an ounce.

8. Columbus says an *arroba* or two. An *arroba* is about twenty-five pounds.

9. A resin used as a spice, chewing gum, and varnish.

10. Columbus puns on *fabla*, which here means both "speech" (*habla*) and "fable."

Jacques Cartier's First Voyage, 1534

*O*N *A*PRIL 20, 1534, *J*ACQUES *C*ARTIER *SET OFF FROM* *F*RANCE *with two ships. While Columbus had hoped to find the Indies by sailing straight west, by the time of Cartier's voyage, Europeans realized that there was a continent in the way. Therefore, Cartier was looking for a relatively narrow water passage from the North Atlantic, through the American continent, to the Pacific—the "Northwest Passage." In the journal entries below, Cartier begins on May 21 in icy waters off the east coast of Newfoundland, not far from Leif Eiriksson's Vínland.*

May 21. With a west wind we bore northeast by east from Cape Bonne Viste to Bird Island, which was entirely circled by broken ice. Despite the ice, we rowed to the island in two boats to catch some birds. There are so many birds there that no one would have believed it without seeing them, because even though the island is only one league in circumference, it is so full of them you would think the birds had been shipped in, and there are a hundred times more of them circling the island in the air. Some of the birds are as big as geese and black or white with beaks like crows' beaks. They stay in the water and can't fly because their wings are no longer than half a hand, but with those wings they fly as fast through water as the other birds through air. They are marvelously fat, and we called them *aponats.*[1] In less than a half hour we loaded them like stones into our boats, and in each of the ships we salted down four or five barrels of them, in addition to what we ate fresh.

May 23–24. . . . Even though the island is fourteen leagues from the mainland, bears[2] swim there to eat the birds. Our people came upon one that was big as a cow and white as a swan, and he leapt into the water in front of them. The next day, which was Pentecost Sunday, as we were sailing toward the land, we came upon the same bear, halfway between the island and the mainland, swimming toward land as fast as we were sailing. He noticed us, and we gave chase in our boats and captured the bear, whose flesh was as tasty as a two-year-old heifer's. . . .

June 12. . . . [W]e sighted a large ship out of La Rochelle[3] that had anchored overnight in Brest Harbor, its men intending to fish there without any real idea of where they were. We rowed up to it in our boats and directed them a league off to the west of St. Jacques River, to what I think is one of the best harbors in the world and which we named the Jacques Cartier Harbor.[4]

If only the land were as good as its harbors! This land should not be called New Land, but rather Rocks-and-Stones-and-Rugged, because on the whole north coast I never saw more than a cartload of soil, and I went ashore several times. And at Blanc Sablon all there is is moss and little thwarted shrubs. I think it must be the land God gave to Cain. The people there are fairly well built, but frightful and wild. They bunch their hair back like a sheaf of hay, stick some kind of nail into it, and tie bird feathers into it. Both men and women wear animal skins, but the women wear theirs tighter and cinch themselves around the waist. And they paint themselves with rust colors. They have boats made from the bark of birch trees for going out on the sea and catching seals.[5] Once I saw those boats, I realized this was not their permanent home, but a place to come to hunt seals and other food. . . .

June 29–30. On the next-to-last day of the month, with the wind from the south by south-southwest, we sailed west until Tuesday morning without coming to land, but toward evening we did sight what looked like two islands behind us, about nine or ten leagues to the west-southwest. And we sailed to the west for some forty leagues until sunrise. As we sailed, we realized that what had looked like two islands was in fact the mainland, lying from south-southeast to north-northwest all the way to a beautiful cape, which we named Cape Orleans.[6] All this land is low and level, unbelievably beautiful, and full of beautiful trees and meadows, but we could not find a harbor because the land is low and because of all the sandbars, so we rowed to land in our boats at several places and also entered a lovely river that was very shallow, where we saw the wild people's boats crossing the river, so we named it River of Boats, but we didn't have anything more to do with the people because a strong wind was blowing from the sea to the shore and we had to row back to the ships. . . .

We rowed to land at four different places to look at the trees, which are wondrously lovely and fragrant. We found cedar, yew, pine, white elm, ash, willow, and many other trees unknown to us—none of them with fruit. The areas that are not wooded are very beautiful and lush with peas,[7] red and white currants, strawberries, raspberries, and wheat similar to rye that looks like it has been sowed and cultivated. This land has the mildest weather imaginable and is very warm. There are many doves and wild pigeons.[8] All that is lacking is harbors. . . .

July 3–6. This cape we named Cape Hope because of the hope we had of finding a passage. . . . On Monday, the sixth of July, after hearing mass, we went in one of our boats to explore another cape or point of land seven or eight leagues farther west to see how that land lay. When we were within a half league of the point, we noticed two fleets of native boats crossing from one point of land to another, and there were more than forty or fifty boats. When one of the fleets arrived at the point, many of the people jumped out, went ashore, raised up a great shout, beckoned for us to come to shore, and waved animal skins at the ends of sticks for us to see.[9]

Since we had only one boat, we didn't want to go ashore, so we rowed back toward the other fleet, which was still out on the sea. When the people on land saw that we were getting away, they loaded into two of their largest boats and came after us, joining with five boats from the fleet that was still at sea. They all came close to our boat, dancing and signaling that they wanted to be friends and shouting in their language, "Napou tou daman asurtat!" and other words we couldn't understand.[10]

Since, as I said, all we had was one boat, we didn't want to put our trust in their signals. We made signs for them to pull back, which they did not want to do. Instead, they rowed and paddled so swiftly that immediately their seven boats had our one boat surrounded. Since all our waving and gesturing could not persuade them to back away, we fired two *passevolants*[11] over their heads. At that, they did turn and start toward land, but then they raised up a huge shout and turned back toward us, as before, and were crowding against our boat when we shot two flaming bolts among them that startled them so much that they took flight and followed us no more.

July 7. The next day a party of wild men came in nine boats to the point and the salt bay where we were staying in our ships. As soon as we realized they were coming, we put out in our two boats to meet them at the point. When they saw us, they fled, making signs to us that they had come to trade. They showed us the pelts they were wearing, which weren't worth much. We made similar signs that we didn't mean them any harm and sent two of our men ashore with knives and other ironware, as well as a red hat for their captain.

Seeing that, some of them also came to shore with the pelts; and they traded and showed great and wondrous joy at obtaining ironware and other items. They danced and performed ceremonies, splashing sea water onto their heads with their hands, and they gave us everything they had and went back to their boats completely naked, making signs to us that they would return the next day with more pelts.

July 8–9. On Thursday, the eighth of the month, since the wind was not good for taking our ships out, we equipped our boats to explore the bay. . . . [After a day and a half of looking for a passage], we realized, to our disappointment and sorrow, that we were reaching the end of the bay. At the end of the bay, above the low lands, rose high, mountainous ground.

Seeing that there wasn't any passage, we started back. As we made our way along the shore, we could see wild men on the banks of a lake, over on the low ground, building fires and making smoke. We rowed toward them, discovered an inlet into the lake from the sea, and drove our boats through the inlet into the lake. Some wild men came to us in one of their boats, bringing chunks of seal meat, cooked, which they put onto sticks. Then they retreated, making signs that they were giving the meat to us.

We sent two men ashore with hatchets, paternoster knives,[12] and other merchandise, which they rejoiced to see. Immediately a whole crowd of them came in their boats to our side of the lake bringing pelts and anything they had to trade. There were more than three hundred of them altogether, men, women, and children. The women who hadn't come over were standing in the water up to their knees, dancing and singing. The women in the group that had rowed to our side came up to us quite freely, stroking our arms with their hands and clasping their hands together and raising them to the sky in gestures of joy. They finally felt so comfortable with us that we traded with them hand to hand for everything they had, which wasn't worth much.

We realized that these people would be easy to convert. They go from place to place fishing and living on the fish they catch. Their land is milder than even Spain and more beautiful than can be imagined, and all as level as a lake. And there are no unforested places, however small or sandy, that aren't filled with wild wheat with ears like rye and grain like oats, and as thick with peas as if they had been sowed and cultivated, white and red currants, strawberries, raspberries, red and white roses, and other herbs of sweet-smelling fragrance. There are also many meadows with fine grasses and a lake full of salmon. More than ever I believe that these people would be easy to convert to our holy faith. In their language they call a hatchet a *cochy* and a knife a *bacan*. We named the bay *Warm Bay*.[13]

July 16–25. . . . Because of the stormy weather and poor visibility, we were held
up in [another] harbor until the twenty-fifth of the month, during which time
a large number of wild people came to fish for mackerel, of which there was a
great plenty. There were more than two hundred men, women, and children
with about forty boats. After having rowed around close to the shore, they
came out alongside our ships. We gave them paternoster knives, glass, combs,
and other items of little value that they rejoiced over, raising their hands to the
sky and singing and dancing in their boats. These people can really be called
wild: they must be the poorest people in the world, because except for their
boats and fishing nets, everything they have is not worth five sous.[14] They all
go naked except for a little pelt they wear to hide their nature and some old
animal skins they throw over themselves. There is nothing about them or their
language like the first people we found. They shave all around their head except for some hair at the top that they let grow as long as a horse tail and tie
close to their head with leather thongs. The only lodging they have is their
boats, which they turn upside down and sleep under on the ground. They eat
their meat almost raw after warming it a little over coals and do the same with
fish.[15] . . .

From what I could understand they only come to the sea during fishing
season. They grow a millet as large as peas.[16] They have plenty of it, just like
in Brazil, and eat it instead of bread. In their language they call it *kagaige*.
They also have plums, which they dry for the winter just the way we do,
called *honesta*, and figs, nuts, pears, apples, and other fruits, and beans,
which they call *sahé*; the nuts, *caheya*. . . . If you show them anything that
they don't have and don't know what is, they shake their heads and say
nouda, which means they don't have any and don't know what it is. They explained by gestures how their own things grow and how they use them. They
never eat anything that tastes of salt. They are amazing thieves and steal
everything they can.

On the twenty-fourth of the month we constructed a thirty-foot cross, with
many of them looking on. Under the cross piece we hung a shield embossed
with three fleurs-de-lys, with tall letters carved in wood over the shield: "Vive
Le Roi de France."[17] We planted this cross in their presence, and they saw us
make and plant it. As soon as it was raised into the air, we all got down on our
knees, clasped our hands, and worshiped it before them. Then we signaled to
them, pointing to the sky, that from there our redemption came. At that, they
made exclamations of wonder, turning and looking at the cross.

After we had gone back to our ships, their captain came out to us, dressed
in an old bearskin and accompanied in the boat by three of his sons and a
brother. They didn't come as close to the ship as usual, and he harangued us,

pointing at the cross and making a cross with two fingers. Then he pointed at the land all around us as if to say that all that land belonged to him and that we should not be planting a cross on it without his permission.

After he had delivered his harangue, we showed him a hatchet and pretended to want to trade it for the bearskin he was wearing. He understood, and little by little, came closer to the ship, because he wanted to have the hatchet. Then one of our men, in one of our boats, grabbed hold of his boat, and two or three of our men jumped onto their boat and made them come onto our ship.

They were astonished, but as soon as they were on board, the Captain assured them that no harm would be done them and gave great signs of affection toward them. He made them eat and drink and enjoy themselves, and, using hand gestures, explained that we had planted the cross as a landmark for entering the harbor, that we planned to come back soon, bringing ironware for them, that we wanted to take two of his sons with us, and that we would bring them back again into that harbor.[18]

Then we dressed the two sons in shirts and livery and red hats and put necklaces of brass on their necks. They were pleased with this new apparel and gave their old rags to the people who were going back to shore. We gave a hatchet and two knives to each of the three who were going back, which they seemed very happy to receive. Then they returned to shore and told the others what had happened.

About noon of the same day, six boats came out to the ship with five or six men in each, to say goodbye to the two whom we had kept. They brought fish to them and made signs to us that they would not tear down the cross. They also delivered several harangues that we did not understand.

The next day, the twenty-fifth of the month, a good wind came. We left the harbor and, once out of the river, bore to the east-northeast.[19]

Translated by John DuVal from Bibliothèque National ms. Moreau 841, facsimile in *A Memoir of Jacques Cartier, Sieur de Limoilou, His Voyages to the St. Lawrence, a Bibliography and a Facsimile of the Manuscript of 1534,* ed. James Baxter (New York, 1906), 262–96.

Discussion Questions

1. What features of the landscape did Cartier describe? What was he interested in? What would be his ideal landscape? How did he choose names for places?

2. How did Cartier describe the various people he met (Micmacs and Iroquoians)?

3. How did Indians and French communicate without interpreters? Were they successful?

4. Why did Cartier erect a cross? What did the Iroquoians think he was doing?

5. Should we consider the Iroquoian chief's sons, Taignoagny and Domagaia, as early modern explorers, like Leif Eiriksson, Columbus, and Cartier?

Notes

1. Penguinlike great auks, which became extinct in the nineteenth century. He also saw smaller auks, razorbills, and northern gannets.

2. Polar bears.

3. A French port. French fishing vessels often ventured near the far North Atlantic coast of North America.

4. This name did not stick. It is now called Cumberland Harbor.

5. Cartier calls seals *loups-marin,* literally, "sea wolves."

6. Cartier is now in the Gulf of St. Lawrence, sailing along the north coast of Prince Edward Island.

7. Probably beans, which were native to the Americas.

8. Probably passenger pigeons, which were extinct by the early twentieth century.

9. These people were Micmac Indians, an Algonquian people native to southeastern Canada and northeastern New England.

10. Scholars of the Micmac language have interpreted Cartier's transcription (of words he did not understand) as Micmac for "we wish to love you."

11. Flare shots or warning shots.

12. Probably beaded or inscribed knives.

13. Gaspé Bay, in northeastern Quebec Province, just below the mouth of the St. Lawrence River.

14. A sou was a small French coin. Five sous was not much.

15. These people were Iroquoians but not part of the Iroquois Confederacy.

16. This was corn (maize). Cartier here discovers that he has exaggerated when he called these Iroquoians "the poorest." This was just their fishing camp.

17. "Long live the king of France."

18. The sons' names were Taignoagny and Domagaia.

19. By leaving the Gulf of St. Lawrence and heading back to the open sea, Cartier misses the fact that he was at the mouth of the St. Lawrence River, the view of which is obstructed by an island, Île d'Anticosti. However, Taignoagny and Domagaia described the river to him on their way back to France, and they all returned the next year. On that second visit, relations between Cartier and the Iroquoians went badly, and Cartier kidnapped Taignoagny and Domagaia along with some others and forcibly carried them back to France, where they died without seeing their homeland again. Although the St. Lawrence proved to be a dead end, it eventually became the heart of New France when Samuel de Champlain founded Quebec on its banks in 1608.

Alvar Núñez Cabeza de Vaca's Shipwreck off the Texas Coast, 1528–1536

*C*ABEZA DE VACA WAS THE TREASURER FOR PÁNFILO DE NARVÁEZ'S EXPEDITION, *which landed near Tampa Bay in April 1528. Narváez led most of the men, including Cabeza de Vaca, to explore the land along the coast and instructed the men in the ships to parallel their progress and eventually pick them up. The ships lost track of those on foot and decided to abandon the search. After Indian attacks, illness, and accidents killed many of his men, Narváez decided that the rest should build rafts to float to Mexico. Tossed around the gulf on their flimsy rafts with no provisions, Narváez and most of the others died. The group that included Cabeza de Vaca was thrown up on an island off the coast of Texas. In the following excerpt, beginning in 1528, Cabeza de Vaca has just sent his four best swimmers from the island to try to swim to Mexico.*

A few days after the four Christians swam away, a season of such bad cold and storms came on that the Indians could not pull up roots and could get no fish from their weirs.[1] The houses gave such poor shelter that people started dying. Five Christians who were at a farm on the coast were so desperate that they ate one another until only one remained, who being left at last all by himself had no one left to eat. Their names were Sierra, Diego López, Corral, Palacios, and Gonçalo Ruiz. Because of this, the Indians were so upset and scandalized that at first, if they had caught sight of him, they would have surely killed him, and we realized we were all in big trouble.

In very little time, of the eighty men in the two parties that had reached the island, only fifteen were left alive.

After all those deaths, a stomach sickness struck the Indians and half of them died. And they believed we were the ones killing them! With this conviction, they got together and agreed to kill those of us who were left, and were about to do it, too, when an Indian who was loyal to me argued that we were not what was killing them, because if we had been all that powerful, we would have made sure that not so many of our own people died as they could plainly see *had* died; we had not been able to find a cure for ourselves, and now only a few of us were left, not doing anybody any harm; so the best thing for them to do was leave us alone. Our Lord granted that the others took this advice and their plan came to nothing.

We named this island *Malhado*, Bad Luck Island.[2] The people we found there are tall and sturdy. The only weapons they have are bows and arrows, which they are very skillful with. The men have one of their nipples pierced through and through—and some of them have both nipples pierced—by a needle which they make for that purpose. Then they pull a bamboo shoot half a palm long and as thick as two fingers through the hole. They also pierce their lower lips and insert a cane shoot half as thick as a finger.

They live on the island from October to the end of February. In November and December they live off the roots I mentioned, which they pull up out of the water. They have weirs, but when the fishing gives out, they just eat the roots. At the end of February they move to other places because then the roots are putting out new plants and aren't good.

These are the people who of all the world love their children most and treat them best. When it happens that a child dies, the parents weep, and the kinfolk weep, and then the whole village. The weeping goes on for an entire year.... The Indians weep for all their dead in this manner, except for old people, who don't count for them, because, they say, old people have had their day, serve no purpose, have quit taking care of children, and just occupy ground.

Their custom is to bury the dead, except for doctors, whom they cremate. As the fire burns, they all dance and have a big party. Then they grind the bones into powder. After a year they perform rites for the dead and all slash themselves and give the kinfolk water to drink with the bone powder mixed into it.

Each man has a specific wife. The doctors are the most privileged and can have two or three, who get along together in good friendship and harmony.

When a man marries off his daughter, from the day the groom marries her, whatever he catches—whether hunting or fishing, all of it—his bride carries to her father's house and doesn't dare keep any of it or eat one bite of it herself. And they get what they eat from the father-in-law's house. During all this time neither father-in-law nor mother-in-law enters into the groom's home, nor may he go into his parents-in-law's or his brother- or sister-in-law's homes. If by any chance they come upon each other anywhere, they go out of their way to avoid each other by a bowshot's distance, keeping their heads down all the while and their eyes on the ground, because they consider it bad luck to see each other or speak to each other. The women are free to communicate and talk with the parents-in-law and relatives. This custom holds on the island as well as the mainland as far as fifty leagues inland.

There is another custom, which is when a child or sibling dies, for three months the people in the house don't hunt for food, but would rather starve. So the kinfolk and neighbors provide what they need to eat. Since so many were dying during the time we were there, most households were suffering terribly from hunger because they still held to this custom and ceremony. And no matter how hard the ones that did go out worked, the weather was too rough for them to get more than a little. That's why the Indians who kept me left the island and went in their canoes to inlets along the mainland where there are plenty of oysters.

For three months of the year that's all they eat, and the water they drink is very bad. They are low on wood and well supplied with mosquitoes. Their houses are made of rope mats over oyster shells. And they sleep on skins, if they happen to have them, laid out on top of the shells.

So there we were until the end of April, when we started going along the coast eating blackberries for a month, during which time the Indians never cease to have parties and religious celebrations.

The Indians on the island wanted to make doctors out of us, without examinations and without asking to see diplomas, because they cure diseases by blowing on the sick person, and with their breath and then their hands they cast out the disease. They ordered us to do that, too, and thus make ourselves useful for something. We laughed and said what a joke—we didn't know how to heal people!

So they stopped giving us food for as long as we wouldn't do what they were telling us to do. Seeing how stubborn we were, one Indian told me I didn't know what I was talking about when I said his knowledge wasn't any use, because stones and things growing in the fields did have virtue and by laying warm stones on somebody's stomach he himself healed and eased the pain; and we after all were men, too, and men with greater virtue and power than he had.

Finally we were reduced to such need that we had to do what they demanded, instead of worrying about whether we would be punished for doing it.

Here is how they do their healing: as soon as they realize they are sick, they call for a doctor, and after they are cured, not only do they give him everything they own, but their kinfolk also look for things to give the doctor. What the doctor does is to make some incisions where the pain is and suck all around the incision. They cauterize with fire, which they claim to be very effective, and I tried it myself, and it worked for me. After this they blow on the place where it hurts, and they think that takes the pain away.

The way we healed was to make the sign of the cross over the sick people and blow on them, say an Our Father and a Hail Mary, and pray as best we could that God our Lord would give them health and breathe into them the will to treat us well.

It pleased God our Lord in his mercy to grant that all those we were praying for and making the sign of the cross over told the others that they were healed and whole. So in that respect the treatment they gave us was good, and they did without food so as to give food to us. And they gave us skins, too, and other little things.

[Some Karankawas canoe Cabeza de Vaca to the mainland, where he makes his living for several years healing and trading. When he finally starts westward in search of Mexico, he reunites with three companions who had been enslaved by coastal Indians, by now the only survivors of the castaways on Bad Luck Island: Alonso del Castillo and Andrés Dorantes—mentioned in the selection above—and Esteban, a man who was brought on the original expedition as a slave and whom Cabeza de Vaca refers to as "The Negro." Together, they walk across Texas and much of New Mexico. Each group of Indians introduces them to the next group, treating them as respected healers. In 1536, they finally near Mexico and see signs of other Spaniards.]

After coming upon clear traces and signs of Christians[3] and realizing how close we were to them, I gave thanks to God our Lord for his willingness to rescue us from such sad and wretched captivity. Every reader can judge the pleasure we felt by considering how long we had been in that country and the trials and dangers we had passed through. That night I asked one of my companions to go in search of the Christians, who were now passing through the very territory that we had recently made safe and which was a three-days' journey away. My companions were unwilling, and said they were too tired and too worn out from work, even though they were each stronger and younger than I and better fitted to go. Since that was what they wanted, the next morning I took with me the Negro and eleven Indians, and we found the Christians' tracks and followed them past three campsites where they had spent the night. The next day I went ten leagues and the morning after that I came upon four Christians on horseback, who were astonished to see me so strangely dressed and in the company of Indians. They stood looking at me for a long time, so stunned that they neither spoke to me nor examined me nor asked me anything. I told them to take me to their captain.

So we traveled another half league to where the captain was, Diego de Alcaraz. After I spoke with him, he said he was lost out there, because it had been several days since he had been able to take any Indians, and there was nowhere to go, because they were beginning to run out of supplies and get hungry. I told him that Dorantes and Castillo were ten leagues behind us, with many people who had brought us. So he sent three horses along with fifty of the Indians he had brought with him. The Negro went with them to guide them, and I stayed there and asked them to witness what year and month it was that I arrived there and how I came there, which they did. From this river to San Miguel, which is legally part of the province they call San Galicia, is thirty leagues.

After five days Andrés Dorantes and Alonso del Castillo arrived with the people who had gone to get them, and they brought with them six hundred more people that the Christians had forced to flee to the mountains or hide all over the country. Those who had come along with me had rousted them out of their hiding places and handed them over to the Christians, whereas they had sent away the people they had brought with them up until then. When they came to me, Alcaraz asked us to summon the people of the villages along the river, who were now hiding all over the mountains and order them to bring food—even though orders weren't necessary, since they were always bringing us everything they could. So we sent messengers to summon them, and six hundred people came, bringing all the corn they could get, in jars sealed with clay that they had hidden and buried. They brought everything they had to us, but we didn't want to take anything but food, and we gave the rest to the Christians to share. After that, we had many bitter arguments with the Christians, because they wanted to make slaves out of the Indians we had brought.

We left them in anger, leaving behind turquoise bows and hides and arrows, as well as the five emeralds,[4] which we forgot and so we lost them, and we gave the Christians many cow hides and other things that we had with us.

We had a good deal of trouble trying to persuade the Indians to go back to their houses and take care of themselves and plant their corn. All they wanted to do was go with us until, as was the custom, they left us with other Indians, because they were afraid that if they turned back without doing that, they would die, but as long as they stayed with us they wouldn't be afraid of the Christians or their lances.

This worried the Christians, who had their interpreter say we were their people and had gotten lost a long time ago and were bad luck and not worth much, and that they themselves were the lords of that land, and people had to obey them and serve them.

But all these claims made little or no impression on the Indians, who talked them over among themselves and said the Christians were lying, because we came from where the sun rose, and they, from where it set; we healed the sick, but they killed the healthy; we came naked and barefoot, but they came in clothes and on horses and with lances; and we weren't greedy—rather everything the Indians gave us we turned around and gave away, leaving nothing for ourselves, whereas these others had nothing on their minds but to steal everything they found and never gave anything to anybody.

That's how they described us and praised our deeds in contrast with those others' deeds. And that's what they said to the Christians' interpreter, too, and they said the same to everybody else through a language that we could understand, known as Primahaitu, which sounds like Basque and which we found used throughout the more than four hundred leagues that we traveled, without any other language we could depend on.

When all was said and done, the interpreter never could persuade the Indians that we were one and the same as the Christians. We had to struggle just to argue them into going back to their homes. We ordered them to look after themselves, to settle their towns, and to sow and cultivate their land, which had become overgrown from not having people in it. I have no doubt that it is the best of the Indian lands—the most fertile and the best for living on. They get to plant their crops three times in one year. The land has many fruits and beautiful rivers and other beautiful bodies of water. There are signs and strong indications of gold and silver mines. The people are very docile. They serve the Christians (those who are friends to them) very willingly. They are very adaptable, much more than the Mexicans,[5] and finally, the land will never fail to be fertile.

As we said goodbye to the Indians, they told us they would do what we ordered and settle their towns again, if the Christians left them alone. And I assert and affirm that if they didn't, the Christians are to blame.

After we sent the Indians away in peace and thanked them for the troubles they had endured with us, the Christians sent us, under guard, to a certain Cebreros, a mayor, and after him, to two others, who took us across mountains and deserts to sever any communication between us and the Indians and keep us from seeing or hearing about what they were in fact doing. Thus it can be seen how men's thoughts deceive them: we were trying to secure their freedom, and when we thought they had it, the opposite happened, because the Christians had it planned to attack the Indians whom we had sent off with assurances of peace. And what they planned, they did.

[For the further adventures of Esteban, read Castañeda's account, later in this volume.]

Translated by John DuVal from Alvar Núñez Cabeza de Vaca, *La relación y comentarios del governador Alvar Núñez Cabeça de Vaca de lo acaescido en las dos jornadas que hizo a las Indias* (Valladolid, 1555), folios 19v–22, 47v–49v.

Discussion Questions

1. How did the Karankawas interpret the unprecedented diseases that were attacking them?

2. Why did Cabeza de Vaca think he might be punished for attempting to heal the sick? How did he interpret his ability to heal?

3. Cabeza de Vaca refers to Esteban as one of the Christians, but most Africans practiced either Islam or a native African religion. Might Esteban have interpreted his experiences differently due to his religious background or enslaved status?

4. Why did Cabeza de Vaca's Indian companions think that the four Spaniards that they knew were not the same kind of people as the Spanish slavers?

5. How did Cabeza de Vaca change as a result of his journey?

Notes

1. The Indians were Karankawas. Weirs are traps.

2. Galveston Island.

3. In this section, Cabeza de Vaca is referring to the other Spaniards, not his group, as "the Christians."

4. People who greeted Cabeza de Vaca in the towns along the way of his last march had given them coral from the sea in the south and turquoise from the north, and specifically to him five emerald arrowheads used for feasts and celebrations.

5. By Mexicans, he means Indians in Mexico.

Jacques Marquette on Descending the Mississippi River with Louis Joliet, 1673

JACQUES MARQUETTE WAS A JESUIT PRIEST, and Louis Joliet was a Québecois merchant. This excerpt from Marquette's journals describes the beginning of their voyage together in search of the Mississippi River, which they did find and descend, although not all the way to its mouth. This was a part church-, part government-sponsored expedition, and while Marquette's goal was to spread the Gospel, Joliet's was to confirm reports of gold mines and discover whether the Mississippi was a northwest passage to the Pacific. Here, in May 1673, the expedition's two canoes leave St. Ignace Mission on the northern shore of Lake Michigan. Although Marquette and Joliet were explorers, by 1673 Europeans and Indians knew much more of each other than they had in earlier centuries.

The day of the Feast of the Immaculate Conception of the Holy Virgin, to whom I had offered up prayers throughout my stay in this land of the Ottawas asking her to obtain God's grace for me to be able to visit the nations along the Mississippi, was the very day when Monsieur Joliet arrived with orders from the Compte de Frontenac, our governor, and Monsieur Talon, our commanding general, to make the discovery with me; so I was all the more delighted, seeing that my plans were about to be accomplished and I was in the happy necessity of risking my life for the salvation of these peoples, especially the Illinois, who during the time when I was living at Point St. Esprit had been pleading with me to bring the word of God to them.[1]

It did not take us long to get our gear ready for a journey we had no idea how long would last. Indian corn and some smoked meat were the only provisions we took with us in two canoes, Monsieur Joliet and I and five other men, determined to do all and endure all for such a glorious enterprise.

So it was that on the 17th of May, 1673, we departed from the St. Ignace Mission in Michilimakinac, where I was living then. The joy we felt at being chosen for this expedition lifted our hearts and turned the ache of having to paddle from morning till night to pleasure. Because we were in search of new lands, we took every possible precaution so that however risky the enterprise, it would not be rash. We learned everything we could from the Indians who had been to those places, and we even traced out a map of the new territories according to what they told us. On it we marked the rivers we were going to have to navigate, the names of the peoples and the places we would have to pass through, the course of the Big River, and what routes we would have to take when we were on it.

Above all, I placed our journey under the protection of the Holy Immaculate Virgin, promising her that if she granted us the grace to discover the Big River, I would name it *Conception* and would give that same name to the first mission I established among the new peoples, which I did indeed do among the Illinois.[2]

With all these precautions, we joyfully plied our oars on Lake Huron, the Illinois Lake, and the Bay of Stinks.[3] The first nation we came to was the Wild Oats Nation.[4] I turned up their river to visit these people, whom we had been preaching the gospel to for several years so that there were many good Christians among them.

The wild oat,[5] from which their name derives because it grows in their lands, is a kind of plant that springs up in swamps and mud-bottomed creeks and is very much like the wild oat that grows among our grains. The ears grow from stalks that are knotty at intervals. They grow up out of the water around June and rise to about two feet above the surface. The grain isn't any thicker than our oat, but it is twice as long and yields more flour.

Here is how the Indians harvest and prepare it for eating. In September, which is the best month for harvesting it, they cross the "fields" of wild oats in their canoes, shaking the ears on all sides into the canoes as they go. If the grain is ripe, it falls out easily, and in little time, they have their supply. But to clear away the chaff and husk and the film that encloses each grain, they smoke-dry it on a wooden grill over a little fire that they keep going for a few days. When the oats are dry, they pack them into a leather pouch which they stick into a hole dug into the ground for that very purpose. Then they stamp on it so long and hard that the grain separates from the chaff and is easy to winnow. After that, they pound it into flour. Or they may boil it without pounding it and season it with grease. Cooked that way, with no better seasoning, these wild oats are almost as fine a delicacy as rice.

I told these Wild Oat people about my plans to travel and discover far-away nations and instruct those nations in the mysteries of our holy faith. They were very surprised and did their best to dissuade me. They claimed I would come upon nations who show strangers no mercy and for no pretext at all smash their skulls in, that the war which had broken out among the various peoples on our route would expose us to inevitable death from bands of warriors who are always at war, that the Big River is very dangerous for people who don't know the difficult passages, that it is full of terrifying monsters who swallow men and canoes in one gulp, that there is one demon who can be heard from a long way off who blocks the passage and sinks all those who dare come near, and finally that the heat in those countries is so extreme that it would surely kill us.

I thanked them for this good advice but told them I could not follow it and that I would be happy to give my life for the salvation of souls, that I was not concerned about this supposed demon, that we would defend ourselves against any sea monsters, and that we would be careful to avoid all the other dangers they were threatening us with.

After bidding them say their prayers to God and giving them some instruction, I left them, and we set out in our canoes.

Translated by John DuVal from Jacques Marquette, *Au Mississippi: la première exploration (1673)*, ed. Alfred Hamy (Paris, 1903), app. 5.

Discussion Questions

1. What was Marquette's purpose in getting to know Indians? Do you think that Joliet and the other Frenchmen on the journey had different purposes?

2. How did Marquette and Joliet prepare for the journey?

3. Why would the Wild Oat people warn Marquette not to journey southward? Do you think they believed their own dire warnings, or were they laying it on thick?

4. Why did Marquette and Joliet go against their advice?

Notes

1. In 1669, Marquette had helped to establish the Mission of St. Esprit on Lake Superior in present-day Wisconsin, which was a mission to Illinois Indians, a group of culturally related nations. In 1671, the mission moved and was renamed St. Ignace Mission, from which he and Joliet departed in 1673.

2. Marquette had many rivals for naming the "Big River," including La Salle, who wanted to name it the Colbert River, after the powerful French minister Jean Baptiste

Colbert, and Iberville, who called it the St. Louis River for the king. "Mississippi," the Algonquian word meaning "Big River," won out in the end. When Marquette founded a mission among the Kaskaskia Indians in 1675, he gave it the name Immaculate Conception. Although most people referred to the mission as Kaskaskia, Immaculate Conception is still the name of a church in Kaskaskia, Illinois, built in the 1710s.

    3. Green Bay.

    4. Menominee Indians.

    5. "Wild oats" are wild rice.

Captain James Cook's Third Voyage, 1776–1780

*O*N HIS THIRD AND FINAL VOYAGE OF EXPLORATION, *British explorer Captain James Cook led the ships* Resolution *and* Discovery *to the Hawaiian Islands. He and his crew were probably the first Europeans to visit those islands, which he named the Sandwich Islands for the fourth earl of Sandwich, a British lord for whom the sandwich was named. From the islands, he sailed to the North American continent and explored the shore from Vancouver Island to the Bering Strait, failing, like Jacques Cartier and countless others, to find a northwest passage. When his ships returned to Hawaii, Cook was killed in a skirmish with some Native Hawaiians. John Webber accompanied the voyage as its official artist.*

John Webber, The Inside of a House in Nootka Sound [Vancouver]. Source: James Cook and James King, A Voyage to the Pacific Ocean, Undertaken by the Command of His Majesty, for Making Discoveries in the Northern Hemisphere (London, 1785), atlas vol., plate 42. Courtesy John Carter Brown Library at Brown University.

Charles Grignion's engraving of Webber's drawing, A Canoe of the Sandwich Islands [Hawaii], Rowers Masked. *Source: James Cook and James King,* A Voyage to the Pacific Ocean, Undertaken by the Command of His Majesty, for Making Discoveries in the Northern Hemisphere *(London, 1785), atlas vol., plate 65. Courtesy John Carter Brown Library at Brown University.*

Discussion Questions

1. According to Webber, he had to give away the buttons from his coat to persuade the residents of the house in Nootka Sound to let him draw the large carved figures. What might their reasoning have been?

2. What details can you see in that house? What do they tell you about life there?

3. What details can you see in the picture of the Hawaiian canoe? How would life in those islands have differed from life in Nootka Sound? What do you think they thought of Cook and his men, who may have been the first Europeans they saw?

4. How do you think the centuries of European exploration before 1776 colored how Cook and Webber interpreted Nootka Sound and the Hawaiian Islands?

5. What can you learn from a drawing that you cannot learn from written sources? What kind of information is missing?

Osage Creation Account
(Black Bear Clan Version), Recorded 1920s

THE OSAGES LIVED IN THE MISSOURI RIVER VALLEY, between the Mississippi River and the Great Plains (and many still live in part of that territory, in what is now Oklahoma). This tale begins after Wa kon ta, the Creator, has instructed the Osages that they are to become a people and they have realized that they must find a home. They are looking down on the earth but can see only water. Remember that this is an oral history and would have been told aloud in the Osage language. This version, transcribed by ethnologist and Omaha Indian Francis La Flesche and either translated by him or by an interpreter, attempts to convey the repetition and cadence of the oral version. Because you may find this document difficult to interpret, it may help to compare it with the other exploration accounts.

The people spoke to one another, saying: "O, younger brothers, look you, it is not possible for the little ones[1] to become a people. Let search be made for a way." They mediated upon continuing the descent. They sat in great perplexity. Then they took the downward course to earth. They found the earth engulfed in water that lay undisturbed. . . .

The people spoke to one another, saying: "O younger brothers, what shall we do?" They said to one another, "it is impossible for the little ones to dwell upon the surface of the water. Let us cause search to be made." The Sho'-ka,[2] who stood near, even as these words were spoken, hastened to the Water-beetle and quickly returned with him. The people spoke to the Water-beetle, saying: "O, grandfather, it is not possible for the little ones to dwell upon the surface of the water. We ask of you to make search for a way out of our difficulty." Verily, at that time and place, it has been said, in this house, the Water-beetle replied: "O, my grandchildren, you say it is not possible for the little ones to dwell upon the surface of the water. You ask me to search for a way out of your difficulty. I shall make search for a way." Thereupon he pushed forth, even against the current. Running swiftly upon the surface of the water, he came to a bend of the water, then spoke, saying: "It is impossible for me to give you help, O, my grandchildren. Although it is not possible for me to help you, I will say to you: my walk of life is upon the surface of the water. The little ones shall make of me their bodies. When the little ones make of me their bodies, they shall be free from all causes of death as they travel the path of life. When the little ones make of me their bodies, they shall cause themselves to be difficult to overcome by death."

[Conversations with the Water-spider, the Water-strider, and the Red-breasted Leech yield similar advice but no help in finding a home.]

Then they spoke to the Great Elk, saying: "O, grandfather, it is not possible for the little ones to dwell upon the surface of the water, O, grandfather. It is not possible for the little ones to make the waters to become dry. We ask you to seek for a way out of our difficulty. It is not possible for the little ones to dwell upon the surface of the water."

Verily, at that time and place, it has been said, in his house, the Great Elk threw himself suddenly upon the water, and the dark soil of the earth he made to appear by his strokes. Then he spoke to the people, saying, "O, elder brothers, I have given you cause to be grateful and happy. When the little ones go toward the setting sun against their enemies and take with them this dark soil as a sign of their supplications, their prayers shall never fail to be heard as they travel the path of life." . . .

[The Great Elk throws himself upon the water three more times, bringing up blue soil, red soil, and yellow soil.]

The dark soil of the earth, he held up to view and spoke to the people, saying: "This dark soil of the earth I have not made without a purpose. When the little ones use it as a sign of their supplications, when they put it upon their faces as a sign of their supplications, and moisten, with their tears, even so much as their eyelids, their prayers shall never fail to be heard as they travel the path of life."

Then he held to view the blue soil of the earth, and spoke to the people, saying: "This blue soil also I have made for you to put upon your faces. When the little ones go toward the setting sun against their enemies and take with them this blue soil as a sign of their supplications, their prayers shall never fail to be heard as they travel the path of life." . . .

[The Great Elk gives similar instructions regarding the red soil and the yellow soil. The Osages then send one of their own, their "younger brother," who has taken the form of a puma,[3] to explore the new land.]

Then after a time the people said to one another: "There are signs that our younger brother is returning. Stumbling, tripping again and again as he hastens, running repeatedly as he hurries homeward. Go, some of you, and speak to him." And some of the brothers hastened to meet him and to speak to him. In response to their inquiries, the Puma spoke, saying: "O, elder brothers, yonder stands a man, O, elder brothers. Verily, a man whose appearance excites fear, a man who is like us in form." Then the people spoke, saying: "O, younger brothers, look you, I have said, we are a people who spare none of our foes, a people who are never absent from any important movement. Whoever this man may be, we shall send him to the abode of spirits. It matters not whose little one he may be, we shall make him to lie low."

In the direction of the man they hastened. They made one ceremonial pause. Then, at the fourth pause, the Puma spoke, saying: "There he stands, O, elder brothers." "It is well," the people replied. "We shall send him to the abode of spirits." Their index fingers they thrust into their mouths, to moisten them and to give them killing power.[4] Verily, at that time and place, it has been said, in this house, the man spoke, saying: "I am a Hon'-ga (a sacred person), O, elder brothers." He stood saying. Then the Puma spoke, saying, "O, elder brothers, he speaks clearly our language." "I am a Hon'-ga," the stranger continued, "who has come from the midst of the stars. O, elder brothers, Young-chief is my name, I who stand here, Radiant-star is my name, I who stand here, Star-that-travels is my name." Then the people replied: "It is well." The stranger continued: "Young-chief is a name you shall use as you travel the path of life. The radiant star also is a name you shall use as you travel the path of life.[5] In giving you these names I give you cause to be grateful and happy, O, elder brothers." "It is well," the people replied. . . .

[The Osages send the Puma out several times to look for ceremonial objects, but most of his trips fail to yield any.]

The people spoke to one another, saying: "There are signs that our younger brother is returning, stumbling again and again in his haste, running from time to time as he hastens homeward. Go, some of you, and speak to him." Then some of the brothers hurried to him and spoke to him, saying: "O, younger brother." To their inquiries the Puma replied: "O, elder brothers, verily, an animal of some kind stands yonder, O, elder brothers, an animal that is formidable in appearance, an animal with cloven feet. O, elder brothers, the animal has horns upon its head, that make it formidable in appearance." Then the people spoke to one another, saying: "O, elder brothers, our younger brother has come home in great alarm. He had seen an animal standing yonder. Verily, an animal that is fear-inspiring in appearance. An animal with cloven feet. The animal has horns upon his head.[6] It is well!" the people exclaimed. "Make haste," they said to one another. "Look you, we are a people who spare none of the foe, a people who are never absent from any important movement. It matters not whose little one that animal may be, we shall send him to the abode of spirits."

They moved forward with quickened footsteps. They made one ceremonial pause. At the fourth pause they came near to the place. Then the Puma spoke, saying: "There it stands, O, elder brothers." The people drew near to the animal, and stood in line, then spoke, saying: "It is a female, O, elder brothers." Verily at that time and place, it has been said, in this house, the people spoke, saying: "We shall make of the animal the sacred articles we need, O, elder brothers. Even its skin we shall consecrate to ceremonial use, O, elder brothers. Behold the length of its back. Even the back of this animal is fit for ceremonial use. Out of its skin we shall make ceremonial robes, to commemorate the consecration of the skin to ceremonial use."

From Francis La Flesche, *Smithsonian Institution, Bureau of American Ethnology, 36th Annual Report* (Washington, DC, 1921), 221–37. The Osages' Hun ka (Earth) subdivision has seven clans, of which the Black Bear Clan is one. The other subdivision is the Tsi shu (Sky).

Discussion Questions

1. What were the Osages looking for as they explored?
2. How do their goals compare to those of other explorers?
3. What did they discover?
4. The creation account was an oral history that was translated and written down in the early twentieth century. Do you think that it had changed over the course of Osage history? How do you think the recording of the account affected it?

Notes

1. "The little ones" is the Osage name for themselves.
2. An Osage emissary.
3. The Puma Clan is an Osage clan.
4. The Creator had given the Osages this power because they did not yet have weapons.
5. These became Osage chief names.
6. A bison.

II

INTERPRETING AND INSTRUCTING
NEW PEOPLES

THIS SECTION REVEALS WHAT HAPPENED after initial European explorations, when different peoples were getting to know one another better. Each wanted to understand new acquaintances and also instruct them in how they should see the world and relations within it. In these documents, consider the ways in which different Europeans, Indians, and Africans tried to figure out how to fit new peoples into their older understandings of the world and, in some cases, bend them to their own interests.

La Relation des Montagnais

Excerpt

P IERRE PASTEDECHOUAN *nous a rapporté que sa grand'mère prenoit plaisir à raconter l'estonnement qu'eurent les Sauvages voyants arriver le vaisseau des François qui aborda le premier en ces pays-cy, ils pensoient que ce fust une Isle Mouvante, ils ne savoient que dire des grandes voiles qui la faisaient marcher, leur estonnement redoubla voyans quantité d'hommes sur le tillac. Les femmes commencèrent à leur dresser des cabanes, ce qu'elles font ordinairement quand de nouveaux hostes arrivent, & quatre canots de Sauvages se hasardèrent d'aborder ces vaisseaux, ils invitent les François à venir dans les cabanes qu'on leur preparoit, mais ils ne s'entendaient pas les uns les autres. On leur donna une barrique de pain ou biscuit, l'ayant emporté et revisité, n'y trouvant point de goust, ils la jetèrent en l'eau.**

*From Paul le Jeune, "Relation de ce qui c'est passé en la Nouvelle France en l'annee 1633, envoyée au R. P. Barth. Jacquinot, Provincial de la Compagnie de Jesus en la province de France," in *Relations des Jésuites, contenant ce qui s'est passé de plus remarquable dans les missions des pères de la compagnie de Jésus dans la Nouvelle-France* (Québec, 1858), 1 (1633 section): 9. Translation begins on p. 67.

The Requerimiento, 1533 Version

*I*N *1511, D*OMINICAN PRIEST *A*NTONIO *M*ONTESINOS PUBLICLY ACCUSED *Spanish conquistadors of sinful cruelty toward Indians. He charged that true Christians would not subject Indians to unjust wars and enslave them, without making any effort to convert them to Christianity. Shocked into action by Montesinos's criticism, King Ferdinand in 1512 commissioned legal scholar Juan López de Palacios Rubios to draft the Requerimiento. The king required that when conquistadors encountered a new people, a representative must read the document aloud to them. The first reading took place in 1514, in what is now Venezuela, in front of a deserted town, because the Indians had already fled. The version here is the one revised slightly for Ferdinand's grandson, Carlos I, and given to Francisco Pizarro in 1533 for his conquests in Peru. For other times when the Requerimiento was read, see Castañeda's account in this volume.*

On behalf of the Emperor and King Don Carlos[1] and of Doña Juana, his mother, Monarchs of Castille, Leon, Aragon, the two Sicilies, Jerusalem, Navarre, Granada, Toledo, Valencia, Galicia, Majorca, Seville, Sardinia, Cordova, Corsica, Murcia, Jaén, Algarve, Algeciras, Gibraltar, the Canary Islands and the Indies, and the islands and mainlands of the Ocean; Count and Countess of Barcelona, Lords of Biscay and Molina, Duke and Duchess of Athens and Neopatria,[2] Count and Countess of Roussillon and Sardinia, Marquises of Oristano and Gociano,[3] Archduke of Austria, Duke and Duchess of Burgundy and Brabant, Count and Countess of Flanders and Tirol, etc., Tamers of Barbarous Nations, we, their servants, do inform and make known to you, to the best of our abilities, that the one and eternal God our Lord created the heavens, the earth, and a man and a woman from whom we and you and all who dwell in the world are procreated and descend as well as all who may come after us. However, because of the vastness of their progeny for the five thousand years and more since the world was created, some people had to go in one direction and others in other directions, and people were divided into many kingdoms and provinces, because as one unity they could not hold together and survive.

God our Lord put one man, who was named Saint Peter, in charge of all these peoples, as supreme lord for all of them to obey; and he was chief over all human lineages wherever men had gone, and under every law, religion, or belief whatsoever. And God gave the whole world to him to be under his rule and jurisdiction, and He ordered that a seat be established for him in Rome, as the fittest location from which to rule the world and judge and govern all peoples—Christians and Muslims, Jews and Gentiles, and of any other religion or belief whatsoever. They called him Pope and Papa, which is to say *Admirable, Great Father, Governor* of all mankind.

Those who were living at the time obeyed this Saint Peter and accepted him as lord and king, supreme over the universe, and so it has been with all others elected after him to the Papal Seat, and so it has continued to be to this day and shall continue to be until the world comes to an end.

One of the former Pontiffs who succeeded to the seat and dignity that I have described, being lord over the world, did give and donate these islands and mainland of this ocean and all that therein lie to the said King and Queen and to all successors to their kingdoms, as is duly written in certain documents, which you may look at if you wish.[4]

Their Majesties are thus monarchs and lords of these islands and of this mainland by virtue of said donation. Other islands and almost all who have received this news have accepted their Majesties as monarchs and lords and obeyed and served them as subjects ought to do, willingly and without resistance; and, without delay, as soon as they were informed of the aforementioned facts, they received and obeyed the priests and holy men whom their Highnesses sent to preach to them and teach them our Holy Faith; and they all of their own free and agreeable accord, without any reward or conditions, became Christian and are so now; and their Highnesses received them gladly and kindly and ordered them to be treated even as their other subjects and vassals; and you are expected and obliged to do the same.

In conclusion, to the best of our abilities we ask and require that you hear and understand this which we have informed you of, that you grant it to be understood, that you deliberate over it for a reasonable amount of time, and that you recognize the Church as exalted mistress over the entire world; and the supreme Pontiff, who is called Pope, in his name; and the Emperor and the

Queen, Doña Juana, our Lord and Lady, in their place, as masters, lords and monarchs of these islands and the mainland by virtue of said donation, and that you agree and make arrangements for these priests and holy men to proclaim and preach unto you the aforementioned faith.

If you do this, you will do well, and do what you are beholden to do and obliged to do; and their Highnesses and we, acting in their names, will receive you with all love and charity, and we shall leave your wives and children and homes to be free and unenslaved for you to do with freely as you wish and as you deem right, and they will not compel you to become Christian, but only if you yourselves, being informed of the truth, would like to be converted to our holy Catholic Faith (as almost all your neighbors on the other islands have done), in which case their Highnesses will extend unto you privileges, allow you exemptions, and give you many thanks.

And if you do not do this or maliciously delay in doing it, we assure you that with God's help we will come upon you and make war upon you everywhere and in every way that we can and will subject you to the yoke and obedience of the Church and their Majesties, and will take from you your bodies, your wives, and your children and make them slaves, and as slaves shall sell them and dispose of them however their Majesties may command, and we shall take your goods and do unto you all the harm and evil that we can, as unto vassals who do not obey and deny their lord and resist and contradict him. And we declare that the deaths and damages that result from your denial are your fault and not their Majesties' fault, or our fault, or the fault of any of the gentlemen who attend us.

And just as we have said and required, we ask that the scribe here present write it down and sign it in testimony and that all here-present act as witness.

Translated by John DuVal from appendix in Luciano Pereña, *La idea de justicia en la conquista de América* (Madrid, 1992), 237–39.

Discussion Questions

1. Why did the Spanish feel compelled to read the Requerimiento?
2. On what authority did they base their claims?
3. What do you think Indians thought upon hearing the Requerimiento read in Spanish, a language they had never heard? After Ferdinand, interpreters were required, if available. What do you think Indians thought upon hearing the Requerimiento interpreted into their own languages?
4. Sixteenth-century Spanish reformer Bartolomé de las Casas wrote that, when he heard the Requerimiento, he didn't know whether to laugh or cry. What do you think he meant?

Notes

1. In addition to being the king of Spain, Carlos I was the Holy Roman Emperor and thus claimed sovereignty over, as you can see, a vast territory.

2. In Greece.

3. In Sardinia.

4. This passage refers to the papal bulls of 1493, in which Pope Alexander VI declared that the lands discovered in the west belonged to Spain.

Pedro de Castañeda de Nájera on the Search for the Seven Cities of Cíbola, 1540

*P*EDRO DE CASTAÑEDA MOVED *from northern Spain to Culiacán, on the west coast of Mexico, where, in the 1530s, he heard rumors of seven great cities to the north, in what is now Arizona and New Mexico. Some who heard the rumors inferred that these cities must be the mythic seven cities of gold, believed to have been founded by seven Portuguese bishops who supposedly had crossed the Atlantic to escape the Muslim invasion of Iberia. Castañeda begins his account with the rumors and the first attempts to find the cities, then tells of his journey north with Francisco Vásquez de Coronado in 1540. Castañeda gives a first-hand account of what happened to the main army. When smaller parties split off, he collected reports from participants when they returned and added them to his account.*

In the year fifteen hundred thirty, when Nuño de Guzmán was president of New Spain,[1] there was an Indian subject to him who was born in the valley (or valleys) of Oxitipar, whom Spaniards called *Tejo*.[2] This Indian said that his father, who had since died, had been a merchant when Tejo was a child and had traveled inland with his wares of luxuriant bird feathers and brought back great quantities of gold and silver, which were plentiful in that land; and he said that he himself had gone with his father once or twice and seen many great towns large enough to compare with Mexico City and the surrounding regions, and seen seven very great towns where there were silver-plated streets. From his own country, he said, it took forty days to travel there, through unpopulated wilderness where all that grew was a little grass, not over three inches high, and that they went as far as the distance between the two oceans, always traveling to the north.

[Guzmán forms an expedition and goes northwest from Mexico City but only makes it as far as Castañeda's town of Culiacán, still far south of the Rio Grande. By 1538, Tejo has died, Guzmán has been removed from his position, and Antonio de Mendoza is viceroy of New Spain. He appoints the ambitious Francisco Vásquez de Coronado governor of Nuevo Galicia, the province on the Pacific coast that includes Culiacán.]

At that time there came to Mexico City three Spaniards, named Cabeza de Vaca, Dorantes, and Castillo Maldonado, and one Negro, all of whom had been lost from the fleet of Pánfilo de Narváez in Florida.[3] They arrived by the road from Culiacán, having crossed the land from one ocean to the other, as those who care to do so may read about in the narrative which the same Cabeza de Vaca addressed to Prince Philip, now king of Spain and our sovereign. They informed the good Don Antonio de Mendoza that in the lands which they had crossed through they had heard much talk of powerful cities, four or five stories high, as well as other things very different from what turned out to be true. The good viceroy informed the governor [Coronado], who hurriedly cut short his visit and departed for his own dominions, taking with him the Negro, whom he had bought, along with the three Franciscan friars. One of these was named Friar Marcos de Niza, a theologian and priest; another, Friar Daniel, a lay brother; and the third, Friar Antonio de Santa María.

As soon as Coronado arrived at the province of Culiacán, he sent the friars and the Negro, whose name was Esteban, in search of that country, because Friar Marcos de Niza had offered to go in search of it, having been in Peru when Don Pedro de Alvarado had traveled there. As the three friars traveled with the Negro, it seems that they were not at all pleased with him because he took along with him the women that people were giving him, and he was acquiring turquoises and making a profit out of everything. Even so, the Indians in the villages they passed through got along better with him, because they had seen him before, so the friars made up their minds to send him on ahead, discovering and pacifying, so when they themselves arrived all they had to do was hear what he had to say and explain what they were looking for.

Once separated from the friars, Esteban became ambitious to win honor and a reputation for courage and daring by discovering, all by himself, those high and mighty cities, so famous throughout the earth. Taking followers with him from the villages, he managed to cross the deserts between the populated regions and Cíbola so far ahead of the friars that he was in Cíbola, eighty leagues beyond the desert, when they were just reaching Chichilticale, where the desert begins. (From Culiacán to where the desert begins is two hundred twenty leagues, and eighty more leagues through the desert, which makes three hundred in all, give or take ten leagues.)[4]

So when Esteban the Negro reached Cíbola, he came loaded with all the turquoises people had given him, along with beautiful women, whom they had also given him. Indians came, too—those who accompanied him and had followed him from every village, believing they could cross the whole earth under his protection and suffer no danger. But because the people there had more sense than the people who followed Esteban, they lodged him in a closed-in space while the rulers and elders heard him speak and tried to understand why he had come to their land.

Once they were sufficiently informed, they consulted with one another for three days. Then, from what the Negro had told them about how two white men sent by a great lord and well versed in the affairs of heaven were coming along behind him to do divine works, they decided he must be a spy or a guide for nations that were coming to conquer them, because it sounded crazy for him to claim that the people in the country he came from were white, when here he was a black man, and they were sending him!

They went back to him, and after more talk, when he asked them for turquoises and women, that seemed too much. So they decided to kill him. And that is what they did do, without killing any of those who had come with him. They took some boys as hostages and let the rest, who were about sixty in all, go free back to their own lands. About sixty leagues from Cíbola as they were fleeing back in terror, they came upon the friars in the desert and told them the sad news. This terrified the friars so much that although they did not trust the people who had gone with the Negro, they opened up their bags and handed them everything they were carrying so that all they had left were their implements for saying mass. With that they turned around with no more sight of Cíbola than what the Indians described and hurried back with their fancy skirts tucked up.

[Influenced by word from the friars that Cíbola is a great and wealthy city, Mendoza sends General Coronado north in 1540 with an army that includes Castañeda and, by his count, three hundred Spaniards and eight hundred Mexican Indians. At the town of Chichilticale, near where the present-day states of Arizona, New Mexico, Sonora, and Chihuahua meet, on the same route that Esteban and the friars had taken, Coronado leaves most of the army and leads a much smaller cavalry force toward Cíbola.]

From there [Chichilticale], they traveled across desert for two weeks until they arrived eight leagues from Cíbola at a river which, because it flowed red and murky, they named the Rio Bermejo.[5] There are barbels[6] in this river, as in Spain. Here they saw the first Indians in that land, two of them, who fled immediately and gave the alarm. The next day some Indians appeared and let out a cry, at a safe distance, and although they could be seen, some of our men were so alarmed that one of them threw his saddle on backwards. Those were new men, but the seasoned veterans mounted, charged, and overran the Indian force. The Indians fled like people who knew the land, and none of them could be taken.

The next day our troop came in good order into the populated region, and as soon as they saw the first town, Cíbola, some of them cursed Brother Marcos with so many curses that God forbid they should be repeated.

It's a rough little rocky town. There are ranches in New Spain which look more impressive from a distance. It is a town of three or four storeys with two hundred warriors. The homes are small and confined, with no courtyards. One courtyard serves a whole neighborhood.

People from the whole region had gathered there, because it is a province of seven towns, some of which are a good bit larger and stronger than Cíbola. These people were drawn up waiting in orderly squadrons on a field in sight of the town. When the interpreters proclaimed the requerimiento to them and they did not reply with offers of peace, but showed themselves more bold, our men shouted "Santiago!" "Santiago!," charged, and dispersed them.[7]

Then they went on to take the town, which was not easy, because the entrance was narrow and winding. As the general was coming in, a large rock knocked him onto the ground, and they would have killed him there if it had not been for Don Garci Lópes de Cárdenas and Hernando de Albarado, who fell upon him and pulled him away, using their bodies to shield him from the rocks, which were not few. But since after the first onslaught of the Spanish there was no resistance, in less than an hour they entered and took the town, and there they found food, which was what they needed most. From that point on, the whole province was set at peace.

[Meanwhile, the main army arrives in the town of Señora and begins preparing to leave for Cíbola.]

Juan Gallego would carry a message back to the viceroy in New Spain, and with him he would take Brother Marcos, who felt unsafe in the region of Cíbola because his account had turned out false in every detail: the kingdoms he described were not discovered, nor were any populous cities, nor heaps of gold, nor the rich jewels that were advertised, nor the brocades, nor any of the things that had been proclaimed from the pulpits. After all this was announced, the people who were staying behind [in Señora] divided up, and the rest loaded up their provisions and, as the general had commanded, left for Cíbola. . . . Melchior Días set out with guides to the northwest in search of the sea coast.[8] . . .

The captain heard talk that the ships were three days' journey down river toward the sea from there, and when they arrived where the ships had been, that is, more than fifteen leagues up river from the harbor mouth, they found these words carved on a tree: "Alarcón arrived here. At the foot of this tree there are letters." They pulled forth the letters and from them learned how long the men had stayed there awaiting news of the expedition and how Alcarón had turned the ships back toward New Spain because they could go no farther north, because that "sea" was in reality only a huge bay which curved back when it reached the "island" of Marqués, which people call *California*, and they explained that California was not an island at all, but a peninsula that curved around that inlet.[9]

When the captain [Días] saw that, he started back up the river without seeing the sea, and searched for means to cross to the other bank and continue upstream along that side. After traveling for five or six days, they thought they could cross with rafts. For that purpose they called upon many of the people from the region. These people, however, were seeking to mount an assault on our people and were on the lookout for a good opportunity. As soon as they knew they wanted to cross, they hurried to make the rafts as fast and diligently as they could in order to ferry our people into the water and drown them there or at least separate them so they couldn't help or reinforce one another.

While the rafts were being made, a soldier who had gone off the trail saw a great number of armed men crossing a ridge on the lookout for when our people would cross. He brought back word of this, and they seized one of the Indians to find out the truth from him. When they pressed him,[10] he admitted the whole plot that was planned for when the crossing would occur: as soon as some of our people had crossed and some were on the river while some were still waiting to cross, the ones on the rafts would try to drown the men they were ferrying across and the rest of them would attack by land from both sides of the river. And with all their strength and numbers, if they had had discretion and discipline, they would have pulled it off. Once it was clear what they intended, the captain had the Indian put to death, secretly. That night our forces threw him out onto the river with a heavy weight so that the Indians wouldn't realize they had been found out.

The next day, when they realized our people had stolen across, they shouted war cries and shot volleys of arrows. But when our cavalrymen reached them, thrusting at them pitilessly with their lances, and our harquebusiers[11] fired at them, they had to take to the mountains, leaving not a man there still alive. Thus the troops crossed safely, our Indian allies paddling one way and our own raftsmen paddling the other.

The horses crossed alongside the rafts, where we will leave them now to tell how the main army advanced toward Cíbola. Because they were traveling under the general's orders and he had left everything in peace, everywhere they found the native people happy and unafraid and willing to accept our leadership.

In the province called Vacapan[12] a great quantity of prickly pears grow, which the natives preserve. They made gifts of these preserves, and when the people of the army ate them, they all fell into a stupor with headaches and fever so that if the natives had wanted to, they could have inflicted great damage on them. It lasted twenty-four hours.

After they left there, they came to Chichilticale. One day after they left there, the scouts saw a herd of cattle[13] going by, and I saw them and followed them. They had huge bodies, long hair, and big, thick, long horns. They raised their heads up with their horns against their backs and ran so fast over rough ground that we couldn't catch up with them and had to let them go.

Three days into the desert on the banks of a river flowing through deep ravines and gorges, we found a horn which the general, after having seen it, had left behind for the men in the army to see, too, because it was six feet long and as thick at its root as a man's thigh and shaped more like the horn of a ram than any other animal. It was a sight to see.

Continuing from there, the army came within a day's journey from Cíbola. In the afternoon a whirlwind of frigid air set in and then a great downpour of snow which threw the troops into confusion. The army kept moving until it reached a place of huge rocks and hollows. Dark night was coming on and danger for the Indian allies, who were mostly from the warm regions of New Spain and felt the cold so cruelly that the next day it was a hard job to get them feeling good enough to ride on horses while the soldiers went on foot.

Thus, with difficulty, the army came to Cíbola, where its general was expecting it and had provided for lodging. There they were all united, except for some captains and troops who had gone out to discover other provinces. . . .

Meanwhile, General Francisco Vásques de Coronado, now that Cíbola was at peace, was finding out from the people of that land what provinces existed in the region and trying to get them to spread the news to their friends and neighbors that Christians had come to their land who wanted nothing else but to be their friends and learn about good lands to settle. And he asked that these friends and neighbors come to see them and talk with them. Thus the people in those parts let him know about the places they had communication with and dealings with. They told about a province of seven towns of the same sort, although somewhat different from theirs, and they said that they themselves didn't have anything to do with them. This province is called Tuscayan.[14] It is twenty-five leagues from Cíbola. The towns are lofty, and the people are warlike with one another.

The general had sent Don Pedro de Tovar there with seventeen horsemen and three or four foot soldiers. With them went a Franciscan friar, Brother Juan de Padilla, who had been a soldier in his youth. When they arrived at the province, they came in so secretly that no one noticed them, because from province to province the land is unpopulated and has no houses, and the people don't venture outside their towns any farther than their fields, especially then, when they had heard news that Cíbola had been taken by fierce men riding on beasts that ate people. For people who had never seen horses, this was big news that filled them with wonder.

When our people arrived under cover of night, they managed to conceal themselves under the ditch in front of the town and could hear the natives talking in their houses. But when morning came, they were visible, and they drew themselves up in order. The townsmen marched out to meet them in ordered ranks and no signs of confusion, bearing bows and shields and clubs. There was opportunity for the interpreters to speak with them and declare the requerimiento so that they could understand them. But nevertheless they drew lines in the ground and ordered our people not to cross them in the direction of their towns.

They did cross some of the lines, talking to the people as they moved. They got so far that one of the Indians lost control and struck a horse on the legs next to the bridle. Brother Juan, angry over the time that was being wasted with them, said to the captain, "Really, I don't see what we're doing here!" Seeing that, they shouted, "Santiago" and charged so suddenly that they knocked down many of the Indians, who scattered in confusion. Some fled into the town; others didn't have a chance to get away. Then the haste with which they came out of the town offering peace and bringing presents was so great that orders were given to gather up the fallen and not do them any more harm.

The captain and those with him set up a royal seat close to the town, and there where they dismounted, the people came offering peace and saying they came to pledge obedience on behalf of the whole province and to ask them to be friends and to receive the presents they were giving, that is, some cotton clothing, though not much, because they do not grow cotton there.

Translated by John DuVal from Pedro de Castañeda de Nájera, "Relación de la jornada de Cíbola," in *The Coronado Expedition, 1540–1542*, ed. George Parker Winship (Washington, DC, 1896), 110–27.

Discussion Questions

1. From here, Coronado's expedition forged on to other pueblos and then another six hundred miles across the plains to present-day Kansas, all in search of the seven cities. What made the Spanish so intent on finding these cities?

2. What do we learn from this account about the dangers of misinterpretation?

3. What did Castañeda think about Esteban? How much can we trust Castañeda's interpretation of Esteban's dealings with the Indians he met?

4. The word *amigos* means "friends" and usually refers to the Indian allies of the Spanish. The translator usually translates it as "Indian allies." With this translation, what might be lost in the reader's perception of these Indians and their relations with the Spaniards? What other word or phrase might be used to translate *amigos* better? Should the same word or phrase always be used?

Notes

1. New Spain was centered in Mexico City and stretched from the southern regions of Central America through the western half of what is now the United States.

2. The name Tejo probably indicated that he was a Tejas Indian, from whom the state of Texas gets its name.

3. These are, of course, Alvar Núñez Cabeza de Vaca, Andrés Dorantes, Alonso del Castillo, and Esteban, the characters in Cabeza de Vaca's account, included earlier in this volume.

4. A Spanish league is about 2.6 miles. At this point, Esteban has gone about one hundred miles beyond where he had traveled before, when he probably got as far as present-day El Paso, Texas. Cíbola was a Zuni pueblo in what is now New Mexico.

5. *Bermejo* means "bright red." This was the river later called the Colorado, which also means "reddish in color."

6. Whiskered fish, in this case probably catfish.

7. "Santiago!" was a battle cry during the Reconquista. Spain's patron saint was Santiago (St. James). For the requerimiento, see pp. 53–56.

8. Melchior Días went looking for the Pacific coast because Hernando de Alarcón had been sent in ships up the west coast of Mexico to deliver supplies to Coronado's army.

9. As Castañeda has realized, Alarcón sailed up into the Gulf of California, which left him at a dead end at the Colorado River. His ships sailed up the river until it was so shallow that they had to turn around and return to Mexico without delivering the supplies.

10. When Castañeda records that they "pressed" the captive, he implies that they tortured him.

11. A soldier armed with a harquebus, a matchlock gun invented in the fifteenth century, notoriously heavy and hard to aim.

12. Probably the land of the Opatas in northern Sonora.

13. Bison.

14. Hopi pueblos of Arizona.

Rock Painting,
Pecos River Valley, Texas, 1500s

A Southwestern Indian drew this pictograph, *probably in the 1500s, after having seen Spaniards for the first time. The pictograph was discovered in what is now Seminole Canyon State Historical Park in southwestern Texas, in a region where there are many rock paintings. In the original, the church is red. The handprint on the right is the artist's signature.*

Discussion Questions

1. What did this artist portray?
2. Does what the artist chose to portray tell you something about what he or she thought was important about the Spaniards?
3. Why do you think the artist drew this picture?
4. Can visual images drawn by people without a written language give us useful insights into their history? What are the limitations of this kind of evidence?

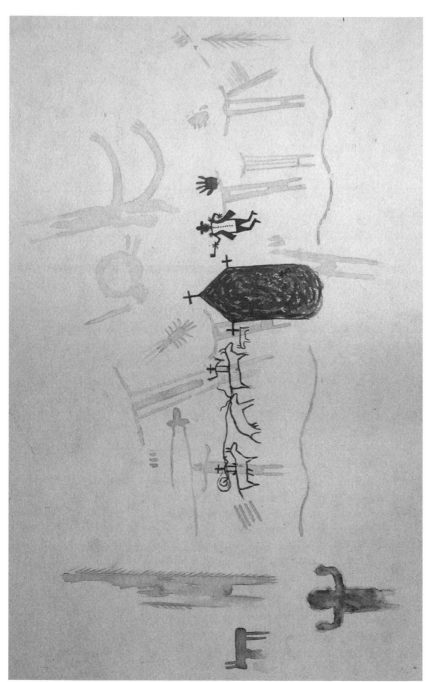

"Vaquero Shelter" (site 41VV77), copied by Forrest Kirkland, 1937, Kirkland 2261-63 (plate 69). *Courtesy of the Texas Archaeological Research Laboratory, University of Texas, Austin.*

Montagnais Indians on Their First Encounter with the French, Early 1500s

*T*HE MONTAGNAIS LIVED NORTH OF THE ST. LAWRENCE RIVER, *on Canada's At-lantic coast. They met Jacques Cartier on his first voyage, in August 1534, as he was heading for home. This is an account of their first meeting with the French, probably French fishermen who came even earlier than Cartier. It was written down in 1633 by a French missionary who got it from a Montagnais man whose grandmother had told it to him.*

Pierre Pastedechouan reported to us that his grandmother took pleasure describing the Indians' astonishment when they saw the first French ship arrive. They thought it must be a moving island. They didn't know what to make of the big sails that made it move. Their surprise redoubled when they saw all the men on deck. The women started getting the houses ready, which is what they customarily do when new guests arrive, and four Indian canoes risked going out to meet the ship. They invited the Frenchmen to come to the cabins they had prepared for them, but they could not understand each other. The Frenchmen gave them a barrel of hardtack, but when they took it home and tried it, they didn't like it and threw it into the water.

In other words, theirs was the same astonishment that the king of Calcutta had felt before that when he saw the first European ships approach his shores. He sent messengers to find out who these people were whom the large wood house had brought, and the messengers reported to their master that the people were amazing, frightful men who dressed in iron, ate bones, and drank blood. (They had seen them wearing their cuirasses,[1] eating hardtack, and drinking wine.)

Our Indians said that the French drank blood and ate wood, also referring to wine and hardtack. Since they couldn't understand what nation the French came from, they gave them a name which has referred to the French ever since: *Ouemichtigouchiou,* that is, a man who works with wood, or one who is in a canoe or boat made of wood. They saw that our ship was made of wood, whereas their little canoes are only made of bark.

Translated by John DuVal from Paul le Jeune, "Relation de ce qui c'est passé en la Nouvelle France en l'annee 1633, envoyée au R. P. Barth. Jacquinot, Provincial de la Compagnie de Jesus en la province de France," in *Relations des Jésuites, contenant ce qui s'est passé de plus remarquable dans les missions des pères de la compagnie de Jésus dans la Nouvelle-France* (Québec, 1858), 1 (1633 section): 9.

Discussion Questions

1. According to this story, what did the Montagnais think of the French?

2. Enumerate the narrative links between the Montagnais Indians who first met Frenchmen and you, the present reader (in other words, who told this story to whom)? How do these links affect the reliability of the narrative as you receive it?

3. Do you think Pierre Pastedechouan's grandmother was making fun of the French? Of her own ancestors?

4. Is this a better source for sixteenth-century native perspectives than Jacques Cartier's account?

Notes

1. Armor.

John Smith on the Powhatans, 1607–1616

*B*E SURE TO READ THE INFORMATION ON POWHATAN HISTORY *in this book's intro-duction before reading this document. After three failed attempts to found a colony at Roanoke (near the present-day border between North Carolina and Virginia), English settlers founded Jamestown in 1607, on Powhatan Indian land in the Chesapeake Bay region. At first, the Powhatans fed the newcomers, but the Indians soon grew tired of the settlers' inability to feed themselves. This account comes from the English captain John Smith, a leader of Jamestown and the colony's main negotiator with the Powhatans. He begins by describing those Indians' political system.*

Although the country people[1] be very barbarous, yet have they among them such government, as that their Magistrates for good commanding, and their people for due subjection, and obeying, excel many places that would be counted very civil. The form of their Common-wealth is a Monarchical government, one as Emperor rules over many Kings or Governors. Their chief ruler is called *Powhatan*, and takes his name of his principal place of dwelling called *Powhatan*. But his proper name is *Wahunsonacock*.[2] Some Countries he has which have been his ancestors', and came unto him by inheritance, as the Country called *Powhatan, Arrohateck, Appamatuck, Pamunkee, Youghtanund*, and *Mattaponient*. All the rest of his territories expressed in the Map, they report have been his several conquests. . . .

His will is a law and must be obeyed: not only as a King, but as half a God they esteem him. His inferior Kings whom they call *Werowances*, are tied to rule by customs, and have power of life and death at their command. . . . They all know their several lands, and habitations, and limits, to fish, fowl, or hunt in, but they hold all of their great Werowance Powhatan, unto whom they pay tribute of skins, beads, copper, pearl, deer, turkeys, wild beasts, and corn. What he commands they dare not disobey in the least thing. It is strange to see with what great fear and adoration, all these people do obey this Powhatan. For at his feet they present whatsoever he commands, and at the least frown of his brow, their greatest spirits will tremble with fear: and no marvel, for he is very terrible & tyrannous in punishing such as offend him.

[In December 1607, Smith is taken prisoner by the Powhatans and held for six or seven weeks. The next section is written in the third person rather than the first person. Smith is still the author, but he apparently drew on others' notes to assist his recollection.]

At last they brought him to Werowocomoco, where was Powhatan their Emperor. Here more than two hundred of those grim Courtiers stood wondering at him, as he had been a monster; till Powhatan and his train had put themselves in their greatest braveries.[3] Before a fire upon a seat like a bedstead, he sat covered with a great robe, made of Rarowcun[4] skins, and all the tails hanging by. On either hand did sit a young wench of 16 or 18 years, and along on each side the house, two rows of men, and behind them as many women, with all their heads and shoulders painted red; many of their heads bedecked with the white down of birds; but every one with something: and a great chain of white beads about their necks. At his entrance before the King, all the people gave a great shout. The Queen of Appamatuck was appointed to bring him water to wash his hands, and another brought him a bunch of feathers, instead of a towel to dry them. Having feasted him after their best barbarous manner they could, a long consultation was held, but the conclusion was, two great stones were brought before Powhatan. Then as many as could laid hands on him, dragged him to them, and thereon laid his head, and being ready with their clubs, to beat out his brains. Pocahontas the King's dearest daughter, when no entreaty could prevail, got his head in her arms, and laid her own upon his to save him from death. Whereat the Emperor was contented he should live to make him hatchets, and her bells, beads, and copper; for they thought him as well of all occupations as themselves. For the King himself will make his own robes, shoes, bows, arrows, pots; plant, hunt, or do anything so well as the rest. . . .

Two days after, Powhatan having disguised himself in the most fearful manner he could, caused Capt. Smith to be brought forth to a great house in the woods, and there upon a mat by the fire to be left alone. Not long after from behind a mat that divided the house, was made the most doleful noise he ever heard; then Powhatan more like a devil than a man with some two hundred more as black as himself, came unto him and told him now they were friends, and presently he should go to Jamestown, to send him two great guns, and a grindstone, for which he would give him the Country of Capahowosick, and forever esteem him as his son Nantaquoud. So to Jamestown with 12 guides Powhatan sent him. That night they quartered in the woods, he still expecting (as he had done all this long time of his imprisonment) every hour to be put to one death or other: for all their feasting. But almighty God (by his divine providence) had mollified the hearts of those stern Barbarians with compassion.

[After Smith's return to Jamestown, Pocahontas and her attendants regularly bring them food. In 1609, Smith sails for England. In 1613, the English at Jamestown kidnap Pocahontas, in an attempt to gain leverage over her father. In a diplomatic marriage approved by the Powhatans and the English, she marries John Rolfe in 1614. In 1616, they and their young son travel to England, where she is received at court and meets Smith for the first time in seven years.]

Hearing [Pocahontas] was at Branford[5] with divers[6] of my friends, I went to see her: After a modest salutation, without any word, she turned about, obscured her face, as not seeming well contented; and in that humor her husband, with divers others, we all left her two or three hours, repenting myself to have written she could speak English. But not long after, she began to talk, and remembered me well what courtesies she had done: saying, "You did promise Powhatan what was yours should be his, and he the like to you; you called him father being in his land a stranger, and by the same reason so must I do you," which though I would have excused, I durst not allow of that title, because she was a King's daughter; with a well set countenance she said, "Were you not afraid to come into my father's country, and caused fear in him and all his people (but me) and fear you here I should call you father; I tell you then I will, and you shall call me child, and so I will be for ever and ever your countryman. They did tell us always you were dead, and I knew no other till I came to Plymouth; yet Powhatan did command Uttamatomakkin to seek you, and know the truth, because your countrymen will lie much."

This Savage,[7] one of Powhatan's Council, being among them held an understanding fellow; the King purposely sent him, as they say, to number the people here, and inform him well what we were and our state. Arriving at Plymouth, according to his directions, he got a long stick, whereon by notches he did think to have kept the number of all the men he could see, but he was quickly weary of that task: Coming to London, where by chance I met him; having renewed our acquaintance, where many were desirous to hear and see his behavior, he told me Powhatan did bid him to find me out, to show him our God, the King, Queen, and Prince, I so much had told them of: Concerning God, I told him the best I could, the King I heard he had seen, and the rest he should see when he would; he denied ever to have seen the

King, till by circumstances he was satisfied he had: Then he replied very sadly, "You gave Powhatan a white Dog, which Powhatan fed as himself, but your King gave me nothing, and I am better than your white Dog."[8]

From John Smith, *The Generall Historie of Virginia, New-England, and the Summer Isles with the names of the Adventuerers, Planters, and Governours from their first beginning Ano 1584 to this present 1624* (London, 1624), 37–38, 47–49, 122–23.

Discussion Questions

1. What kind of political structure did the Powhatans have? How much power did their leader, Powhatan, have? Does his power conflict with modern-day images of Indian societies?

2. As you read Smith's account of his famous rescue by the princess Pocahontas (and the information on Powhatan history in this book's introduction), do you get the impression, as some scholars claim, that Smith made the story up, that he is telling the truth and Powhatan and Pocahontas had planned the event ahead of time, or that Pocahontas suddenly and spontaneously changed the mind of the king?

3. How did Smith interpret their actions?

4. In England, what did Pocahontas and Uttamatomakkin accuse the English of? What do you think Uttamatomakkin reported when he returned home?

Notes

1. The Powhatan Indians.
2. Powhatan was Wahunsonacock's title, but the English usually referred to him simply as Powhatan.
3. Finery.
4. Raccoon.
5. In Middlesex, England.
6. Many.
7. Uttamatomakkin was also known as Tomocomo.
8. Pocahontas died at Gravesend, England, shortly after this meeting, in March 1617.

John Eliot's Translation of the Bible into the Massachusett Language, 1663

*T*HIS WAS THE FIRST COMPLETE CHRISTIAN BIBLE PRINTED IN THE AMERICAS, *in Cambridge, Massachusetts, in 1663. It is a translation from English into Massachusett, an Algonquian Indian language. Because Massachusett had no written form, the British and Indian translators had to invent the spelling of every single word by trying to indicate the pronunciation of Massachusett with English letters and according to rules for pronouncing English. Puritan missionary John Eliot led the effort to make this translation because, to Protestants, reading the Bible for oneself was a direct link to God.*

Discussion Questions

1. What do you think the Massachusett Indians thought of the process of translating the Bible? Of the Bible itself? Do you think most could read it?

2. Try reading some of the first page of Genesis out loud. How does it sound to you? What words aren't translated? Why not?

3. There is evidence that copies of the Massachusett Bible were burned during Metacom's War (King Philip's War), in which some New England Indians fought against the English. Why might people have burned the Bibles?

4. After that bloody war, another Puritan minister, Cotton Mather, wrote that "the great things of our Holy Religion brought unto them in [Indian languages], unavoidably arrive in Terms that are scarcely more intelligible to them than if they were entirely English." What did Mather mean by saying this, and how might Eliot have countered?

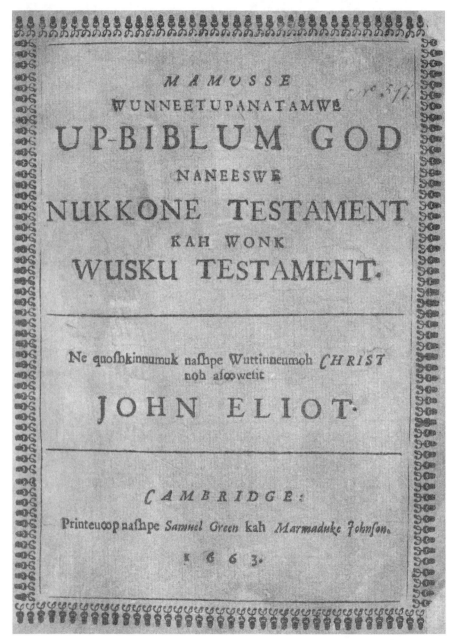

MAMUSSE
WUNNEETUPANATAMWE
UP-BIBLUM GOD
NANEESWE
NUKKONE TESTAMENT
KAH WONK
WUSKU TESTAMENT.

Ne quoſhkinnumuk naſhpe Wuttinneumoh *CHRIST*
noh aſoowefit

JOHN ELIOT·

CAMBRIDGE:

Printeuoop naſhpe *Samuel Green* kah *Marmaduke Johnſon.*

1 6 6 3.

Title page, The Holy Bible, Containing the Old Testament and the New *(Cambridge, MA, 1663). Courtesy the Library Company of Philadelphia.*

NEGONNE OOSUKKUHWHONK ℳOSES,

Ne asoweetamuk

GENESIS.

CHAP. I.

a Pſal.
33.6.
& 136.
5.
Act.14.
15.
& 17.
24.
Hebr.
11.3.
b 2Cor.
4.6.

Eske kutchiſſik *a* ayum God
Keſuk kah Onke.

2 Kah Ohke mô matta kuhkenauunncunkquttinnꝏ kah monteagunninno, kah pohkenum woſkeche mꝏnôi, kah Naſhauanit popomthau woſkeche nippekontu.

3 Onk nꝏwau God *b* wequaiaj, kah mô wequai.

4 Kah wunnaumun God wequai ne en wunnegen : Kah wutchadchaübe-ponumun God noeu wequai kah noeu pohkenum.

5 Kah wutuſſoweétamun God wequai Keſukod, kah pohkenum wutuſſoweétamua Nukon : kah mô wunnonkꝏꝏk kah mô mohtompog negonne keſuk.

e Pſal.
136.5.
Jer.10.
12. &
51.15.

6 Kah nꝏwau God *c* ſepakehtamꝏudj nôeu nippekontu, kah chadchapemꝏudj itathauweit nippe wutch nippekontu.

7 Kah ayimup God ſepakehtaméoonk, kah wutchadchabeponumunnap naſhaueu nippe agwu, uttiyeu agwu ſepakehtaméoonk, kah naſhaueu nippekontu uttiyeu ongkouwe ſepakehtaméoonk, kah mônkô n nih.

d Jer.
51.15.

e Pſal.
33.7.
& 136.
5.
Job 38.
8.

8 Kah wuttiſſoweétamun God *d* ſepakehtamo onk Keſukquaſh, kah mô wunnonkꝏꝏk, kah mô mohtompog nahohtoeu keſukok.

9 Kah nꝏwau God moémꝏidj *e* nippe ut agwu keſukquaſh kah paſukqunnu, kah pahkemoidj nanabpeu, kah mônkô n nih.

10 Kah wuttiſſoweétam n God nanabpi ohke, kah môcémꝏ nippe wuttiſſoweta nun Kehtoh, & wunnaumun God ne en wunnegen.

11 Kah nꝏwau God dtanueékej ohke moſkeht, moſkeht ſkanném̃unáꝏk ſkanném̃unaſh, & meechammue mahtugquaſh meechum̃inꝏk meeſhn̄mꝏnk niſh nog paſuk neane wuttinnuſuonk , ubbuukum niuuꝏk et woſkeche ohke, kah mônkô n nih.

12 Kah ohke dtannegeaup moſket, kah moſket ſkánném̃enuhꝏk ſkanné nu aſh, niſh noh paſuk neane wuttinnu ſuonk, kah m̃atug meechammêꝏk, ubbu ſkahm inn̄ꝏꝏk wuthogkut niſh noh paſuk neane wuttiinnuſuonk, kah wunnaaman God ne en wunnegen.

13 Kah mo wunnonkꝏꝏk, kah mo mohtompog ſhwekeſukod.

14 Kah nꝏwau God, *f* Wequanantégi nuohettich ut wuſepakehtamꝏonganit keſukquaſh, & pohſhéhettich ut naſhauwe keſukod, kah ut naſhauwe nukkonut, kah kukkineaſuongauůhhettich , kah uttꝏcheycůhettich, kah keſukodtuꝏwuhhettich, ka'a kodtumnꝏꝏwuhhettich.

fDeut.
4.19.
Pſal.
136.7.

15 Kah n̄ nag wequanantéganuóhettich ut ſépakehtamꝏwonganit wequaſumóhettich ohke, onk mô n nih.

16 Kah ayum God nesſuñaſh milliyeuaſa wequananteganaſh, wequananteg mohiag nananumꝏnꝏ keſukod, wequananteg peaſik nanananaꝏmꝏ nukon, kah anoggtog.

17 Kah upponuh God wuſepakehtamꝏonganit keſukquaſh , woh wequohſumwog ohke.

18 Onk wohg wunnanaanumůnneau keſukod kah nukon , kah pohſhémꝏ naſhaueu wequai, kah naſhaueu pohkénum, kah wunnaumun God ne en wunnegen.

gJer.
31.35.

19 Kah mô wunnonkꝏꝏk kah mo mohtompog yaou quinukok.

20 Kah nꝏwau God, moonahettich nippekontu pomónutcheg pomantamwae, kah puppinſhaäuſſog pumunahettich ongkouwe oakec woſkeche wuſepahkehtamꝏonganit keſukquaſh.

21 Kah kezheau God matikkenuautcheh Pꝏtäꝏpoh, kah niſh noh pomantanôe óäas nob pompámayit uttiyeu mꝏnacheg nippekontu, niſh noh paſuk neane wuttinnuſſuonk, kah niſh nꝏh ꝏnuppohwhunin puppinſhaaſh, niſh noh paſuk neane wuttinnuſſuonk, kah wunnau nun God ne en wannegen.

22 Kah ꝏnanumꝏh nahhôg God nꝏwau, Miſſ. ſneetuſnittegk, b kah muttaanꝏk, kah nunwapeg'k nippe u: kehtohhannie, kah puppin ſhſſog muttáanhettich ohket.

h Gen.
8.17.
& 9. 1,

23 Kah mo wunoi kꝏok kꝏ mo mohtompog napanna auita ſhſhikqui rakok.

24 Kah nꝏwau God, Paſ ꝏwaheonch o'ke óäs pomantanw̃ieu, niſh noh paſuk nea ne wuttiinnu iſa, neeti ſhog, puuaijéchag

A kah

Olaudah Equiano on
Encountering Europeans, 1740s

WHEN HE WAS IN HIS FORTIES, OLAUDAH EQUIANO, also known as Gustavus Vassa, published his autobiography to advocate for the abolition of slavery and for black human rights. The book told of Equiano's boyhood in West Africa, his enslavement in the Americas, and how he bought his freedom. Once free, Equiano moved to London and became a leader in the abolition movement. His autobiography was a bestseller in England and the United States. At this point in the story, he has been captured by African slave raiders and brought to the coast. His account of meeting his first white men conveys the confusion and fear of a child captured into slavery.

The first object which saluted my eyes when I arrived on the coast was the sea, and a slave ship, which was then riding at anchor, and waiting for its cargo. These filled me with astonishment, which was soon converted into terror when I was carried on board. I was immediately handled and tossed up to see if I were sound by some of the crew; and I was now persuaded that I had gotten into a world of bad spirits, and that they were going to kill me. Their complexions too differing so much from ours, their long hair, and the language they spoke (which was very different from any I had ever heard) united to confirm me in this belief. Indeed such were the horrors of my views and fears at the moment, that, if ten thousand worlds had been my own, I would have freely parted with them all to have exchanged my condition with that of the meanest slave in my own country. When I looked round the ship too and saw a large furnace or copper boiling, and a multitude of black people of every description chained together, every one of their countenances expressing dejection and sorrow, I no longer doubted of my fate; and, quite overpowered with horror and anguish, I fell motionless on the deck and fainted. When I recovered a little I found some black people about me, who I believed were some of those who brought me on board, and had been receiving their pay[1]; they talked to me in order to cheer me, but all in vain. I asked them if we were not to be eaten by those white men with horrible looks, red faces, and loose hair. They told me I was not; and one of the crew brought me a small portion of spirituous liquor in a wine glass; but, being afraid of him, I would not take it out of his hand. One of the blacks therefore took it from him and gave it to me, and I took a little down my palate, which, instead of reviving me, as they thought it would, threw me into the greatest consternation at the strange feeling it produced, having never tasted any such liquor before.

Soon after this the blacks who brought me on board went off, and left me abandoned to despair. I now saw myself deprived of all chance of returning to my native country, or even the least glimpse of hope of gaining the shore, which I now considered as friendly; and I even wished for my former slavery in preference to my present situation, which was filled with horrors of every kind, still heightened by my ignorance of what I was to undergo. I was not long suffered to indulge my grief; I was soon put down under the decks, and there I received such a salutation in my nostrils as I had never experienced in my life: so that, with the loathsomeness of the stench, and crying together, I became so sick and low that I was not able to eat, nor had I the least desire to taste any thing. I now wished for the last friend, death, to relieve me; but soon, to my grief, two of the white men offered me eatables; and, on my refusing to eat, one of them held me fast by the hands, and laid me across I think the windlass,[2] and tied my feet, while the other flogged me severely. I had never experienced any thing of this kind before; and although, not being used to the water, I naturally feared that element the first time I saw it, yet nevertheless, could I have got over the nettings, I would have jumped over the side, but I could not; and, besides, the crew used to watch us very closely who were not chained down to the decks, lest we should leap into the water: and I have seen some of these poor African prisoners most severely cut for attempting to do so, and hourly whipped for not eating. This indeed was often the case with myself.

In a little time after, amongst the poor chained men, I found some of my own nation, which in a small degree gave ease to my mind. I inquired of these what was to be done with us; they gave me to understand we were to be carried to these white people's country to work for them. I then was a little revived, and thought, if it were no worse than working, my situation was not so desperate: but still I feared I should be put to death, the white people looked and acted, as I thought, in so savage a manner; for I had never seen among any people such instances of brutal cruelty; and this not only shown towards us blacks, but also to some of the whites themselves. One white man in particular I saw, when we were permitted to be on deck, flogged so unmercifully with a large rope near the foremast, that he died in consequence of it; and they tossed him over the side as they would have done a brute. This made me fear these people the more; and I expected nothing less than to be treated in the same manner.

I could not help expressing my fears and apprehensions to some of my countrymen: I asked them if these people had no country, but lived in this hollow place (the ship): they told me they did not, but came from a distant one. "Then," said I, "how comes it in all our country we never heard of them?" They told me because they lived so very far off. I then asked where were their women? Had they any like themselves? I was told they had: "and why," said I, "do we not see them?" They answered, because they were left behind. I asked how the vessel could go? They told me they could not tell; but that there were cloths put upon the masts by the help of the ropes I saw, and then the vessel went on; and the white men had some spell or magic they put in the water when they liked in order to stop the vessel. I was exceedingly amazed at this account, and really thought they were spirits. I therefore wished much to be from amongst them, for I expected they would sacrifice me: but my wishes were vain; for we were so quartered that it was impossible for any of us to make our escape.

From Olaudah Equiano, *The Interesting Narrative of the Life of Olaudah Equiano, or Gustavus Vassa, the African, Written by Himself* (London, 1789), 1: 70–77. One historian has suggested that Equiano was actually born in South Carolina and compiled his record of Africa and the middle passage from what other slaves told him. Whether first- or secondhand, the account is based on information from West Africans.

Discussion Questions

1. What was Equiano's first impression of these alien people?
2. How did he interpret their actions?
3. Does Equiano's book seem like an effective abolitionist tool?
4. Compare this account with the other accounts of first encounters you have read. How did circumstances affect interpretations of new peoples?

Notes

1. They had delivered Equiano to the slave ship.
2. The mechanism that raised the anchor. Equiano later became an accomplished sailor.

Pontiac's Speech to an Ottawa, Potawatomi, and Huron Audience, 1763

DESPITE EXTENSIVE INDIAN INVOLVEMENT IN THE SEVEN YEARS' WAR, which you can read about in Washington's and Bougainville's accounts, no Indians were invited to participate in the Treaty of Paris of 1763. Sources of trade dwindled, and British colonists poured into the Ohio Valley. In 1763, Pontiac, an Ottawa war leader, began spreading the message of the Delaware (Loup) prophet, Neolin, who advocated a new interpretation of Indian-European relations. We receive this account through multiple interpretations: that of Neolin (presumably in his native Delaware language), the language Pontiac used that day (perhaps Ottawa), French (probably written down by the French Canadian soldier and notary Robert Navarre), and now in English.

An Indian [Neolin] of the Loup[1] Nation wanted to meet the Master of Life, which is the name all the Indians call God. He decided, without telling anyone in his nation or village, to go on a journey to Paradise, where he knew the Great Master lived. But since he didn't know the way to get there and knew no one who had been there and could show him the road, he tried magic, hoping to pull forth good omens from his dreams.

All Indians, as a general rule, put great faith in their dreams, and it is very hard to free them from this superstition, as this story proves. In his dream, the Loup Indian imagined that all he had to do was start out, and after many, many steps, he would arrive at the heavenly dwelling place, so very early the next day he did start. He dressed and equipped himself for hunting, not forgetting to take his weapons and a large cooking pot.

And thus he set out on his journey to Heaven to see the Master of Life.

The first seven days went well according to his plans. He walked with good courage, always firm in the confidence that he could reach his goal. Eight days went by without anyone appearing to block his way. On the evening of the eighth day, as the sun was setting where it always sets, he stopped at an opening into a little meadow where he saw a good place to spend the night along the bank of a creek. As he was setting up camp, he noticed at the other end of the meadow three paths, all very wide and well trodden down, and this seemed strange to him. Nevertheless, he kept working, setting up shelter and starting a fire. As he cooked his supper, he realized that the farther the sun went down and the darker the day grew, the lighter the three paths became. This surprised him, and frightened him, too.

He hesitated, considering what to do—stay where he was or get away from there and camp somewhere else. But as he reflected, he remembered his magic, or rather, his dream, and that the only reason he had started out on this journey was to see the Master of Life, and this thought led him to feel and believe that one of the three paths was the one he had to take to get where he wanted to go.

[Neolin tries two of the paths but comes upon huge fires on both.]

So he had to go back and take the third path. He walked on it for a whole day without seeing a thing to hold him back, when all of a sudden there appeared before him an astonishingly white mountain, which amazed him and brought him to a halt. Nevertheless, he firmed his resolve and kept going, determined to see what this mountain could be.

When he reached the foot of the mountain, the path gave out, and it grieved him not to be able to keep going. As he stood there, he looked around and saw a woman of the mountain. She was dazzlingly beautiful, and her clothes were so white the whiteness of the snow seemed dull next to them.

She was sitting down, and she spoke to him in his own language: "You seem surprised not to find the path to where you want to go. I know that for a long time you have wanted to see and speak with the Master of Life. That is why you set out on this journey: to see him. The path to his home is on this mountain, and to climb the mountain, you must abandon everything you have, take off all your clothes, and leave everything at the foot of the mountain. No one will stop you. Go wash in the river over there, and afterwards you will climb."

Step by step, the Loup Indian obeyed the words of the woman. But there remained one difficulty: how to get to the top of the mountain, which rose straight up, without a path, as sheer as ice. He asked her what he should do to get to the top, and she answered that if he really wanted to see the Master of Life, he had to climb, and with no more help than his hand and his left foot.

This seemed impossible to the Loup, but with the woman's encouragement, he began to climb, and with great difficulties, he did succeed. When he got to the top he was surprised not to see anybody anymore. The woman had disappeared. He found himself without a guide, facing three villages that stood in front of him. He did not recognize them, and they seemed differently constructed from his own, more beautiful and better ordered.

After meditating for a while on what he ought to do next, he started out toward the village that seemed most promising to him.

When he reached halfway from the edge of the mountaintop, he remembered that he was naked and was afraid to go on, but a voice he recognized told him to keep walking and that he should not be afraid because he had washed and now that he had washed he could walk in confidence.

He had no more difficulty and walked all the way to what he thought must be the village gate. He stopped and waited for it to open so that he could enter. As he was gazing at the lovely outside of the village, the door opened. He saw a handsome man all dressed in white coming toward him. The man took him by the hand and said that he was going to grant his wish to speak to the Master of Life. The Loup allowed himself to be led, and they came together to a place of unequaled beauty, which the Indian could not cease to wonder at. There he saw the Master of Life, who took him by the hand, gave him a hat embroidered all over with gold, and bade him sit down on it. The Loup hesitated for fear of spoiling the hat, but he was ordered to sit, and he obeyed without a word.

When the Loup was seated, God said to him, "I am the Master of Life, and I know what you want to learn and whom you wish to speak with. Listen well to what I am about to say to you, for your own sake and for all the Indians. I am the one who made Heaven and Earth, the trees, the lakes, the rivers, and all people and everything you see and everything you have seen on Earth. Because I made all this and because I love you all, you must do what I say and what I love and not do what I hate. I do not at all love for you to drink yourselves senseless the way you do. When you fight among yourselves, you do not do right, and I hate it. You take two wives or chase after the wives of other men, and that is not right. I hate it. You should have only one wife and keep her until death. When you want to go to war you juggle and sing magical incantations, thinking you speak to me. You don't. You speak to Manietout,[2] an evil spirit who breathes nothing but evil into you and whom you listen to because you don't know me well.

"The land where you live—I made it for you and not for other people. Why do you put up with the Whites[3] on your lands? Is it because you can't get along without them? I know that the people you call the Children of your Great Father[4] supply your needs, but if you were not evil, as you are, you would do without them and you could live just as you lived before you met them. Before the people you call your Brothers came to your lands, didn't you live by the bow and arrow? You didn't need guns or powder or those other things. Nevertheless, you caught animals to eat and dressed in their skins, but when I saw you giving your-selves to evil, I withdrew the animals into the depths of the forests so that you would need your Brothers to supply your needs and clothe yourselves. All you have to do is become good and do what I want and I will send the animals back for you to live on.

"I do not forbid you to allow the Children of your Father[5] among you. I love them. They know me and pray to me, and I give them their needs and every-thing they bring with them. But as for those who have come to trouble your lands: drive them out, make war on them. I do not love them. They do not know me and are my enemies and the enemies of your Brothers. Send them back to the lands I made for them, and let them stay there.

"Here is a prayer which I give to you in writing to learn by heart and teach to the Indians and to the children." The Loup answered that he did not know how to read. The Master of Life answered that when he went back to the Earth all he had to do was give the writing to the village chief, who would read it and teach it by heart to him and all the Indians and that they must recite it evening and morning without fail. "You must tell all the Indians, drink no more than a cup of wine a day or at most two cups. Have no more than one wife. Do not chase after other men's wives or after the unmarried women. Do not fight among yourselves. Do not practice magic, but prayer, because when you prac-ticed magic you conversed with the Evil Spirit. Drive from your lands those Redcoat dogs who will do you nothing but harm. When you need something, address your prayers to me, and I will give to you as I give to your Brothers. Do not sell to your Brothers what I have placed on Earth for food. In short, be good, and you will receive free all that you need. When you meet one another, give greetings, and give your left hand, because it is the heart's hand. Above all things, Loup Indian, I command you to pray every day, morning and night, the prayer that I give you."

The Loup promised to do what the Master of Life told him and to speak for him to the other Indians, and that in the future the Master of Life would be happy with them.

Then the same man who had brought him by the hand came to take him again and guide him back to the foot of the mountain, where he told him to take up his belongings again and go back to his village. This the Loup Indian did, and when he arrived, he astonished the people of his nation and his vil-lage, because they had not known what had become of him, and they asked him where he had been. Since he had been ordered not to speak to anyone until he spoke to the village chief, he simply made signs to them with his hands that he had been on high. As soon as he entered the village, he went straight to the chief's house and gave him the prayer and the law that the Mas-ter of Life had given him.

This adventure was soon known throughout the village, and people came to hear the words of the Master of Life and carried it to the next village, and those people came to see the famous traveler and spread the news from village to village until it reached Pontiac, who believed it just as we believe an article of faith; and he instilled it into the minds of his Council, who listened to it as to an oracle and told him that he only had to say the word, and all of them were ready to do what he demanded.

Translated by John DuVal from Robert Navarre[?], "Journal ou dictation d'une conspiration, faite par les sauvages contre les Anglais, et du siège du fort de Detroix par quatre nations différentes le 7 mai, 1763, " in *Journal of Pontiac's Conspiracy*, ed. M. Agnes Burton (Detroit, 1912), 23–33.

Discussion Questions

1. Pontiac "demanded" that Indians of different nations form a pan-Indian confederacy to fight the British, which many in the Ohio Valley did (eventually persuading the British to issue the Proclamation of 1763, which forbade most British settlement west of the Appalachians). What in Pontiac's tale of Neolin's journey might persuade Indians to join the confederacy?

2. Compare what the Master of Life said here about the whites with what the oldest of the Natchez elders said about the French in Simon Antoine Le Page Du Pratz's account of the Natchez, later in this volume.

3. At what points in the narrative does the voice of the French author seem to intrude on the voice of Pontiac as the French author narrates what Pontiac said?

4. At what point in the narrative does the voice of Pontiac, the war leader, seem to intrude on the voice of Neolin, the Loup prophet?

Notes

1. The Loup, or Wolf, Indians were the Delawares or Lenni Lenape.

2. Manitou was the name for spirits in Algonquian cultures.

3. The French term is *les Blancs*. Early Spanish and French documents rarely used terms of color to differentiate between Europeans and Native Americans. Native Americans did sometimes use "red" for themselves and "white" for the English or for all Europeans.

4. The Children of their Great Father were their "brothers," the French.

5. The French. It is unclear whether Neolin himself advocated exempting the French, but Pontiac knew they would be important for supplying a war against the British.

III

FOUNDING AND GOVERNING

O NE OF THE REMARKABLE CHARACTERISTICS OF THE COLONIAL ERA was the un-precedented number of new societies that people founded. In this sec-tion, you can compare how different people went about designing their ideal societies. Try to infer what they valued most in a society and what those val-ues tell us about the people designing the society. Of course, model societies rarely turned out as their planners intended.

La Relation de Samuel de Champlain

Excerpt

*S*ELON LA DIVERSITÉ DES HUMEURS LES INCLINATIONS SONT DIFFÉRENTES: *& cha-cun en sa vocation a une fin particulière. Les uns tirent au profit, les autres à la Gloire, & aucuns au bien public. Le plus grand est au commerce, & princi-palement celui qui se fait sur la mer. De là vient le grand soulagement du peuple, l'opulence & l'ornement des Républiques. C'est ce qui a eslevé l'ancienne Rome à la Seigneurie & domination de tout le monde. Les Vénitiens à une grandeur es-gale à celle des puissants Rois. De tout temps il a fait foisonner en richesses les villes maritimes, dont Alexandrie & Thir sont si célèbres : & une infinité d'autres, lesquelles remplissent le profond des terres après que les nations étrangères leur ont envoyé ce qu'elles ont de beau & de singulier. C'est pourquoy plusieurs Princes se sont efforcés de trouver par le Nort, le chemin de la Chine, afin de faciliter le commerce avec les Orientaux, esperans que ceste route seroit plus briefve & moins périlleuse.**

---

*From Samuel de Champlain, *Les Voyages du sieur de Champlain de Saintongeois, capitaine ordinaire pour le Roi, en la marine* (Paris, 1613), 1–6. Translation begins on p. 94.

Great Law of the Iroquois League, c. 1300s (recorded late 1800s)

A ROUND THE FOURTEENTH CENTURY, IN WHAT IS NOW NEW YORK, *Pennsylvania, and southeastern Canada, five Iroquoian nations—the Cayugas, Mohawks, Oneidas, Onondagas, and Senecas—were suffering from constant warfare. One day a spirit or prophet named Dekanawidah (the Peacemaker) came to the five nations with a plan for a Great Peace, in which they would form a confederacy. The nations agreed and became the "People of the Longhouse," comparing their confederacy to an Iroquois longhouse, in which many people lived together peacefully. Over the centuries, the Iroquois passed down (and amended) the Great Law of the Iroquois League through oral tradition and wampum bead belts and strings. In the late 1800s, a Mohawk man named Seth Newhouse wrote down this version, with assistance from Albert Cusick, an Onondaga-Tuscarora.*

1. I am Dekanawidah and with the Five Nations' Confederate Lords I plant the Tree of the Great Peace. I plant it in your territory, Adodarhoh,[1] and the Onondaga Nation, in the territory of you who are Fire Keepers . . . and all the affairs of the Five Nations shall be transacted at this place before you, Adodarhoh, and your cousin Lords, by the Confederate Lords. . . .

6. I, Dekanawidah, appoint the Mohawk Lords the heads and the leaders of the Five Nations Confederacy. The Mohawk Lords are the foundation of the Great Peace and it shall, therefore, be against the Great Binding Law to pass measures in the Confederate Council after the Mohawk Lords have protested against them. . . .

7. Whenever the Confederate Lords shall assemble for the purpose of holding a council, the Onondaga Lords shall open it by expressing their gratitude

to their cousin Lords and greeting them, and they shall make an address and offer thanks to the earth where men dwell, to the streams of water, the pools, the springs and the lakes, to the corn and the fruits, to the medicinal herbs and trees, to the forest trees for their usefulness, to the animals that serve as food and give their pelts for clothing, to the great winds and the lesser winds, to the thunderers, to the sun, the mighty warrior, to the moon, to the messengers of the Creator who reveal his wishes and to the Great Creator who dwells in the heavens above, who gives all the things useful to men, and who is the source and the rule of health and life. . . .

9. All the business of the Five Nations Confederate Council shall be conducted by the two combined bodies of Confederate Lords. First the question shall be passed upon by the Mohawk and Seneca Lords, then it shall be discussed and passed by the Oneida and Cayuga Lords. Their decisions shall then be referred to the Onondaga Lords (Fire Keepers) for final judgment.[2] . . .

11. If through any misunderstanding or obstinacy on the part of the Fire Keepers, they render a decision at variance with that of the Two Sides, the Two Sides shall reconsider the matter and if their decisions are jointly the same as before they shall report to the Fire Keepers who are then compelled to confirm their joint decision. . . .

14. When the Council of the Five Nation Lords shall convene they shall appoint a speaker for the day. He shall be a Lord of either the Mohawk, Onondaga or Seneca Nation. The next day the Council shall appoint another speaker, but the first speaker may be reappointed if there is no objection, but a speaker's term shall not be regarded more than for the day.

15. No individual or foreign nation interested in a case, question or proposition shall have any voice in the Confederate Council except to answer a question put to him or them by the speaker for the Lords.

16. If the conditions which shall arise at any future time call for an addition to or change of this law, the case shall be carefully considered and if a new beam seems necessary or beneficial, the proposed change shall be voted upon and if adopted it shall be called, "Added to the Rafters."[3]

17. A bunch of a certain number of shell (wampum) strings each two spans in length shall be given to each of the female families[4] in which the Lordship titles are vested. The right of bestowing the title shall be hereditary in the family of women legally possessing the bunch of shell strings and the strings shall be the token that the women of the family have the proprietary right to the Lordship title for all time to come, subject to certain restrictions hereinafter mentioned. . . .

19. If at any time it shall be manifest that a Confederate Lord has not in mind the welfare of the people or disobeys the rules of this Great Law, the men or women of the Confederacy, or both jointly, shall come to the Council and

upbraid the erring Lord through his War Chief. If the complaint of the people through the War Chief is not heeded the first time it shall be uttered again and then if no attention is given a third complaint and warning shall be given. If the Lord is contumacious the matter shall go to the council of War Chiefs. The War Chiefs shall then divest the erring Lord of his title by order of the women in whom the titleship is vested. When the Lord is deposed the women shall notify the Confederate Lords through their War Chief, and the Confederate Lords shall sanction the act. The women will then select another of their sons as a candidate and the Lords shall elect him. . . .

20. If a Lord of the Confederacy of the Five Nations should commit murder the other Lords of the Nation shall assemble at the place where the corpse lies and prepare to depose the criminal Lord. If it is impossible to meet at the scene of the crime the Lords shall discuss the matter at the next Council of their nation and request their War Chief to depose the Lord guilty of crime, to "bury" his women relatives[5] and to transfer the Lordship title to a sister family. . . .

24. The Lords of the Confederacy of the Five Nations shall be mentors of the people for all time. The thickness of their skin shall be seven spans—which is to say that they shall be proof against anger, offensive actions and criticism. Their hearts shall be full of peace and good will and their minds filled with a yearning for the welfare of the people of the Confederacy. With endless patience they shall carry out their duty and their firmness shall be tempered with a tenderness for their people. Neither anger nor fury shall find lodgment in their minds and all their words and actions shall be marked by calm deliberation. . . .

26. It shall be the duty of all of the Five Nations Confederate Lords, from time to time as occasion demands, to act as mentors and spiritual guides of their people and remind them of their Creator's will and words. They shall say:

> "Hearken, that peace may continue unto future days! Always listen to the words of the Great Creator, for he has spoken. United people, let not evil find lodging in your minds, for the Great Creator has spoken and the cause of Peace shall not become old." . . .

37. There shall be one War Chief for each Nation and their duties shall be to carry messages for their Lords and to take up the arms of war in case of emergency. They shall not participate in the proceedings of the Confederate Council but shall watch its progress and in case of an erroneous action by a Lord they shall receive the complaints of the people and convey the warnings of the women to him. . . .

42. Among the Five Nations and their posterity there shall be the following original clans: Great Name Bearer, Ancient Name Bearer, Great Bear, Ancient Bear, Turtle, Painted Turtle, Standing Rock, Large Plover,[6] Little Plover, Deer, Pigeon Hawk, Eel, Ball, Opposite-Side-of-the-Hand, and Wild Potatoes. These clans distributed through their respective Nations, shall be the sole owners and holders of the soil of the country and in them is it vested as a birthright.

43. People of the Five Nations members of a certain clan shall recognize every other member of that clan, irrespective of the Nation, as relatives. Men and women, therefore, members of the same clan are forbidden to marry.

44. The lineal descent of the people of the Five Nations shall run in the female line. Women shall be considered the progenitors of the Nation. They shall own the land and the soil. Men and women shall follow the status of the mother. . . .

50. The Royal women of the Confederacy heirs of the Lordship titles shall elect two women of their family as cooks for the Lord when the people shall assemble at his house for business or other purposes. It is not good nor honorable for a Confederate Lord to allow his people whom he has called to go hungry.

51. When a Lord holds a conference in his home, his wife, if she wishes, may prepare the food for the Union Lords who assemble with him. This is an honorable right which she may exercise as an expression of her esteem.

52. The Royal women, heirs of the Lordship titles, shall, should it be necessary, correct and admonish the holders of their titles. Those only who attend the Council may do this and those who do not shall not object to what has been said nor strive to undo the action. . . .

55. Every five years the Five Nations Confederate Lords and the people shall assemble together and shall ask one another if their minds are still in the same spirit of unity for the Great Binding Law and if any of the Five Nations shall not pledge continuance and steadfastness to the pledge of unity then the Great Binding Law shall dissolve. . . .

57. The Lords of the Confederacy shall eat together from one bowl the feast of cooked beaver's tail. While they are eating they are to use no sharp utensils for if they should they might accidentally cut one another and bloodshed would follow. All measures must be taken to prevent the spilling of blood in any way. . . .

59. A bunch of wampum shells on strings, three spans of the hand in length, the upper half of the bunch being white and the lower half black, and formed from equal contributions of the men of the Five Nations, shall be a token that the men have combined themselves into one head, one body and one thought, and it shall also symbolize their ratification of the peace pact of the Confederacy, whereby the Lords of the Five Nations have established the Great Peace.

The white portion of the shell strings represent the women and the black portion the men. The black portion, furthermore, is a token of power and authority vested in the men of the Five Nations.

This string of wampum vests the people with the right to correct their erring Lords. In case a part or all of the Lords pursue a course not vouched for by the people and heed not the third warning of their women relatives, then the matter shall be taken to the General Council of the women of the Five Nations. If the Lords notified and warned three times fail to heed, then the case falls into the hands of the men of the Five Nations. The War Chiefs shall then, by right of such power and authority, enter the open council to warn the Lord or Lords to return from their wrong course. If the Lords heed the warning they shall say, "we will reply tomorrow." If then an answer is returned in favor of justice and in accord with this Great Law, then the Lords shall individually pledge themselves again by again furnishing the necessary shells for the pledge. Then shall the War Chief or Chiefs exhort the Lords urging them to be just and true.

Should it happen that the Lords refuse to heed the third warning, then two courses are open: either the men may decide in their council to depose the Lord or Lords or to club them to death with war clubs. . . . Should the men in their council adopt the second course, the War Chief shall order his men to enter the council, to take positions beside the Lords, sitting between them wherever possible. When this is accomplished the War Chief holding in his outstretched hand a bunch of black wampum strings shall say to the erring Lords: "So now, Lords of the Five United Nations, harken to these last words from your men. You have not heeded the warnings of the women relatives, you have not heeded the warnings of the General Council of women and you have not heeded the warnings of the men of the nations, all urging you to return to the right course of action. Since you are determined to resist and to withhold justice from your people there is only one course for us to adopt." At this point the War Chief shall let drop the bunch of black wampum and the men shall spring to their feet and club the erring Lords to death. Any erring Lord may submit before the War Chief lets fall the black wampum. Then his execution is withheld. . . .

63. Should two sons of opposite sides of the Council Fire agree in a desire to hear the reciting of the laws of the Great Peace and so refresh their memories in the way ordained by the founder of the Confederacy, they shall notify Adodarhoh. He then shall consult with five of his coactive Lords and they in turn shall consult their eight brethren. Then should they decide to accede to the request of the two sons from opposite sides of the Council Fire, Adodarhoh shall send messengers to notify the Chief Lords of each of the Five Nations. . . . When all have come and have assembled, Adodarhoh, in conjunction with his cousin Lords, shall appoint one Lord who shall repeat the laws of the Great Peace. . . .

65. I, Dekanawidah, and the Union Lords, now uproot the tallest pine tree and into the cavity thereby made we cast all weapons of war. Into the depths of the earth, down into the deep underearth currents of water flowing to unknown regions we cast all the weapons of strife. We bury them from sight and we plant again the tree. Thus shall the Great Peace be established and hostilities shall no longer be known between the Five Nations but peace to the United People. . . .

73. The soil of the earth from one end of the land to the other is the property of the people who inhabit it. By birthright the Oñgwehonweh[7] are the owners of the soil which they own and occupy and none other may hold it. The same law has been held from the oldest times. The Great Creator has made us of the one blood and of the same soil he made us and as only different tongues constitute different nations he established different hunting grounds and territories and made boundary lines between them. . . .

80. When the Confederate Council of the Five Nations has for its object the establishment of the Great Peace among the people of an outside nation and that nation refuses to accept the Great Peace, then by such refusal they bring a declaration of war upon themselves from the Five Nations. Then shall the Five Nations seek to establish the Great Peace by a conquest of the rebellious nation. . . .

83. When peace shall have been established by the termination of the war against a foreign nation, then the War Chief shall cause all the weapons of war to be taken from the nation. Then shall the Great Peace be established and that nation shall observe all the rules of the Great Peace for all time to come.

84. Whenever a foreign nation is conquered or has by their own will accepted the Great Peace their own system of internal government may continue, but they must cease all warfare against other nations. . . .

86. Whenever a foreign nation is conquered and the survivors are brought into the territory of the Five Nations' Confederacy and placed under the Great Peace the two shall be known as the Conqueror and the Conquered. . . . The conquered nation shall have no voice in the councils of the Confederacy in the body of the Lords. . . .

92. If a nation, part of a nation, or more than one nation within the Five Nations should in any way endeavor to destroy the Great Peace by neglect or violating its laws and resolve to dissolve the Confederacy, such a nation or such nations shall be deemed guilty of treason and called enemies of the Confederacy and the Great Peace. It shall then be the duty of the lords of the Confederacy who remain faithful to resolve to warn the offending people. They shall be warned once and if a second warning is necessary they shall be driven from the territory of the Confederacy by the War Chiefs and his men.

93. Whenever a specially important matter or a great emergency is presented before the Confederate Council and the nature of the matter affects the entire body of the Five Nations, threatening their utter ruin, then the Lords of the Confederacy must submit the matter to the decision of their people and the decision of the people shall affect the decision of the Confederate Council. . . .

99. The rites and festivals of each nation shall remain undisturbed and shall continue as before because they were given by the people of old times as useful and necessary for the good of men.

From Arthur C. Parker, "The Constitution of the Five Nations," *New York State Museum Bulletin* 184 (1916): 30–60.

Discussion Questions

1. According to the Iroquois framers, what makes a good confederacy? What safeguards did they put in place? What do those safeguards tell you about their worries?

2. How did the Iroquois divide power by gender?

3. What attitude did the confederacy members have toward other nations? Does Section 80 remind you of the Requerimiento?

4. What parts of the Great Law might have changed or been added in the five hundred years between when it was first made and when this version was written down?

Notes

1. When Dekanawidah proposed the plan to the chiefs, all agreed except for an Onondaga chief named Adodarhoh. To win over Adodarhoh, the others offered him a position of particular importance in the confederacy.

2. The Mohawks and Senecas were the "older brothers," while the Oneidas and Cayugas were the "younger brothers."

3. The references to beams and rafters reflect the metaphor of the confederacy as a longhouse.

4. Iroquois families were matrilineal. There were forty-eight (later fifty) royal (*royaneh*) families, each of which chose a male leader as its civil chief and member of the Confederate Council.

5. To end the rights of that family.

6. A water bird.

7. The Iroquois Confederacy members were the Oñgwehonweh, the "original people."

Samuel de Champlain on Founding Quebec, 1608

*I*N THE EARLY 1500S, FRENCH SHIPS MADE MANY TRIPS TO EXPLORE, *fish, and trade off the coast of Newfoundland. As business increased, King Henry IV decided that there should be a permanent French colony there. French navigator Samuel de Champlain here describes the events that led to his founding of Quebec City on the banks of the St. Lawrence, the river that Jacques Cartier had discovered on his second voyage in 1535. Based on the fur trade with neighboring Micmac, Montagnais, Abenaki, and eventually Huron Indians, Quebec became the first permanent French town in North America and the capital of New France.*

Inclinations differ according to the diversity of humors,[1] and in the choice of a vocation each individual has his own particular purpose. Some are drawn to profit, others to glory, and some to public service; most to commerce, and mainly commerce at sea, from which come many comforts for people and opulence and adornment for states. This is what raised ancient Rome to lordship and dominion over all the world and lifted the people of Venice to a grandeur equal to that of powerful kings. From all time it has heaped seaport cities such as famous Alexandria and Tyre[2] and countless others with wealth which they in turn spread throughout the earth after foreign nations have sent them what they have of strange and beautiful treasures. This is why many princes have tried to find the northern passage to China: in order to facilitate commerce with people of the East and in the hopes that this route would be shorter and less dangerous.

[After enumerating the unsuccessful attempts by explorers of various nations to find the elusive Northwest Passage, Champlain continues.]

Despite all these vicissitudes and incertitudes, Lord de Monts[3] wanted to try something unhoped for, and he requested a commission from His Majesty. Realizing that what had ruined previous enterprises was lack of funding for the entrepreneurs, who in one year, or in two, could not get acquainted with the lands and the peoples who live there or find seaports suitable to live in, he proposed to His Majesty a method for financing the attempt without drawing on Royal funds. This would be that he be granted, to the exclusion of all others, the territory's skin and fur trade. This was granted, and he went to great, excessive personal expense. He took with him a great number of men of varying conditions, and there he had lodgings built for his people.[4]

These expenses continued for three straight years. Afterwards, moved by the envy and importunity of certain Basque and Breton merchants, the Council revoked his license, with considerable loss for Monsieur de Monts, who saw his work all come to nothing and had to abandon everything, including all the implements with which he had furnished his settlement.[5]

However, he had submitted a report to the King concerning the fertility of the land; and I submitted one on the methods for finding a passage to China without the encumbrances of Northern glaciers or the oppressions of the torrid zone through which our sailors sail twice going to and twice coming from China with immense difficulty and incredible danger. His Majesty therefore commanded Monsieur de Monts to outfit a new expedition and to send men again to continue what he had begun.

This he did. And this time, because of the uncertainty of his commission, he chose a different place,[6] to avoid giving umbrage once again to the envious. He was also motivated by the hope of finding more advantages inland, where people are more civilized and it is easier to plant the Christian faith and establish the kind of order necessary for preserving a country than along the seacoasts, where savages usually live. Also, he wanted to assure inestimable profit for the King there, and it is to be believed that the nations of Europe will want to deal with people of civilized manners rather than with the fierce and envious humors of people living along the coasts or in barbarous countries.

Translated by John DuVal from Samuel de Champlain, *Les Voyages du sieur de Champlain de Saintongeois, capitaine ordinaire pour le Roi, en la marine* (Paris, 1613), 1–6.

Discussion Questions

1. What did Champlain see as the motives for having a colony?
2. According to Champlain, what choices were more likely to make a colony successful?

3. What kind of relationship did he want New France to have with the native peoples of the region?

4. What kinds of native people did Champlain want to do business with? What do his remarks reveal about his beliefs regarding Indians?

Notes

1. Champlain stamps his narrative with scientific authority by referring to the four so-called *humors* of the human body—blood, phlegm, black bile, and yellow bile—to which scholars since ancient times had ascribed varying human personality traits.

2. Alexandria and Tyre are both great ancient cities on the Mediterranean. Tyre (in present-day Lebanon) was founded at least three thousand years ago by the Phoenicians and is noted for its resistance to invasions by Nebuchadnezzar and Alexander the Great. Alexandria (in present-day Egypt) was named for Alexander the Great and was founded more than two thousand years ago.

3. Pierre de Gua, Lord de Monts, to whom King Henry IV gave the charter and fur trade monopoly for New France in 1598.

4. This first colony was in Acadia (Nova Scotia).

5. The competing merchants had successfully persuaded the king to revoke Lord de Monts's monopoly and reopen the fur trade.

6. This new choice was on the St. Lawrence River.

John Winthrop on Founding New England, 1630

*A*LTHOUGH THIS DOCUMENT WAS NOT SIGNED OR DATED, *historians assume that Puritan leader John Winthrop wrote it during his 1630 voyage to New England on the* Arabella *or perhaps just before leaving England. Because he was on his way to serve as governor of the Massachusetts Bay Colony, he was particularly concerned about his colony's purpose. Most of the European accounts you have read so far have been from Catholics. Like John Eliot, Winthrop was a Protestant who believed in the importance of individual access to the Bible.*

Christian Charity: A Model Hereof

We are a company professing ourselves fellow members of Christ. . . . For the work we have in hand, it is by a mutual consent through a special overruling providence, and a more than ordinary approbation of the churches of Christ to seek out a place of cohabitation and consortship under a due form of government both civil and ecclesiastical. . . .

The end is to improve our lives, to do more service to the Lord, the comfort and increase of the body of Christ whereof we are members, that ourselves and posterity may be the better preserved from the common corruptions of this evil world to serve the Lord and work out our salvation under the power and purity of his holy ordinances.

For the means whereby this must be effected, . . . we must not content ourselves with usual ordinary means; whatsoever we did or ought to have done when we lived in England, the same must we do and more also where we go.

That which the most in their churches maintain as a truth in profession only, we must bring into familiar and constant practice, as in this duty of love, we must love brotherly without dissimulation, we must love one another with a pure heart fervently, we must bear one another's burdens,[1] we must not look only on our own things, but also on the things of our brethren, neither must we think that the lord will bear with such failings at our hands as he doth from those among whom we have lived, and that for 3 reasons:

1. In regard of the more near bond of marriage, between him and us, wherein he hath taken us to be his after a most strict and peculiar manner which will make him the more jealous of our love and obedience so he tells the people of Israel, you only have I known of all the families of the Earth therefore will I punish you for your transgressions.[2]
2. Because the lord will be sanctified in them that come near him. We know that there were many that corrupted the service of the Lord, some setting up altars before his own, others offering both strange fire and strange sacrifices also; yet there came no fire from heaven, or other sudden judgment upon them as did upon Nadab and Abihu who yet we may think did not sin presumptuously.[3]
3. When God gives a special commission he looks to have it strictly observed in every article. When he gave Saul a commission to destroy Amaleck he indented with him upon certain articles, and because he failed in one of the least, and that upon a fair pretence, it lost him the kingdom, which should have been his reward, if he had observed his commission.[4] Thus stands the cause between God and us: we are entered into covenant with him for this work, we have taken out a commission, the Lord hath given us leave to draw our own articles. . . . Now if the Lord shall please to hear us, and bring us in peace to the place we desire, then hath he ratified this covenant and sealed our commission [and] will expect a strict performance of the articles contained in it, but if we shall neglect the observation of these articles which are the ends we have propounded, and dissembling with our God, shall fall to embrace this present world and prosecute our carnal intentions, seeking great things for ourselves and our posterity, the Lord will surely break out in wrath against us, be revenged of such a perjured people, and make us know the price of the breach of such a covenant.

Now the only way to avoid this shipwreck and to provide for our posterity is to follow the counsel of Micah, to do justly, to love mercy, to walk humbly with our God,[5] for this end, we must be knit together in this work as one man, we must entertain each other in brotherly affection, we must be willing to abridge ourselves of our superfluities, for the supply of others' necessities, we must uphold a familiar commerce together in all meekness, gentleness, patience and liberality, we must delight in each other, make others' conditions our own, rejoice together, mourn together, labor, and suffer together, always having before our eyes our commission and community in the work, our community as members of the same body, so shall we keep the unity of the spirit in the bond of peace,[6] the Lord will be our God and delight to dwell among us, as his own people and will command a blessing upon us in all our ways, so that we shall see much more of his wisdom power goodness and truth than formerly we have been acquainted with. We shall find that the God of Israel is among us, when ten of us shall be able to resist a thousand of our enemies, when he shall make us a praise and glory, that men shall say of succeeding plantations: the lord make it like that of New England. For we must consider that we shall be as a City upon a Hill,[7] the eyes of all people are upon us, so that if we shall deal falsely with our God in this work we have undertaken and so cause him to withdraw his present help from us, we shall be made a story and a by-word through the world,[8] we shall open the mouths of enemies to speak evil of the ways of God and all professors for God's sake; we shall shame the faces of many of God's worthy servants, and cause their prayers to be turned into curses upon us till we be consumed out of the good land where we are going. . . . Beloved there is now set before us life and good, death and evil, in that we are commanded this day to love the Lord our God, and to love one another, to walk in his ways and to keep his commandments and his ordinance, and his laws, and the articles of our covenant with him that we may live and be multiplied, and that the Lord our God may bless us in the land whither we go to possess it. But if our hearts shall turn away so that we will not obey, but shall be seduced and worship other Gods, our pleasures, and profits, and serve them; it is propounded unto us this day, we shall surely perish out of the good Land whither we pass over this vast Sea to possess it.[9]

From John Winthrop, *Winthrop Papers* (Boston, 1931), 2: 282–95.

Discussion Questions

1. According to Winthrop, what were the reasons for founding New England?

2. How do these reasons compare to those from other accounts you have read?

3. Winthrop saw New Englanders as God's chosen people—what are the advantages and disadvantages of being a chosen people?

4. Do you think that believing they were God's chosen people helped or hurt the Puritans in their new home?

Notes

1. These phrases come from the Christian Bible: Romans 12:10, I Peter 1:22, and Galatians 6:2.

2. Amos 3:2.

3. Leviticus 10:1–2. Nadab and Abihu, sons of Aaron, offered unholy fire.

4. I Samuel 15:1–29. God had commanded Saul to destroy Amalek and spare none of its men, women, children, or animals. Saul killed all but the king and a few animals, but God punished him for not following his command exactly.

5. Micah 6:8.

6. Ephesians 4:3.

7. Matthew 5:14.

8. Deuteronomy 28:37. From here forward, Winthrop seems to be adopting the role of Moses in Deuteronomy, leading the chosen people.

9. Deuteronomy 30:15–18.

Laws for the Province
of Pennsylvania, 1682

---

*W*ILLIAM PENN WAS A WEALTHY ENGLISHMAN *who joined the Society of Friends (Quakers) as a young man, shocking his father and many of his friends. Wanting to found a colony in the Americas where Friends could worship freely, Penn obtained a grant from English king Charles II, who owed him money, to establish the proprietary colony of Pennsylvania with Penn as the first governor. In 1682, he and his advisers drew up the frame of government and the first laws for the new colony.*

Laws agreed upon in England by the Governor and Divers[1] of the Freemen of Pennsylvania, To be further Explained and Confirmed there by the first Provincial Council and General Assembly that shall be held in the said Province, if they see meet.[2]

1. That the Charter of Liberties declared, granted and confirmed the five and twentieth day of the second month called April, 1682, before divers witnesses by William Penn, Governor and Chief Proprietor of Pennsylvania, to all the freemen and planters of the said province, is hereby declared and approved, and shall be forever held for a fundamental in the government thereof, according to the limitations mentioned in the said charter.

2. That every inhabitant in the said province that is or shall be a purchaser of one hundred acres of land or upwards, his heirs and assigns; and every person who shall have paid his passage, and taken up one hundred acres of land at one penny an acre, and have cultivated ten acres thereof; and every person that hath been a servant or bondsman, and is free by his service, that shall have taken up his fifty acres of land,[3] and cultivated twenty thereof; and

every inhabitant, artificer or other, resident in the said province, that pays scot and lot[4] to the government, shall be deemed and accounted a *freeman* of the said province; and every such person shall and may be capable of electing or being elected representatives of the people in Provincial Council or General Assembly in the said province.

3. That all elections of members or representatives of the people and freemen of the province of Pennsylvania, to serve in Provincial Council or General Assembly, to be held within the said province, shall be free and voluntary: and that the elector that shall receive any reward or gift in meat, drink, money, or otherwise, shall forfeit his right to elect: and such person as shall directly or indirectly give, promise or bestow any such reward as aforesaid, to be elected, shall forfeit his election, and be thereby incapable to serve, as aforesaid. And the Provincial Council and General Assembly shall be the sole judges of the regularity or irregularity of the elections of their own respective members.

4. That no money or goods shall be raised upon, or paid by any of the people of this province, by way of a public tax, custom or contribution, but by a law for that purpose made: and whosoever shall levy, collect or pay any money or goods contrary thereunto, shall be held a public enemy to the province, and a betrayer of the liberty of the people thereof.

5. That all courts shall be open, and justice shall neither be sold, denied nor delayed.

6. That in courts all persons of all persuasions may freely appear in their own way, and according to their own manner, and there personally plead their own cause themselves, or if unable, by their friends. And the first process shall be the exhibition of the complaint in court fourteen days before the trial. . . .

7. That all pleadings, processes and records in courts shall be short, and in English, and in an ordinary and plain character, that they may be understood, and justice speedily administered.

8. That all trials shall be by twelve men, and as near as may be, peers or equals, and of the neighborhood, and men without just exception. . . .

9. That all fees[5] in all cases shall be moderate, and settled by the Provincial Council and General Assembly, and be hung up in a table in every respective court: and whosoever shall be convicted of taking more, shall pay twofold, and be dismissed his employment, one half of which shall go to the party wronged.

10. That all prisons shall be workhouses for felons, vagrants and loose and idle persons, whereof one shall be in every county.

11. That all prisoners shall be bailable by sufficient sureties, unless for capital offences, where the proof is evident, or the presumption great.

12. That all persons wrongfully imprisoned, or prosecuted at law, shall have double damages against the informer or prosecutor.

13. That all prisons shall be free, as to fees, food and lodging.

14. That all lands and goods shall be liable to pay debts, except where there be legal issue,[6] and then all the goods, and one third of the land only. . . .

16. That seven years quiet possession [of land] shall give an unquestionable right, except in cases of infants, lunatics, married women, or persons beyond the sea.

17. That all briberies and extortions whatsoever shall be severely punished. . . .

19. That all marriages (not forbidden by the law of God, as to nearness of blood and affinity by marriage) shall be encouraged; but the parents or guardians shall be first consulted, and the marriage shall be published before it be solemnized, & it shall be solemnized by taking one another as husband and wife before credible witnesses. . . .

27. And to the end that all officers chosen to serve within this province, may with more care and diligence answer the trust reposed in them, it is agreed, that no such person shall enjoy more than one public office at one time.

28. That all children within this province of the age of twelve years shall be taught some useful trade or skill, to the end none may be idle, but the poor may work to live, and the rich, if they become poor, may not want.

29. That [indentured] servants be not kept longer than their time; and such as are careful be both justly and kindly used in their service, and put in fitting equipage at the expiration thereof, according to custom.

30. That all scandalous and malicious reporters, backbiters, defamers and spreaders of false news, whether against magistrates or private persons, shall be accordingly severely punished, as enemies to the peace and concord of this province. . . .

34. That all treasurers, judges, masters of the rolls, sheriffs, justices of the peace, and other officers or persons whatsoever, relating to courts of trials of causes, or any other service in the government, and all members elected to serve in Provincial Council and General Assembly; and all that have right to elect such members, shall be such as profess faith in Jesus Christ, and that are not convicted of ill fame, or unsober and dishonest conversation, and that are of one and twenty years of age at least: and that all such so qualified, shall be capable of the said several employments and privileges, as aforesaid.

35. That all persons living in this province, who confess and acknowledge the One Almighty and Eternal God, to be the creator, upholder and ruler of the world, and that hold themselves obliged in conscience to live peaceably and justly in civil society, shall in no ways be molested or prejudiced for their religious persuasion or practice in matters of faith and worship, nor shall they be compelled at any time to frequent or maintain any religious worship, place or ministry whatever.

36. That according to the good example of the primitive Christians, and for the ease of the creation, every first day of the week called the Lord's Day, people shall abstain from their common daily labor, that they may the better dispose themselves to worship God according to their understandings.

37. That as a careless and corrupt administration of justice draws the wrath of God upon magistrates, so the wildness and looseness of the people provoke the indignation of God against a country; therefore: that all such offences against God, as swearing, cursing, lying, profane talking, drunkenness, drinking of healths, obscene words, incest, sodomy, rapes, whoredom, fornication and other uncleanness (not to be repeated), all treasons, misprisons, murders, duels, felonies, sedition, mayhems, forcible entries and other violence to the persons and estates of the inhabitants within this province: all prizes, stageplays, cards, dice, May-games, gamesters, masques, revels, bull-baitings, cockfightings, bear-baitings and the like, which excite the people to rudeness, cruelty, looseness and irreligion, shall be respectively discouraged and severely punished, according to the appointment of the governor and freemen in Provincial Council and General Assembly, as also all proceedings contrary to these laws, that are not here made expressly penal.

38. That a copy of these laws shall be hung up in the Provincial Council and in public courts of justice, and that they shall be read yearly at the opening of every Provincial Council and General Assembly and court of justice, and their assent shall be testified by their standing up after the reading thereof. . . .

Signed and sealed by the governor and freemen aforesaid, this fifth day of the third month, called May [*sic*], one thousand six hundred eighty and two.

From William Penn, *The Frame of the Government of the Province of Pennsilvania in America: Together with Certain Laws Agreed upon in England by the Governour and Divers Free-men of the Aforesaid Province* (London, 1682), 7–11.

Discussion Questions

1. What rights (economic, political, judicial, and religious) did Pennsylvania's residents receive?

2. William Penn was a reformer. What do these laws tell you about the kind of reforms that Penn desired for England?

3. What similarities and differences do you see between these laws and the Great Law of the Iroquois League? Other accounts you have read? The United States today?

4. If you were establishing the rules for a new society, which of these laws would you include? Which would you alter or omit?

Notes

1. Many.

2. The version that the Pennsylvania legislature eventually approved was a compromise set of laws that provided for a stronger legislature and weaker governor than Penn's original proposal.

3. People who could not afford passage from England to Pennsylvania could become indentured servants, paying for passage by making a contract to work without pay for a certain number of years. At the end of their service, they were to receive fifty acres of land in Pennsylvania.

4. Taxes.

5. Charged by lawyers and other officers of the court.

6. Legitimate children.

Creek Leaders Meet the Trustees of Georgia, 1734

*S*OON AFTER JAMES OGLETHORPE FOUNDED THE NEW COLONY OF GEORGIA, *he re-turned to London. Chief Tomochichi, his wife, Senawchi, and several other Creek Indians accompanied him to establish diplomatic relations with the king of England. In this painting, the Creek delegation is meeting the Georgia trustees. In the center, Oglethorpe is shaking the hand of a Creek boy, dressed in fancy English clothes. The Creek woman, in an English dress, is Senawchi. The interpreter (the only Englishman without a wig) is trader John Musgrove, the husband of prominent Creek-English woman Mary Musgrove. The eagle in the bottom right corner was a gift from the Creeks to the king.*

Discussion Questions

1. How did the Creeks dress for a diplomatic occasion?
2. How did the British dress for a diplomatic occasion?
3. What kinds of power did each side display?
4. What else interests you about the scene?

William Verelst, Trustees of Georgia (1734–35), detail. Courtesy Winterthur Museum.

Father Junípero Serra
Writes from San Diego, 1770

IN THE 1700s, OVER THREE HUNDRED THOUSAND INDIANS lived in what is now California. They fished, hunted, and encouraged wild growth through irrigation and pruning, but, unlike most Indians, they did little farming. Those living near San Diego Bay were the Ipai and Tipai. Since the 1500s, the Spanish had explored Alta California (the Pacific coast north of today's Mexican state of Baja California). Only in the 1760s, when reports circulated of proposed Russian and British colonies, did the Spanish send settlers. Former university professor Junípero Serra would establish missions, and Baja California governor Gaspar de Portolá would run the presidios (military posts). Between April and July 1769, Serra, Portolá, and the others arrived at San Diego Bay. In this letter, Father Serra reports what happened next.

Glory be to Jesus, Mary, Joseph
To the Reverend Preaching Father and Guardian, Friar Juan Andrés:
My lord and venerable father,
    Because of the great distance and the lack of communication where I now am, my letters will have to be few, but I have not and will not neglect any opportunity to write you. The last time was at the beginning of July last year when the packet[1] *San Antonio* (which people call *The Prince*) left the harbor here with the letter in which I wrote to your Reverence describing my arrival in good health and without mishap. Now that some soldiers and their captain are leaving here to travel overland, I write to tell you that I still enjoy good health because God gives it, and that on the fourteenth of July the Franciscan Preaching Fathers, Juan Crespí and Francisco Gómez, set out by land from

here for the harbor of Monterey with a troop of soldiers;[2] and we stayed here: Franciscan Fathers Juan Viscayno, Fernando Parrón, and I.

Our duties were to be divided so that Father Murguía (whom you had written would be arriving on the *San Joseph*) and Father Parrón would be priests for here; Father Crespí and I, for Monterey; and Fathers Viscayno and Gómez for San Buenaventura.[3]

On the sixteenth of July this San Diego Mission[4] was founded in this port, according to the proper forms. In the first of its record books we named ourselves, that is, Father Fernando [Parrón] and me, its priests. So we have been and so we continue, and Franciscan Father Juan Viscayno is staying with us as in his own home while waiting for the founding of his mission.

During that time, when there were few who remained well and many sick and the place and lodgings were uncomfortable and there were no interpreters for speaking with confidence to these poor wretches,[5] nothing much got done beyond handing out the materials for their salvation.[6] Those who at first had accepted us because of the soldiers, when they saw us so reduced in numbers, lying on our sick beds, and continually having to bury our people, decided that they could easily get rid of us. On the Feast of the Assumption of Our Lady,[7] they saw four of our few soldiers leave us to go down to the beach to change the guard and escort Father Fernando back, who had gone to say mass for those on the boat the previous Saturday.

They burst in suddenly, and as soon as the four soldiers who were still there realized what was happening, they grabbed their weapons. Fighting broke out and people were being wounded—ours and theirs—but the worst blow was to a Spanish boy from the diocese of Guadalajara who had come to work for me in Loreto and to serve wherever I traveled and wherever I settled. At the first shot he raced into my wooden shack spilling so much blood from his temples and mouth that I hardly had time to absolve him and help him to a good death. In less than a quarter of an hour he died at my feet choking on his own blood. In the time that passed, while I still held him dead and my little hut became a sea of blood, the gunshots and the arrows continued. We had only four men shooting, and the heathen[8] had more than twenty. I stayed with the dead boy, thinking it was likely that I would soon accompany him, but begging God that, without the loss of a single soul, this would be a triumph for the Catholic Faith. And that's what happened, thank God, because when the heathen saw many of their own party bleeding, all of them fled, and it looks like none of them died, so they can still be baptized.

By now their wounds are healed, and since then we have been at peace. Besides the dead boy, three of us were wounded: Father Viscayno, a blacksmith from Guadalajara named Chacón, and a Christian Indian from the San Ignacio Mission.[9] Father Viscayno's wound was from an arrow without an arrowhead, a stray shot that went through some burlap cloth hanging outside and went on to wound him in the right hand where the ring and middle fingers meet. The doctor pulled out a few splinters. His fingers still feel a little numb and don't have full mobility.

One time I had started to baptize a child when, right in the middle, they grabbed the baby out of the godfather's hands. And the parents had agreed to the baptism beforehand! It did not take place, but it will, with God's help.

The twenty-fourth of January of this year, the whole expedition from Monterey arrived, and with it, the two priests, Fathers Crespí and Father Gómez.[10] They had suffered much trouble and hardship, but they had not had to put up with any hostility in that heathen territory so thickly populated with unbelievers, as is all the land from here to the harbor of our patron saint, San Francisco. These same priests have beheld the land with their own eyes and are taking the same opportunity as I am to write your Reverence. Therefore, I will not pause to recount to you what is truly worthy of being narrated and published so as to inspire everybody to join in the spiritual conquest of this new world so that many thousands of souls may soon be given to God.

Now, my dearly beloved Guardian Father, I see and witness with my own eyes what I formerly wrote Your Reverence: that if Your Reverence and the Venerable Discretorium accept and request the hundred priests and nuns which the Royal Council offered Franciscan Father Pablo, and if you send them all to California and not hold back even one, I will find places for all of them, and I can add that even they will not be enough. But if they don't want to suffer any hardships, even one will be more than enough. . . .

With all my heart I commend myself to every individual of this holy community down to the humblest servant, and I beg all of you to commend us to God and pray for the conversion of all these poor heathen to our holy Catholic Faith; and if it is not too bold of me, who am nothing, to ask it of such a grave community, I would beg you to say a Hail Mary to our Divine Lady thanking her for delivering us on the day of her Assumption and asking her to continue her kind assistance. I held her image in one hand and in the other her divine crucified son when the arrows were raining down, and I thought that with them as my defense I would not die, or I would die well, although a great sinner.

Other than prayers, I don't know what to ask of Your Reverence or of the holy College. When something does arrive, who knows where I will be. Thus whatever Your Reverence would like to send should go to this new mission, founded in obedience to Your Reverence, with you, Your Reverence, presiding. May all our Presiding Fathers, whatever the cost, cherish it, and may it grow excellent with time. In conclusion, may God Our Lord keep Your Reverence in his holy love and grace for many years.

Mission of the Lord San Diego de Alcalá in his port of San Diego, among the heathen of Alta California, 10 February 1770.

Your affectionate servant and humble subject kisses Your Reverence's hand,
Friar Junípero Serra

Translated by John DuVal from Junípero Serra to Father Juan Andrés, February 10, 1770, in *Writings of Junípero Serra*, ed. Antonine Tibesar (Washington, DC, 1966), 1: 148–54.

Discussion Questions

1. What did Serra mean by "the spiritual conquest of this new world"?
2. The Spanish had only been at San Diego for a short time when the Ipais attacked. Why did they do so?
3. If an Ipai were writing this report instead of Serra, how do you think he or she might report on what happened before, during, and after the raid?
4. Serra prays that the San Diego Mission will "grow excellent with time." After he wrote this letter, a much larger attack in 1775 destroyed the mission, the Franciscans rebuilt it, Mexico gained its independence from Spain in 1821 and then lost Alta California to the mostly Protestant United States in 1848, and the city of San Diego grew to over one million people. Do you think Serra would say it has grown excellent?

Notes

1. A ship that carries mail.
2. Portolá led this expedition that intended to establish a presidio and mission at Monterey Bay, on the coast of the present-day state of California.
3. The San Buenaventura Mission was finally founded in 1782, in what is now the city of Ventura, between Los Angeles and Santa Barbara.
4. San Diego, sometimes spelled Santiago, is Spanish for St. James, the patron saint of Spain.
5. The Ipai Indians.
6. Franciscan missionaries brought crucifixes, rosaries, and pictures of the Virgin Mary. They could not persuade any Ipais to be baptized.
7. August 15, 1769.
8. Serra uses the words *gentiles* (heathens) for unbaptized Indians and *neophytes* for those who were baptized but not fully converted.
9. San Ignacio Mission was a more established mission, founded in 1728 in the central part of Baja California.
10. Father Crespí had intended to establish a mission at Monterey Bay, but the expedition had wandered around without provisions and unable to find the bay until Portolá decided they should return to San Diego.

Catherine the Great's Response to a Petition to Establish a Russian Colony, 1788

*I*N 1783, RUSSIAN EXPLORER AND MERCHANT GRIGORII IVANOVICH SHELIKHOV *established the first colony in the Aleutians, on Kodiak Island. There, he lived with his wife, children, and crew for almost two years in a small fort, trading Russian goods for sea otter furs from native Aleuts. Back in Russia, in February 1788, he and his business partner, Ivan Golikov, petitioned Empress Catherine the Great for official sanction for their colony; a trade monopoly in the Aleutians; permission to trade with the Spanish colonies, Japan, China, Korea, India, and the Philippines; a twenty-year no-interest loan; and one hundred Russian soldiers. Probably bribed, the Commission on Commerce heartily recommended that the empress grant the petition and give each man a sword and a medal in recognition of his patriotic service. This document is the Empress Catherine's response.*

Remarks of Empress Catherine II on the Report of the Commission on Commerce Regarding Sailing and Trade in the Pacific Ocean, April–August 1788.

1. 200,000 for twenty years without interest! No loan has had lower interest, even when the Senate was giving out money and land to the willing. With sufficient security or credible security guarantee, the money can be obtained from other sources. At the moment there is no money in the Treasury. Such a loan resembles the story of a man who wanted to teach an elephant to speak within a thirty-year period. When asked why it would take so long, he said that by thirty years either the elephant, or he, or the person who lent him the money to train the elephant would be dead.

2. A hundred soldiers for the company over there is like thousands for here. Soldiers are needed in Siberia, too.

3. Golikov and Shelikhov request permission to trade exclusively within the newly discovered lands. This would establish a real monopoly, which goes against my principles. They claim they arranged everything well, but no one from the island region has verified that.

Note: New discoveries have a lot of needs, and will cause problems, especially if every discovery turns into a monopoly. The examples with American villages prove to be negative and unprofitable to the state.

4. A specific order that would protect them, their clerks, and workers against all ills and offenses is not necessary, since every subject should already be protected by the general law against all ills.

Note: Check the ordinances pertaining to the paying of taxes in the Aleutian Islands. If no ordinance is found, then forbid merchants to collect the tax that is unauthorized by the lawful ruler.

Note: Forbid the merchants who mess around the islands to go there and trade.

Note: Award Golikov and Shelikhov with swords, insignia, and commendations.[1]

Note: Since Golikov and Shelikhov are really "good people," they request the rights for exclusive trade, but they have forgotten that there might be other good people in the world.[2]

Note: It is unfair to deprive all merchants of the right to trade just because some of them have been reckless.[3] This vice is not universal, and it is not appropriate to issue a decree because of their vice.

Note: European trade companies are all going bankrupt, and soon the English and Dutch companies will go under like the French company did.[4]

Note: If these exclusive trading rights are granted by the Commission on Commerce to Golikov and Shelikhov, then the hundred-headed monster (i.e., monopoly) will gradually advance into Russia. After this request numerous requests based on greed and other passions would also emerge. Exclusive rights for the Pacific commerce would be followed by a monopoly on Caspian Sea trade, etc., etc., and all other trades, branches and companies would become monopolies as well, because one exception from the established regulations would mean thousands and more similar exceptions.

Note: Where do the islanders get iron and copper—on the islands or the mainland? . . .

Note: Order the Court to submit all retained notes concerning Okhotsk and Irkutsk. If there is everyday correspondence, send in copies, because the notes attached to the report have been insufficient, even useless, and there are no maps.[5]

Note: As for the Kuril Islands,[6] it is necessary to resolutely confirm that they will not dispute with China over the territory. Similarly, do not disturb islands belonging to any other countries.

Note: Wide expansion into the Pacific will not be useful. Trade is one thing, taking possession of territories is something else.

Note: The [Commission's] notes [on the proposal] say little to nothing about the American mainland.

Translated by Natalia Shchegoleva from Empress Catherine's notes, April–August 1788, in *Russkie otkrytiia v Tikhom okeane I severnoi Amerike v XVIII veke* (Moscow, 1948), 281–82. For Golikov and Shelikhov's petition, see the same volume, 265–69.

Discussion Questions

1. What did Empress Catherine the Great think of the idea of colonizing in the Americas?

2. What reasons did she give for rejecting the petition?

3. At the time, Russia was at war with both Turkey and Sweden. Do you think these wars affected the empress's decision?

4. In 1799, after the deaths of Catherine and Shelikhov, Tsar Paul chartered and gave a twenty-year trade monopoly in the Aleutians and Alaska to the Russian American Company, headed by Golikov and Natalia Alekseeva Shelikhova (Shelikhov's widow). Should the tsar have listened to Catherine's reasoning?

Notes

1. This was the only recommendation by the Commission on Commerce that the empress adopted.

2. The commission had assured her that the petitioners were "good people."

3. The commission had alleged that granting this exclusive right would keep out reckless merchants.

4. John Law's Compagnie de l'Ouest had leased the colony of Louisiana from France in 1717, attracted large numbers of investors with outrageous promises of Louisiana's wealth, and fled France with their money.

5. Okhotsk and Irkutsk are Russian harbors, from which the petitioners proposed to get equipment and goods. The empress must particularly have doubted the accessibility of Irkutsk, which is near Lake Baikal, over one thousand miles from the Pacific coast.

6. A string of islands stretching from Japan northeast to the Kamchatka Peninsula.

IV

SOCIAL AND ECONOMIC LIFE

IN THIS SECTION, WE EXAMINE HOW PEOPLE LIVED AND MADE THEIR LIVINGS in North American colonies. As the colonies developed, people within them and in the Indian nations on the continent farmed, traded, and performed other work that supported them and sustained their societies. In these documents, consider how different people lived and how their choices were limited or expanded by others.

Método de Gobierno que se Observa en Esta Misión de la Purísima Concepción

Excerpt

1. TODOS LOS DÍAS DE FIESTA SEAN DE DOS CRUCES, *que obligan a los Indios, o sean de una cruz se dice Misa, y deben concurrir todos a oírla; con la diferencia, que la Víspera del día de dos Cruces se repica al medio día, a la noche, y antes de la Misa; pero el día de una Cruz no se repica al medio día, sino solamente de la noche, y antes de la Misa.* *

*From *Guidelines for a Texas Mission: Instructions for the Missionary of Mission Concepción in San Antonio: Transcript of the Spanish Original and English Translation*, ed. Benedict Leutenegger (San Antonio, 1976), 3–49, original at College of Our Lady of Guadalupe, Zacatecas, Mexico. Translation begins on p. 150.

Thomas Campanius Holm's Engraving of New Sweden, 1640s

In 1637, Dutch traders seeking to evade the Dutch West India Company's monopoly decided to base their trading operations in Sweden and establish "New Sweden" in the Delaware Valley. They named their trading post "Fort Cristina" (now Wilmington, Delaware) for the Swedish queen. Soon, Swedish merchants took over the venture and sent Swedes and Finns to farm the colony. The Dutch seized the colony in 1655. The Swedish artist Thomas Campanius Holm made this engraving of European traders and Delaware (Lenni Lenape) Indians to illustrate his 1702 history of New Sweden. Holm based his history on his grandfather's description of 1640s New Sweden.

Discussion Questions

1. Can you tell from the engraving that Holm never visited the Americas?
2. What seems correct? What did he get wrong?
3. What kind of colony did Holm imagine?
4. What might people in Sweden have thought when they saw the engraving (fifty years after they lost the colony)?

Thomas Campanius Holm, Kort beskrifning om provincien Nya Swerige uit America *(1702),* frontispiece. Courtesy the Library Company of Philadelphia.

Hans Sloane Observes Jamaica, 1687–1689

JAMAICA WAS ORIGINALLY INHABITED BY TAINOS, who met Columbus on his second voyage, in 1494. The English took the island from Spain in the 1650s, although a community of escaped slaves continued to hold part of the island for several more decades. Beginning in the 1660s, the English imported African slaves to work sugar plantations in Jamaica. Hans Sloane was born in Ireland and studied chemistry, botany, and medicine in London and Paris. In 1687, he set off for Jamaica as the physician to the colony's new governor. After the governor died, Sloane returned to London, bringing back notes, drawings, and dried specimens of plants and animals. He became a central figure in London's scientific community and served as the president of the Royal Society from 1727 (succeeding Isaac Newton) to 1741. The specimens that Sloane collected on this trip and in his later endeavors became the first collections of the British Museum.

The meat of the inhabitants of Jamaica is generally such as is in England, as beef, pork, and fish, salted and preserved, and sent from hence and Ireland, flour, peas, salted mackerels, etc. from these places and New England or New York, on which not only the masters feed, but also they are obliged to furnish their servants both whites and blacks with three pounds of salt-beef, pork, or fish, every week, besides cassava bread,[1] yams, and potatoes. . . .

Swine are of two sorts, one running wild in the country amongst the woods, which feed on the fallen fruits, etc. and are sought out by hunters with gangs of dogs, and chiefly found in the more unfrequented, woody, inland parts of the island. After pursuit, and that they are wearied by the dogs, when they come to a bay, they are shot or pierced through with lances, cut open, the bones taken out, and the flesh is gashed on the inside into the skin, filled with salt and exposed to the sun, which is called jerking. It is so brought home to their masters by the hunters, and [tastes] much as bacon, if broiled on coals. These hunters are either blacks or whites, and go out with their dogs, some salt and bread, and lie far remote from houses, in huts, in the woods, for several days, in places where swine come to feed on the fruits. . . .

Turtle (tortoises) are of several sorts, those of the sea, called green turtle from their fats being of that color, feed on conches or shellfish, are very good victuals, and sustain a great many, especially of the poorer sort of the island. . . .

Manatee is taken in this island, very often in calm bays, by the Indians. It is reckoned extraordinary good victuals. . . .

[Cassava] bread is eaten dry as ours, or dipped in water, on which it immediately swells, and has no very pleasant taste this way, though dry it has none at all. Dipped in sugared water this bread is still more pleasant, and if it be a little toasted afterwards, it [tastes] yet better. If dipped in wine, it will not swell as if dipped in water. It will keep a long time without corruption, so that it is taken as provision for the sloops trading to the Spanish Main, etc. This bread is worth about seven shillings and six pence the hundred weight, sometimes double that, according to its scarcity. People who feed altogether on this, live as long, and in as good health as they who feed on any other sort of bread.

Plantains is the next most general support of life in the island. They are brought in from the plantain-walk, or place where these trees are planted, a little green; they ripen and turn yellow in the house, when, or before they are eaten. They are usually roasted, after being first cleared of their outward skins, under the coals. They are likewise boiled in Oglios or Pepper-Pots,[2] and prepared into a paste like dumplings, and several other ways. A drink is also made of them.

The next succedaneum for bread, in this place, are potatoes. They are roasted under the coals, or boiled, and are eaten as the former.

Yams are likewise used here in lieu of bread, and are prepared as the others, only because they are very large, they are usually cut in pieces.

Grains in use here are, 1. Guinea-corn.[3] 'Tis prepared and used as rice, and tastes as well, and is as nourishing. It is usually the food of poultry and pigeons.

2. Indian corn or maize, either toasted or boiled, is fed on by the slaves, especially the young ears of it, before ripe, are roasted under the coals and eaten; this is thought by them very delicious, and called mutton; but 'tis most used for feeding cattle and poultry.

3. Rice is here planted by some Negroes in their own plantations,[4] and thrives well, but because it requires much beating, and a particular art to separate the grain from the husk, 'tis thought too troublesome for its price, and so neglected by most planters.

Peas, beans, and pulse[5] of sorts different from those of Europe, are here very common. They are eaten when green, as ours of Europe, and when dry, boiled, [and] afford the Negroes very good and strong provision.

Flour from New York is counted the best, but this as well as all other flour, and biscuit, are subject to be spoiled with weevils, or small scarabs, if long kept.

Chocolate is here used by all people, at all times, but chiefly in the morning; it seems by its oiliness chiefly to be nourishing, and by the eggs mixed with it to be rendered more so. The custom, and very common usage of drinking it came to us from the Spaniards, although ours here is plain, without spice. I found it in great quantities nauseous and hard of digestion, which I suppose came from its great oiliness, and therefore I was very unwilling to allow weak stomachs the use of it, though children and infants drink it here as commonly as in England they feed on milk. Chocolate colors the excrements of those feeding on it of a dirty color.

The common use of this, by all people in several countries in America, proves sufficiently its being a wholesome food. The drinking of it actually warm, may make it the more stomachic, for we know by anatomical preparations, that the tone of the fibers are strengthened by dipping the stomach in hot water, and that hot liquors will dissolve what cold will leave unaffected.[6]

Besides these ordinary provisions, the raccoon, a small quadruped, is eaten. Rats are likewise sold by the dozen, and when they have been bred amongst the sugar-canes, are thought by some discerning people very delicious victuals. Snakes or serpents and cossi (a sort of worms) are eaten by the Indians and Negroes. . . .

The better sort of people lie as in England, though more on quilts, and with few, if any coverings; they hold here that lying exposed to the land breezes is very unhealthy, which I do not believe to come so much from the qualities of the air, either manifest or more obscure, as from this, that the air is, when one goes to sleep here, very hot, the sunbeams having heated it so long, it retains this heat for some considerable time in the night, which afterwards sweating away, it grows towards morning very cold, and affects one so much as by the coldness sometimes to awake one if sleeping. This must of necessity check insensible transpiration, and so may be the cause of many diseases. To avoid this, Negroes and Indians sleep not without a fire near them.

Hammocks are the common beds of ordinary white people. They were in use amongst the Indians, and are much cooler than beds, so cool as not to be lain in without clothes, especially if swung, as is usually the custom here. . . .

Indians and Negroes lie on the floors, most generally on mats made of bulrushes . . . with very little or no coverings, and a small fire near them in the cottages. Hence they and ordinary white servants, who lie not in beds, are not said to go to bed, but to go and sleep: and this phrase has generally obtained all over the plantations.

Beds are sometimes covered all over with gauze to hinder the mosquitoes or gnats from buzzing about, biting or awaking those lying in them. This is chiefly after rain.

It is esteemed here the wholesomest way to go to bed early, and rise early.

The heat of the air exhausting the spirits, no wonder if some of the edge of mankind to venery be taken off; it is thought by some men, that they are be-witched or charmed by the air, by others that that desire in women by this heat is augmented, but I believe neither, for what I could find [from] several peo-ple this appetite is the same as in other places, neither are men more be-witched or charmed here than in Europe; but I believe people being here more debauched than in England, the consequences may be more taken notice of; and I am apt to think that a great many dropsies may come from this, noth-ing depauperating the blood like excessive venery. I once saw a very great dropsy fall on a strong young man, occasioned by one night's very excessive debauchery. . . .

Their agriculture is but very small, their soil being as yet so fruitful as not to need manuring or dunging their land, although they begin to lay by their dung for future use, they seeing by the example of their neighbors in Barba-dos, that they may need it. And even they themselves here have in some places failed of sugarworks, as near the Angels, where the ground had been cultivated or manured before their coming to the island. . . .

They clear ground likely to be useful by felling the trees as near the root as they can, the timber if near their work, they cut into smaller pieces, split it, and use it in the stokeholes as firewood to boil up the sugars, if not they gather the branches, put them in heaps, and fire them here and there in the field, whereby the field is not only cleared, but made rich with the ashes. The most part of fields are not stubbed up, but the roots of the trees, with about three, four, or five foot of the trunks stand in the field, and sometimes the fallen body of the tree lies along till it decays and rots. A field being so cleared, Ne-groes with hoes make smaller or deeper holes, at nearer or farther distances according to the thing to be planted, and another coming after throws in the seed, or plants the root, and covers it with earth. . . .

The inhabitants of Jamaica are for the most part Europeans, some Creoles, born and bred in the island Barbados, the Windward Islands, or Surinam, who are the masters, and Indians, Negroes, Mulatos, Alcatrazes, Mestises, Quaterons, etc., who are the slaves.[7]

The Indians are not the natives of the island, they being all destroyed by the Spaniards, of which I have said something before, but are usually brought by surprise from the Mosquitoes or Florida,[8] or such as were slaves to the Spanish, and taken from them by the English. They are very often very much checkered in their skin, by cupping with calabashes,[9] are of an olive color, have long black lank hair, and are very good hunters, fishers, or fowlers, but are naught at working in the fields or slavish work, and if checked or drubbed are good for nothing, therefore are very gently treated, and well fed.

The Negroes are of several sorts, from the several places of Guinea,[10] which are reckoned the best slaves. Those from the East Indies or Madagasins are reckoned more worth than others in that they are seasoned to the island.

Clothing of the island is much as in England, especially of the better sort; that of the Indians and Negroes is a little canvas jacket and breeches, given them at Christmas. It seems to me the Europeans do not well, who coming from a cold country, continue here to clothe themselves after the same manner as in England, whereas all inhabitants between the Tropics go even almost naked, and Negroes and Indians live almost so here, their clothes serving them but a very small part of the year. . . .

The buildings of the Spaniards on this island were usually one story high, having a porch, parlor, and at each end a room, with small ones behind for closets, etc. They [were] built with posts put deep in the ground; on the sides their houses were plastered up with clay on reeds, or made of the split trunks of Cabbage-Trees nailed close to one another, and covered with tiles, or Palmetto thatch. The lowness, as well as fixing the posts deep in the earth, was for fear their houses should be ruined by earthquakes, as well as for coolness.

The houses built by the English are for the most part brick, and after the English manner, which are neither cool, nor able to endure the shocks of earthquakes. The kitchens, or cook rooms here, are always at a small distance from their houses, because of the heat and smell, which are both noisome and troublesome. There are no chimneys or fireplaces in their houses, but in the cook room. This word is used to signify their kitchen and is a sea word, as many others of that country.

The houses of considerable planters are usually removed from their sugar, or other works, that they may be free from the noise and smells of them, which are very offensive. The Negroes' houses are likewise at a distance from their masters, and are small, oblong, thatched huts, in which they have all their moveables or goods, which are generally a mat to lie on, a pot of earth to boil their victuals in, either yams, plantains, or potatoes, with a little salt mackerel, and a calabash or two for cups and spoons. . . .

The air here being so hot and brisk as to corrupt and spoil meat in four hours after 'tis killed, no wonder if a diseased body must be soon buried. They usually bury twelve hours after death at all times of the day and night.

The burial place at Port Royal[11] is a little way out of town, in a sandy soil, because in the town or church it is thought unhealthy for the living. Planters are very often buried in their gardens, and have a small monument erected over them, and yet I never heard of any of them who walked after their deaths for being buried out of consecrated ground. . . .

The Negroes from some countries think they return to their own country when they die in Jamaica, and therefore regard death but little, imagining they shall change their condition by that means from servile to free, and so for this reason often cut their own throats. Whether they die thus, or naturally, their country people make great lamentations, mournings, and howlings about them expiring, and at their funeral throw in rum and victuals into their graves, to serve them in the other world. Sometimes they bury it in gourds, at other times spill it on the graves.

They have every one his wife, and are very much concerned if they prove adulterous, but in some measure satisfied if their masters punish the man who does them the supposed injury, in any of his hogs, or other small wealth. The care of the masters and overseers about their wives is what keeps their plantations chiefly in good order, whence they ever buy wives in proportion to their men, lest the men should wander to neighboring plantations, and neglect to serve them. The Negroes are much given to venery, and although hard wrought, will at nights, or on feast days dance and sing; their songs are all bawdy, and leading that way. They have several sorts of instruments in imitation of lutes, made of small gourds fitted with necks, strung with horse hairs, or the peeled stalks of climbing plants. . . . They have likewise in their dances rattles tied to their legs and waists and in their hands, with which they make a noise, keeping time with one who makes a sound answering it on the mouth of an empty gourd or jar with his hand. . . .

They are fruitful, and go after the birth of their children to work in the field, with their little ones tied to their backs, in a cloth on purpose, one leg on one side, and the other on the other of their mother, whence their noses are a little flatted against the mother's back, which amongst them is a beauty. The same is the reason of the broadness of their and Indians' faces. . . . Their children called piccaninnies or rather *Pequeños-Niños*[12] go naked till they are fit to be put to clean the paths, bring firewood to the kitchen, etc., when a boy overseer, with his wand or white rod, is set over them as their task-master.

They are raised to work so soon as the day is light, or sometimes two hours before by the sound of a conch-shell and their overseer's noise, or in better plantations by a bell. They are suffered to go to dinner at twelve, when they bring wood [back] lest they should come idle out of the field home, return to the field at one, and come home at night. . . .

They have Saturdays in the afternoon, and Sundays, with Christmas holidays, Easter called Little or Piccaninny Christmas, and some other great feasts allowed them for the culture of their own plantations to feed themselves from potatoes, yams, and plantains, etc., which they plant in ground allowed them by their masters, besides a small plantain walk they have by themselves.

They formerly on their festivals were allowed the use of trumpets after their fashion, and drums made of a piece of a hollow tree, covered on one end with any green skin, and stretched with thouls or pins. But making use of these in their wars at home in Africa, it was thought too much inciting them to rebellion, and so they were prohibited. . . .

The trade of Jamaica is either with Europe or America. That of Europe consists in bringing thither flour, biscuit, beef, pork, all manner of clothing for masters and servants, as osnabrigs,[13] blue cloth, liquors of all sorts, etc. Maderia wine is also imported in great quantities from the island of that name, by vessels sent from England on purpose, on all which the merchant is supposed to gain generally 50 percent profit. The goods sent back again, or exported from the island, are sugars, most part muscavados,[14] indigo, cotton wool, ginger, pimento all-spice or Jamaica-Pepper, fustic-wood, princewood, lignum vitae, arnotto, logwood, and the several commodities they have from the Spaniards of the West Indies (with whom they have a private trade) as sarsaparilla, cacao-nuts, cochineal, etc., on which they get considerable profit.[15] . . .

There are also many Negroes sold [privately] to the Spaniards, who are either brought lately from Guinea, or bad servants, or mutinous in plantations. They are sold to very good profit, but if they have many cicatrices, or scars on them, the marks of their severe corrections, they are not very saleable.

The commodities the English have in return, besides money, most usually are cacao, sarsaparilla, pearls, emeralds, cochineal, hides, etc.

The trade of Jamaica with the Dutch at Curacao is chiefly for provisions which are wanted very much on that island. The island of Curacao is very small, and very little provision grows on it. The chief advantage the Dutch have of it is that 'tis a place whereto goods are brought to trade with the Spaniards privately on the continent of America, for which purpose 'tis very advantageously seated. . . .

There is likewise a trade with this island from New England and New York. It consists usually in an exchange of rum, molasses, sugar, and money, for horses, beef, pork, flour or rusk.[16] . . .

The religion of those of the island, either Europeans or descended from them (Creoles), is as in England, and the same proportion of dissenters are there as in England.

The Indians and Negroes have no manner of religion by what I could observe of them. 'Tis true they have several ceremonies, as dances, playing, etc., but these for the most part are so far from being acts of adoration of a God, that they are for the most part mixed with a great deal of bawdry and lewdness.

The Negroes are usually thought to be haters of their own children, and therefore 'tis believed that they sell and dispose of them to strangers for money, but this is not true, for the Negroes of Guinea being divided into several captainships, as well as the Indians of America, have wars, and besides those slain in battles many prisoners are taken, who are sold for slaves, and brought hither. But the parents here, although their children are slaves forever, yet have so great a love for them, that no master dare sell or give away one of their little ones, unless they care not whether their parents hang themselves or no. . . .

I have seen sugar made at several plantations; they make it by bruising the canes between iron rollers, in a mill drawn by oxen, the figure whereof is to be seen in Piso[17] and several [other] authors. The juice is conveyed into the boiling house, where in a cistern is mixed about two handfuls of lime, with one hundred and fifty gallons of juice, and then both are let into six coppers one after another, where it is boiled and scummed. The scum is conveyed to the still-house, only that of the fifth copper is put into a jar, that it may be again boiled, in the first copper, because it is purer than the rest, and so will yield sugar. In the sixth, with a little oil or grease, to lay its huffing and boiling over, it is boiled up to sugar, and so cooled in troughs, and carried into pots, where, by a stick run through it, a hole is made, whereby the molasses is drained from it, and leaves the sugar white. This molasses mixed with water, as well as scum or juice from bad canes, is carried into the distilling house; where, after fermentation, when it begins to subside, they in the night time distil it till thrown into the fire it burns not. This in the day time is re-distilled, and from low-wines is called high wines or rum.

From Hans Sloane, *A Voyage to the Islands Madera, Barbados, Nieves, S. Christophers and Jamaica* (London, 1707), 1: xv–lxi.

Discussion Questions

1. What kinds of things interest Sloane? How would you describe his tone?
2. What adaptations did British people make to the climate of Jamaica? What did they not change?
3. What sorts of tasks did different people perform in Jamaica?
4. Why does Sloane think that Indians and Africans have "no manner of religion"?

Notes

1. Cassava bread is made from meal of the tropical cassava's tuberous root.
2. Oglios and pepper pots are stews.

3. Guinea corn, also called *durra*, is the grain of a sorghum plant native to Africa.

4. Rice came to the Americas from West Africa, so some African slaves were familiar with its cultivation and preparation.

5. Pulse is beans, peas, lentils, or any such legumes.

6. Sloane brought some chocolate back to England and began prescribing it mixed with warm milk as a "stomachic," a medicine to ease stomachaches.

7. Sloane's vocabulary reflects the Spanish *casta* system for classifying people. According to the system, mulattos had one black and one white parent, mestizos had one white and one Indian parent, and quadroons had one black grandparent and three white grandparents. A Creole is anyone born in the islands with ancestry from Europe and/or Africa.

8. "Brought by surprise" is Sloane's euphemism for slave raids on the Mosquito Coast of what is now Nicaragua and the Atlantic coast of what is now the southeastern United States.

9. A calabash is a gourd or squash.

10. "Guinea" was a huge region in West Africa, stretching along the Atlantic coast from modern-day Senegal to Cameroon.

11. Port Royal, Jamaica, was a major port city. A 1692 earthquake destroyed it.

12. *Pequeños niños* means little children. Its corruption in English, "piccaninnies," became a derisive term for black children.

13. Osnabrig was a coarse linen cloth originally made in the German town of Osnabrück; later it became a generic term for rough cloth.

14. Muscavados is unrefined sugar.

15. Fustic wood is a yellow wood used for making dye. Princewood and lignum vitae are hardwoods. Arnotto is an orange-red dye. Logwood makes a black dye and a medical astringent. Sarsaparilla is a root used for medicinal purposes, including the treatment of syphilis. Cacao nuts are the seeds that make chocolate. Cochineal is a red dye made from dried insects (the "cossi" that Sloane mentioned earlier). Sloane's reference to "private trade" between Jamaica and the Spanish West Indies (and, in a later paragraph, Dutch Curaçao) implies a violation of England's Navigation Acts.

16. Rusk is a hard bread made for traveling.

17. Willem Piso's 1648 book *Historia naturalis Brasiliae.*

Saukamappee on the Coming of Horses, Guns, and Smallpox, 1700s

---

SAUKAMAPPEE WAS A NAHATHAWAY (CREE) INDIAN. When he was living with the Piegans (one of the Blackfoot nations), he welcomed David Thompson, a young Hudson's Bay Company apprentice, to stay with him for the winter of 1787. That winter, Saukamappee told Thompson some of his history. Thompson described Saukamappee as "at least 75 to 80 years of age; his height about six feet, two or three inches, broad shoulders, strong limbed, his hair gray and plentiful, forehead high and nose prominent, his face slightly marked with the smallpox, and altogether his countenance mild, and even, sometimes playful." Saukamappee's tale of the plains begins when he is a boy in the early 1700s.

The Piegans were always the frontier tribe, and upon whom the Snake Indians[1] made their attacks; these latter were very numerous, even without their allies, and the Piegans had to send messengers among us to procure help. Two of them came to the camp of my father, and I was then about his age (pointing to a lad of about sixteen years). He promised to come and bring some of his people, the Nahathaways with him, for I am myself of that people, and not of those with whom I am [living]. My father brought about twenty warriors with him. There were a few guns amongst us, but very little ammunition, and they were left to hunt for the families. Our weapons were a lance, mostly pointed with iron, some few of stone, a bow and a quiver of arrows; the bows were of larch, the length came to the chin; the quiver had about fifty arrows, of which ten had iron points, the others were headed with stone. He carried his knife on his breast and his axe in his belt. Such were my father's weapons, and those with him had much the same weapons. I had a bow and arrows and a knife, of which I was very proud. We came to the Piegans and their allies. They were camped in the Plains on the left bank of the river (the north side) and were a great many. We were feasted, a great War Tent was made, and a few days passed in speeches, feasting and dances. A War Chief was elected by the chiefs, and we got ready to march. Our spies had been out and had seen a large camp of the Snake Indians on the Plains of the Eagle Hill, and we had to cross the river in canoes, and on rafts, which we carefully secured for our retreat. When we had crossed and numbered our men, we were about 350 warriors (this he showed by counting every finger to be ten, and holding up both hands three times and then one hand). They had their scouts out, and came to meet us. Both parties made a great show of their numbers, and I thought that they were more numerous than ourselves.

After some singing and dancing, they sat down on the ground, and placed their large shields before them, which covered them. We did the same, but our shields were not so many, and some of our shields had to shelter two men. Theirs were all placed touching each other; their Bows were not so long as ours, but of better wood, and the back covered with the sinews of the bison which made them very elastic, and their arrows went a long way and whizzed about us as balls do from guns. They were all headed with a sharp, smooth, black stone (flint) which broke when it struck anything. Our iron-headed arrows did not go through their shields, but stuck in them. On both sides several were wounded, but none lay on the ground; and night put an end to the battle, without a scalp being taken on either side, and in those days such was the result, unless one party was more numerous than the other. The great mischief of war then was, as now, by attacking and destroying small camps of ten to thirty tents, which are obliged to separate for hunting.

I grew to be a man, became a skillful and fortunate hunter, and my relations procured me a wife. She was young and handsome and we were fond of each other. We had passed a winter together, when messengers came from our allies to claim assistance.

By this time the affairs of both parties had much changed; we had more guns and iron-headed arrows than before;[2] but our enemies the Snake Indians and their allies had Misstutim[3] on which they rode, swift as the deer, on which they dashed at the Piegans, and with their stone Pukamoggan[4] knocked them on the head, and they had thus lost several of their best men. This news we did not well comprehend and it alarmed us, for we had no idea of horses and could not make out what they were.[5] Only three of us went and I should not have gone, had not my wife's relations frequently intimated, that her father's medicine bag would be honored by the scalp of a Snake Indian. When we came to our allies, the great War Tent [was made] with speeches, feasting and dances as before; and when the War Chief had viewed us all, it was found between us and the

Stone Indians[6] we had ten guns and each of us about thirty balls, and powder for the war, and we were considered the strength of the battle. After a few days march our scouts brought us word that the enemy was near in a large war party, but had no horses with them, for at that time they had very few of them. When we came to meet each other, as usual, each displayed their numbers, weapons and shields, in all which they were superior to us, except our guns which were not shown, but kept in their leather cases, and if we had shown [them], they would have taken them for long clubs. For a long time they held us in suspense; a tall chief was forming a strong party to make an attack on our center, and the others to enter into combat with those opposite to them. We prepared for the battle the best we could. Those of us who had guns stood in the front line, and each of us [had] two balls in his mouth, and a load of powder in his left hand to reload.[7]

We noticed they had a great many short stone clubs for close combat, which is a dangerous weapon, and had they made a bold attack on us, we must have been defeated as they were more numerous and better armed than we were, for we could have fired our guns no more than twice; and were at a loss what to do on the wide plain, and each chief encouraged his men to stand firm. Our eyes were all on the tall chief[8] and his motions, which appeared to be contrary to the advice of several old chiefs. All this time we were about the strong flight of an arrow from each other. At length the tall chief retired and they formed their long usual line by placing their shields on the ground to touch each other, the shield having a breadth of full three feet or more. We sat down opposite to them and most of us waited for the night to make a hasty retreat. The War Chief was close to us, anxious to see the effect of our guns. The lines were too far asunder for us to make a sure shot, and we requested him to close the line to about sixty yards, which was gradually done, and lying flat on the ground behind the shields, we watched our opportunity when they drew their bows to shoot at us; their bodies were then exposed and each of us, as opportunity offered, fired with deadly aim, and either killed, or severely wounded, every one we aimed at. . . .

The War Chief now called on all the other Chiefs to assemble their men and come to the tent. In a short time they came. All those who had lost relations had their faces blackened; those who killed an enemy, or wished to be thought so, had their faces blackened with red streaks on the face, and those who had no pretensions to the one, or the other, had their faces red with ochre. We did not paint our faces until the War Chief told us to paint our foreheads and eyes black, and the rest of the face of dark red ochre, as having carried guns, and to distinguish us from all the rest. Those who had scalps now came forward with the scalps neatly stretched on a round willow with a handle to the frame; they appeared to be more than fifty, and excited loud shouts and the war whoop of victory. When this was over the War Chief told them that if anyone had a right to the scalp of an enemy as a war trophy it ought to be us, who with our guns had gained the victory, when from the numbers of our enemies we [all] were anxious to leave the field of battle; and that ten scalps must be given to us; this was soon collected, and he gave to each of us a scalp. . . .

After all the war ceremonies were over, we pitched away in large camps with the women and children on the frontier of the Snake Indian country, hunting the bison and red deer which were numerous, and we were anxious to see a horse of which we had heard so much. At last, as the leaves were falling we heard that one was killed by an arrow shot into his belly, but the Snake Indian that rode him got away; numbers of us went to see him, and we all admired him; he put us in mind of a stag that had lost his horns; and we did not know what name to give him. But as he was a slave to man, like the dog, which carried our things; he was named the Big Dog. . . .

The terror of that battle and of our guns has prevented any more general battles, and our wars have since been carried by ambuscade and surprise, of small camps, in which we have greatly the advantage, from the guns, arrow shods of iron, long knives, flat bayonets and axes from the traders. While we have these weapons, the Snake Indians have none, but what few they sometimes take from one of our small camps which they have destroyed, and they have no traders among them.

[Here Saukamappee tells of one of these smaller attacks on a Snake/Shoshone camp, which, unbeknownst to Saukamappee and his comrades, was suffering an outbreak of smallpox, part of the continentwide epidemic of 1775–1782.]

Next morning at the dawn of day, we attacked the tents, and with our sharp flat daggers and knives, cut through the tents and entered for the fight; but our war whoop instantly stopped, our eyes were appalled with terror; there was no one to fight with but the dead and the dying, each a mass of corruption. We did not touch them, but left the tents, and held a council on what was to be done. We all thought the Bad Spirit had made himself master of the camp and destroyed them. . . .

The second day after, this dreadful disease broke out in our camp, and spread from one tent to another as if the Bad Spirit carried it. We had no belief that one man could give it to another, any more than a wounded man could give his wound to another. We did not suffer so much as those that were near the river, into which they rushed and died.[9] We had only a little brook and about one third of us died, but in some of the other camps there were tents in which everyone died. When at length it left us, and we moved about to find our people, it was no longer with the song and the dance; but with tears, shrieks, and howlings of despair for those who would never return to us. War was no longer thought of, and we had enough to do to hunt and make provision for our families, for in our sickness we had consumed all our dried provisions.

From David Thompson, *David Thompson's Narrative of His Explorations in Western America, 1784–1812*, ed. Joseph Burr Tyrrell (Toronto, 1916), 328–37.

Discussion Questions

1. What was warfare on the plains like before the arrival of guns and horses? How did guns change warfare?

2. Why did the Snake (Shoshone) Indians not have guns?

3. How do you think Plains life was going to change once Indians there acquired more horses?

Notes

1. The people whom Saukamappee calls the Snake Indians were the Shoshones, people of the Uto-Aztecan language group who lived west of the Piegans, mostly in present-day Idaho, Utah, and Nevada.

2. By this time, they were getting guns and other manufactures from the Hudson's Bay Company.

3. Horses (literally, "big dogs").

4. Clubs.

5. Horses arrived in the Southwest with Coronado in the 1500s and came in large numbers when the Spanish founded Santa Fe. From there, they spread to Indians in the pueblos, on the southern plains, and gradually toward the Blackfeet and Cree.

6. These were the Assiniboines or Nakotas, a Siouan people of the northern plains who had come to assist the Piegans.

7. The guns were single-shot muskets.

8. The "tall chief" is the enemy (Snake/Shoshone) chief. The "War Chief" is leading Saukamappee's party.

9. This was a desperate attempt to cure themselves.

Benjamin Franklin
Becomes a Printer, 1714–1723

*B*ENJAMIN FRANKLIN'S MOTHER, ABIAH FOLGER FRANKLIN, *was born in Massachusetts in the 1660s. In 1689, she married the widower Josiah Franklin, who had moved with his family to Boston from England. Together, they had ten children, including their youngest son, Benjamin, in 1706. Benjamin Franklin, of course, went on to become a successful author, newspaper publisher, inventor, diplomat, and member of the committee that drafted the Declaration of Independence. Franklin first wrote this section of his autobiography in 1771, when he was sixty-five years old, and he revised it periodically over the last twenty years of his life. We begin with young Benjamin's education.*

My elder brothers were all put apprentices to different trades. I was put to the grammar school at eight years of age, my father intending to devote me, as the tithe[1] of his sons, to the service of the church. . . . I continued, however, at the grammar school not quite one year, though in that time I had risen gradually from the middle of the class of that year to be the head of it, and farther was removed into the next class above it. . . . But my father in the meantime, from a view of the expense of a college education, which having so large a family he could not well afford, and the mean living many so educated were afterwards able to obtain—reasons that he gave to his friends in my hearing—altered his first intention, took me from the grammar school, and sent me to a school for writing and arithmetic, kept by a then famous man, Mr. George Brownell, very successful in his profession generally, and that by mild, encouraging methods. Under him I acquired fair writing pretty soon, but I failed in the arithmetic, and made no progress in it. At ten years old I was taken home to assist my father in his business, which was that of a tallow-chandler and soap-boiler, a business he was not bred to, but had assumed on his arrival in New England, and on finding his dying trade would not maintain his family, being in little request. Accordingly I was employed in cutting wick for the candles, filling the dipping mold and the molds for cast candles, attending the shop, going of errands, etc. I disliked the trade, and had a strong inclination for the sea, but my father declared against it. . . .

I continued thus employed in my father's business for two years, that is, till I was twelve years old; and my brother John, who was bred to that business, having left my father, married, and set up for himself at Rhode Island, there was all appearance that I was destined to supply his place and become a tallow-chandler. But my dislike to the trade continuing, my father was under apprehensions that if he did not find one for me more agreeable, I should break away and get to sea, as his son Josiah had done to his great vexation. He therefore sometimes took me to walk with him, and see joiners, bricklayers, turners, braziers, etc., at their work, that he might observe my inclination, and endeavor to fix it on some trade or other on land. It has ever since been a pleasure to me to see good workmen handle their tools; and it has been useful to me, having learnt so much by it as to be able to do little jobs myself in my house when a workman could not readily be got, and to construct little machines for my experiments while the intention of making the experiment was fresh and warm in my mind. My father at last fixed upon the cutler's trade,[2] and my uncle Benjamin's son Samuel, who was bred to that business in London, being about that time established in Boston, I was sent to be with him some time on liking. But his expectations of a fee with me displeasing my father, I was taken home again.

From a child I was fond of reading, and all the little money that came into my hands was ever laid out in books. Pleased with the *Pilgrim's Progress*, my first collection was of John Bunyan's works in separate little volumes. I afterward sold them to enable me to buy R. Burton's Historical Collections; they were small chapmen's books and cheap, 40 or 50 in all. My father's little library consisted chiefly of books in polemic divinity, most of which I read, and have since often regretted that, at a time when I had such a thirst for knowledge, more proper books had not fallen in my way, since it was now resolved I should not be a clergyman. *Plutarch's Lives* there was, in which I read abundantly, and I still think that time spent to great advantage. There was also a book of Defoe's, called an *Essay on Projects*, and another of Dr. Mather's, called *Essays to Do Good*, which perhaps gave me a turn of thinking that had an influence on some of the principal future events of my life.[3]

This bookish inclination at length determined my father to make me a printer, though he had already one son (James) of that profession. In 1717 my brother James returned from England with a press and letters to set up his business in Boston. I liked it much better than that of my father, but still had a hankering for the sea. To prevent the apprehended effect of such an inclination, my father was impatient to have me bound to my brother. I stood out some time, but at last was persuaded and signed the indentures, when I was yet but twelve years old. I was to serve as an apprentice till I was twenty-one years of age, only I was to be allowed journeyman's wages during the last year. In a little time I made great proficiency in the business, and became a useful hand to my brother. I now had access to better books. An acquaintance with the apprentices of booksellers enabled me sometimes to borrow a small one, which I was careful to return soon and clean. Often I sat up in my room reading the greatest part of the night, when the book was borrowed in the evening and to be returned early in the morning, lest it should be missed or wanted.

And after some time an ingenious tradesman, Mr. Matthew Adams, who had a pretty collection of books, and who frequented our printing-house, took notice of me, invited me to his library, and very kindly lent me such books as I chose to read. I now took a fancy to poetry, and made some little pieces; my brother, thinking it might turn to account, encouraged me, and put me on composing occasional ballads. One was called "The Lighthouse Tragedy," and contained an account of the drowning of Captain Worthilake, with his two daughters: the other was a sailor's song, on the taking of *Teach* (or Blackbeard) the pirate. They were wretched stuff, in the Grub-Street-ballad style[4]; and when they were printed he sent me about the town to sell them. The first sold wonderfully, the event being recent having made a great noise. This flattered my vanity; but my father discouraged me by ridiculing my performances, and telling me verse-makers were generally beggars. So I escaped being a poet, most probably a very bad one; but as prose writing has been of great use to me in the course of my life, and was a principal means of my advancement, I shall tell you how, in such a situation, I acquired what little ability I have in that way.

There was another bookish lad in the town, John Collins by name, with whom I was intimately acquainted. We sometimes disputed, and very fond we were of argument, and very desirous of confuting one another, which disputatious turn, by the way, is apt to become a very bad habit, making people often extremely disagreeable in company by the contradiction that is necessary to bring it into practice; and thence, besides souring and spoiling the conversation, is productive of disgusts and, perhaps, enmities where you may have occasion for friendship. I had caught it by reading my father's books of dispute about religion. Persons of good sense, I have since observed, seldom fall into it, except lawyers, university men, and men of all sorts that have been bred at Edinborough.

A question was once, somehow or other, started between Collins and me, of the propriety of educating the female sex in learning, and their abilities for study. He was of opinion that it was improper, and that they were naturally unequal to it. I took the contrary side, perhaps a little for dispute's sake. He was naturally more eloquent, had a ready plenty of words, and sometimes, as I thought, bore me down more by his fluency than by the strength of his reasons. As we parted without settling the point, and were not to see one another again for some time, I sat down to put my arguments in writing, which I copied fair and sent to him. He answered, and I replied. Three or four letters of a side had passed, when my father happened to find my papers and read them. Without entering into the discussion, he took occasion to talk to me about the manner of my writing [and] observed that, though I had the advantage of my antagonist in correct spelling and pointing[5] (which I owed to the printing-house), I fell far short in elegance of expression, in method and in perspicuity, of which he convinced me by several instances. I saw the justice of his remarks and thence grew more attentive to the manner in writing, and determined to endeavor at improvement.

About this time I met with an odd volume of the *Spectator*.[6] It was the third. I had never before seen any of them. I bought it, read it over and over, and was much delighted with it. I thought the writing excellent, and wished, if possible, to imitate it. With this view I took some of the papers, and, making short hints of the sentiment in each sentence, laid them by a few days, and then, without looking at the book, tried to complete the papers again, by expressing each hinted sentiment at length, and as fully as it had been expressed before, in any suitable words that should come to hand. Then I compared my *Spectator* with the original, discovered some of my faults, and corrected them. . . . My time for these exercises and for reading was at night, after work or before it began in the morning, or on Sundays, when I contrived to be in the printing-house alone, evading as much as I could the common attendance on public worship which my father used to exact of me when I was under his care, and which indeed I still thought a duty, though I could not, as it seemed to me, afford time to practice it.

When about 16 years of age I happened to meet with a book, written by one Tryon, recommending a vegetable diet.[7] I determined to go into it. My brother, being yet unmarried, did not keep house, but boarded himself and his apprentices in another family. My refusing to eat flesh occasioned an inconveniency, and I was frequently chided for my singularity. I made myself acquainted with Tryon's manner of preparing some of his dishes, such as boiling potatoes or rice, making hasty pudding, and a few others, and then proposed to my brother, that if he would give me, weekly, half the money he paid for my board, I would board myself. He instantly agreed to it, and I presently found that I could save half what he paid me. This was an additional fund for buying books. But I had another advantage in it. My brother and the rest going from the printing-house to their meals, I remained there alone, and, dispatching presently my light repast, which often was no more than a biscuit or a slice of bread, a handful of raisins or a tart from the pastry-cook's, and a glass of water, had the rest of the time till their return for study, in which I made the greater progress, from that greater clearness of head and quicker apprehension which usually attend temperance in eating and drinking. . . .

My brother had, in 1720 or 1721, begun to print a newspaper. It was the second that appeared in America, and was called the *New England Courant*. The only one before it was the *Boston News-Letter*.[8] I remember his being dissuaded by some of his friends from the undertaking, as not likely to succeed, one newspaper being, in their judgment, enough for America. At this time (1771) there are not less than five-and-twenty. He went on, however, with the undertaking, and after having worked in composing the types and printing off the sheets, I was employed to carry the papers through the streets to the customers.

He had some ingenious men among his friends, who amused themselves by writing little pieces for this paper, which gained it credit and made it more in demand, and these gentlemen often visited us. Hearing their conversations, and their accounts of the approbation their papers were received with, I was excited to try my hand among them; but, being still a boy, and suspecting that my brother would object to printing anything of mine in his paper if he knew it to be mine, I contrived to disguise my hand, and, writing an anonymous paper, I put it in at night under the door of the printing-house. It was found in the morning, and communicated to his writing friends when they called in as usual. They read it, commented on it in my hearing, and I had the exquisite pleasure of finding it met with their approbation, and that, in their different guesses at the author, none were named but men of some character among us for learning and ingenuity. I suppose now that I was rather lucky in my judges, and that perhaps they were not really so very good ones as I then esteemed them.

Encouraged, however, by this, I wrote and conveyed in the same way to the press several more papers, which were equally approved; and I kept my secret till my small fund of sense for such performances was pretty well exhausted, and then I [divulged] it, when I began to be considered a little more by my brother's acquaintance, and in a manner that did not quite please him, as he thought, probably with reason, that it tended to make me too vain. And, perhaps this might be one occasion of the differences that we began to have about this time. Though a brother, he considered himself as my master, and me as his apprentice, and accordingly expected the same services from me as he would from another, while I thought he demeaned me too much in some he required of me, who from a brother expected more indulgence. Our disputes were often brought before our father, and I fancy I was either generally in the right, or else a better pleader, because the judgment was generally in my favor. But my brother was passionate, and had often beaten me, which I took extremely amiss; and, thinking my apprenticeship very tedious, I was continually wishing for some opportunity of shortening it, which at length offered in a manner unexpected.[9]

One of the pieces in our newspaper on some political point, which I have now forgotten, gave offense to the Assembly. [My brother James] was taken up, censured, and imprisoned for a month, by the speaker's warrant, I suppose, because he would not [divulge] his author. I too was taken up and examined before the council; but, though I did not give them any satisfaction, they contented themselves with admonishing me, and dismissed me, considering me, perhaps, as an apprentice, who was bound to keep his master's secrets.

During my brother's confinement, which I resented a good deal, notwithstanding our private differences, I had the management of the paper; and I made bold to give our rulers some rubs in it, which my brother took very kindly, while others began to consider me in an unfavorable light, as a young genius that had a turn for libeling and satire. My brother's discharge was accompanied with an order of the House (a very odd one), that *"James Franklin should no longer print the paper called the New England Courant."*

There was a consultation held in our printing-house among his friends, what he should do in this case. Some proposed to evade the order by changing the name of the paper; but my brother, seeing inconveniences in that, it was finally concluded on as a better way, to let it be printed for the future under the name of BENJAMIN FRANKLIN; and to avoid the censure of the Assembly that might fall on him as still printing it by his apprentice, the contrivance was that my old indenture should be returned to me, with a full discharge on the back of it, to be shown on occasion, but to secure to him the benefit of my service, I was to sign new indentures for the remainder of the term, which were to be kept private. A very flimsy scheme it was; however, it was immediately executed, and the paper went on accordingly, under my name for several months.

At length, a fresh difference arising between my brother and me, I took upon me to assert my freedom, presuming that he would not venture to produce the new indentures. It was not fair in me to take this advantage, and this I therefore reckon one of the first errata of my life; but the unfairness of it weighed little with me, when under the impressions of resentment for the blows his passion too often urged him to bestow upon me, though he was otherwise not an ill-natured man: perhaps I was too saucy and provoking.

When he found I would leave him, he took care to prevent my getting employment in any other printing-house of the town, by going round and speaking to every master, who accordingly refused to give me work. I then thought of going to New York, as the nearest place where there was a printer; and I was rather inclined to leave Boston when I reflected that I had already made myself a little obnoxious to the governing party, and, from the arbitrary proceedings of the Assembly in my brother's case, it was likely I might, if I stayed, soon bring myself into scrapes; and farther, that my indiscreet disputations about religion began to make me pointed at with horror by good people as an infidel or atheist. I determined on the point, but my father now siding with my brother, I was sensible that, if I attempted to go openly, means would be used to prevent me. My friend Collins, therefore, undertook to manage a little for me. He agreed with the captain of a New York sloop for my passage, under the notion of my being a young acquaintance of his that had got a naughty girl with child, whose friends would compel me to marry her, and therefore I could not appear or come away publicly. So I sold some of my books to raise a little money, was taken on board privately, and as we had a fair wind, in three days I found myself in New York, near 300 miles from home, a boy of but 17, without the least recommendation to, or knowledge of, any person in the place, and with very little money in my pocket.

[While in New York, Franklin obtained a job with a printer in Philadelphia and soon traveled to that city, where he lived most of his life.]

From Benjamin Franklin, *The Autobiography of Benjamin Franklin*, ed. John Bigelow (New York, 1890), 13–36.

Discussion Questions

1. What paths were open to a working-class boy in early eighteenth-century New England? What opportunities would Franklin's sisters have had?
2. How does Franklin portray his accomplishments and character?
3. How did he become a writer?
4. What were the dangers of a printing profession?

Notes

1. A tithe was the tenth of one's income owed to God. See Leviticus 27:30–2.
2. A cutler makes and repairs knives.
3. Franklin mentions the English Protestant preacher John Bunyan (1628–1688), the author of *Pilgrim's Progress*, *Grace Abounding*, and other works; R. Burton, the

pseudonym under which Nathaniel Crouch (c. 1632–1720) published pocket-size chapbooks; Greek biographer Plutarch (c. 46–120), author of *The Lives of the Noble Grecians and Romans*; English novelist Daniel Defoe (c. 1660–1731); and New England Puritan minister Cotton Mather (1663–1728).

4. Publishers in London's Grub Street put out low-end books and pamphlets.

5. Punctuation.

6. The *Spectator* was a daily journal from London, which published higher-quality essays than most of what Franklin had been reading.

7. Thomas Tryon (1634–1703) was an English advocate of vegetarianism, temperance, nonviolence, and the abolition of slavery.

8. Two other newspapers were started in the British mainland colonies in 1719, so the *Courant* was probably the fourth, not the second.

9. Franklin's note: "I fancy his harsh and tyrannical treatment of me might be a means of impressing me with that aversion to arbitrary power that has stuck to me through my whole life."

Eliza Lucas to Mrs. Boddicott, 1740

ELIZA LUCAS WAS BORN IN THE BRITISH WEST INDIES COLONY of Antigua in 1722 and was educated in London. In 1738, when Eliza was fifteen years old, her father, George Lucas, moved his family from Antigua to South Carolina in part because of the brewing war with Spain (the War of Jenkins' Ear). George soon returned to defend the island, leaving Eliza, her mother, and her sister Polly behind. With her father away and her brothers in England, Eliza managed the Lucases' Carolina plantations. The business included importing and raising supplies, exporting rice and other products, and managing the labor of the plantations' slaves. Eliza's father sent her indigo seeds, and she experimented with growing them and processing them into dye. She exported her first indigo crop to England in 1744, and indigo soon became one of South Carolina's major exports. Here, Eliza writes to a friend in England.

To my good friend Mrs. Boddicott
May 2, 1740
Dear Madam,

I flatter myself it will be a satisfaction to you to hear I like this part of the world as my lot has fallen here, which I really do. I prefer England to it 'tis true but think Carolina greatly preferable to the West Indies, and was my Papa here I should be very happy. We have a very good acquaintance from whom we have received much friendship and civility. Charles Town, the principal one in this province, is a polite agreeable place. The people live very genteelly and very much in the English taste. The country is in general fertile and abounds with venison and wild fowl; the venison is much higher flavored than in England but 'tis seldom fat.

My Papa and Mama's great indulgence to me leaves it to me to choose our place of residence either in town or in country, but I think it more prudent as well as most agreeable to my Mama and self to be in the country during my father's absence. We are 17 miles by land and 6 by water from Charles Town where we have about 6 agreeable families around us with whom we live in great harmony. I have a little library well furnished (for my papa has left me most of his books) in which I spend part of my time. My music and the garden which I am very fond of take up the rest of my time that is not employed in business of which my father has left me a pretty good share, and indeed 'twas unavoidable as my Mama's bad state of health prevents her going through any fatigue. I have the business of 3 plantations to transact which requires much writing and more business and fatigue of other sorts than you can imagine, but lest you should imagine it too burthensome to a girl at my early time of life give me leave to assure you I think myself happy that I can be useful to so good a father and by rising very early I find I can go through much business, but lest you should think I shall be quite moaped[1] with this way of life I am to inform you there is two worthy ladies in Charles Town, Mrs. Pinckney[2] and Mrs. Cleland, who are partial enough to me to be always pleased to have me with them, and insist upon my making their houses my house when in town and press me to solace a little much oftener than 'tis in my power to accept . . . but I sometimes am with one or the other for 3 weeks or a month at a time and then enjoy all the pleasures Charles Town affords. But nothing gives me more than subscribing myself,

dear Madam,
your most affectionate and most obliged humble servant,
Eliza Lucas

Pray remember me in the best manner to my worthy friend Mr. Boddicott.

From Letterbook of Eliza Lucas, afterwards Mrs. Charles Pinckney, 1739–1762, Pinckney Family Papers, South Carolina Historical Society, Charleston, microfiche SCHS 38-21, sheet #14.

Discussion Questions

1. What did Lucas value in her new home?
2. What do you think she missed?

3. What might Mrs. Boddicott, back in England, have thought of Lucas's letter?

4. Are you surprised that a seventeen-year-old girl was running three plantations? Why was she in charge? What kinds of tasks do you think she performed?

Notes

1. Moaped (usually spelled moped) means bored or melancholy.

2. This Mrs. Pinckney died in January 1744, and Eliza Lucas married her widower, the forty-five-year-old Charles Pinckney, the following May.

Runaway Advertisements, Mid-1700s

THE FOLLOWING ADVERTISEMENTS WERE PLACED BY MASTERS whose workers had run away. The ads come from Christoph Saur's German-language newspaper Pensylvanische Berichte, *published in Philadelphia; the* North Carolina Gazette, *published in New Bern; the* Maryland Gazette, *published in Annapolis; and the* Virginia Gazette, *published in Williamsburg. Some were runaway slaves of African descent, while others were European servants who had run away before completing their indentures.*

Ran away from the subscribers, on Roanoke River, a Negro fellow, named Thomas Boman, a very good blacksmith, near six feet high, has a little blemish in one of his eyes, good set of teeth, well-made sensible fellow, and slow of speech; he can read, write, and cypher[1]; carried away with him about fifty or sixty pounds in cash, and a grey roan horse, bridle and saddle, a pair of money-scales and weights, and one pair of sheets; three coats, one a broadcloth or serge, one a bearskin cape-coat, of a grey color, one a homespun coat, a blue jacket, and a great many other clothes. Whoever will apprehend the said fellow and secure him, so that the owners may get him, shall be paid by the subscribers 12 pistoles,[2] besides what the law allows, and one fourth part of the money he has when taken.—Robert West, sr.; Robert West, jr.

Note: 'Tis supposed he is gone towards South Carolina, as he was seen over Tar River.[3]

Ran away from the subscriber, a Negro fellow, named Frank; he is a short thick fellow, speaks good English, and is a sensible negro. Had on when he went away, a very good thick jacket, and carried a woman's gown with him; is branded on the left buttock with a R. Is an old offender,[4] and a great thief. Whoever brings him to me, shall have thirteen shillings and four pence, proclamation money, reward, besides the country allowance, paid by: Samuel Johnston.

Note: All persons are forbid, at their peril, to harbor him.[5]

Ran away from the subscriber, living in Westmoreland County; a servant man named Edmund Cryer, an English man, born at Leeds in Yorkshire, about 5 feet 8 inches high, a thin visage and pale complexion, his hair cut off, and his apparel unknown. He is a shoemaker by trade, and carried his tools with him. He was seen crossing the River from Boyd's Hole [Virginia] to Maryland, about three days after his elopement. He has been about four years in the country, and this is the third attempt he has made to get out. Whoever apprehends the said servant, so that he may be convey'd safe home, shall have two pistoles reward.—Richard Lee.[6]

Peter Conrad, residing in New Hanover Township, announces that a German servant ran away from him on the 10th of this month, by the name of Carl Witt, by trade a blacksmith, he is between 30 and 40 years old, of medium stature and with a fresh complexion. He was wearing a blue/bluish coat, a striped linen jacket, a fine linen shirt, good shoes and stockings, a white cap, a new fine hat. Took a watch. A boy of 15 went away with him, he is wearing a blue jacket. Whoever detains and confines them in a way that their master can get them back shall have 40 shillings and payment of reasonable expenses from the abovementioned Peter Conrad.[7]

Five Pistoles Reward. Ran away from the subscriber, in Fairfax County, in Virginia, on the 8th of September last, an English indented servant woman, named Elizabeth Bushup, about 23 Years of age, of a low stature, fair skin, black eyes, black hair, a scar on her breast, and loves drink; had on when she went away, a calico gown and petticoat, a pair of stays, a hoop coat, a black furr'd hat, a pair of calamanco shoes, a muslin apron, and several other things too tedious to mention. It is suspected she was carried away, by Capt. Tipple's boatswain, from Potomac River to Pawtucket, where the ship lies, or that he has left her at the mouth of the River. Whoever takes up the said servant, and brings her to her master, shall have five pistoles reward, besides what the law allows, and five pistoles more if it can be proved that the said boatswain conceals her.—Gerrard Alexander.[8]

Ran away from the subscriber, living in Norfolk, a young Mulatto fellow, named Joe, alias Josiah Sally. He is a sailor, and had on when he went away, a blue fear-nothing jacket, trousers, an old hat and wig, yarn stockings, and shoes. Whoever will apprehend and bring him to me, or secure him so that I may have him again, shall have a pistole reward, besides what the law allows.— Charles Steuart.[9]

Ran away from the subscriber, living in King-William County, on the 16 day of June, 1753, a Mulatto wench, named Molly, about 26 years of age, of a middle stature, long visage, and freckled, has a drawling speech, a down look, and has been chiefly brought up to carding and spinning. She was first supposed to be harbored in New-Kent County, by some of her relations, but not hearing of her since the first week after her elopement, it is supposed she has either got to some of the neighboring provinces, or gone beyond sea. Whoever will apprehend her, so that she may be had again, shall have ten pistoles reward; or if she is beyond sea, whoever declares the name of the skipper and vessel that carried her, so that the offender may be brought to justice, shall have twenty pistoles reward.—Ferdinando Leigh.[10]

Friedrich Stein in Lancaster announces that a German servant ran away from him by the name of Philip Andreas Pitzler, a saddler, about 28 years old, 5 feet, 4 inches tall; speaks good English, good French, and Latin, has long black hair, and ties it back. When he left, he was wearing a bearskin coat, leather pants, one white and one striped shirt, woven stockings, good shoes, and a felt hat. Whoever takes him in and confines him so that his master can get him back shall have four pounds as well as reasonable expenses.[11]

Joseph Williams in Merian Township on the way from Philadelphia to Cannestocker [Canistoga], near the Inn Zum Hirsch, announces that a German servant ran away from him, his name is Friederich Wandel, 19 years old, is of tall stature, and has thin legs, the inside of the ankle of his left foot is slightly thicker than the other one, and is often sore, has a narrow pale face, short black hair, speaks fairly good English; when he left, he was wearing a black-and-white patterned new jacket, lined with brown flannel in the front and white flannel in the back, with pewter buttons on wood, the sleeves are too short, a worn, turned-up pointed hat, a home-made linen shirt with red letters at the front opening, leather pants without buttons at the knees, old shoes with laces. He says he can make baskets, and because his father Georg Wandel appeared several times and wanted to free his son with money but never brought any money, his master believes that his father fetched him or had him fetched on the night of June 17; if that isn't the case, he may have wanted to visit secretly his cousin Jacob Wandel, a hair-sieve[12] maker near Bethlehem at the Delaware Fork. Whoever takes this servant in and confines him so that his master can get him back shall have five pounds as well as reasonable expenses.[13]

Martin Kirschner in Bern Township in Berks County announces that on June 16 a maidservant ran away from him. Her name is Anna Margaretha Müllerin, she is from Bamberg, 34 years old; when she left, she was wearing an old quilted coat, and a half-fulled brown skirt, and a half-linen bodice of the same material, and a linen striped bodice. She is of short stature, and the skin of her face is pockmarked, and there is a noticeable mark on one of her calves. Whoever finds her and returns her or confines her so that he can get her back shall have three pounds as well as reasonable expenses.[14]

Discussion Questions

1. What do you think the masters of Thomas Boman and Frank meant when they described their slaves as "sensible"?

2. Who do you think was most likely to get away? Who was most likely to get caught? Why do you think Benjamin Franklin's brother did not print an ad seeking him after Benjamin skipped out on his indenture?

3. What kinds of things did people take? Why? How did their masters know what they had?

4. Do you see any differences in how masters described different types of laborers?

Notes

1. To cipher is to do arithmetic.
2. A Spanish gold coin worth a little over eighteen shillings (£1 is twenty shillings).
3. *North Carolina Gazette*, March 13, 1742.
4. R stands for "runaway." "Old offender" means he has run away many times.
5. *North Carolina Gazette*, March 13, 1742.
6. *Maryland Gazette*, May 23, 1745.
7. Translated by Sabine Schmidt from *Pensylvanische Berichte*, October 16, 1745.
8. *Maryland Gazette*, November 7, 1745.
9. *Virginia Gazette*, December 24, 1751.
10. *Virginia Gazette*, November 7, 1754.
11. Translated by Sabine Schmidt from *Pensylvanische Berichte*, November 16, 1754.
12. A very fine sieve, with a bottom made of horsehair.
13. Translated by Sabine Schmidt from *Pensylvanische Berichte*, November 16, 1754.
14. Translated by Sabine Schmidt from *Pensylvanische Berichte*, November 16, 1754.

Mary Christina Martin's Case before the German Society of Pennsylvania, 1772

*P*HILADELPHIANS OF GERMAN DESCENT FOUNDED *the German Society of Penn-sylvania (GSP) in 1764 to assist German immigrants. Many Germans came as indentured servants, a particularly vulnerable status. The GSP could be help-ful in preventing masters from unfairly extending indentures. Although Christina Martin was Dutch, she too turned to the GSP for help. If she had been German, her hearing would have been conducted in German, but the GSP did all business with non-Germans in English. These are the minutes of the meeting.*

Saturday, October 24, 1772

The Officers of the German Society met at Rudolph Burners.

Appeared Mary Christina Martin the Widow of George Martin who with his said Wife and Six Children, embarked at Rotterdam[1] in the Ship *Minerva*, Captain Johnstone. Her Husband died on his Passage—She says that her Hus-band agreed for Nine Guineas[2] a Freight—and that he had 40 Guineas Hol-lanish advanced him in Holland by Mssrs. Crauford & Co.—That at her ar-rival in Philadelphia, three of her Sons were sold at £30 each which is equal to £90 and her two younger Children, a Girl of 8 Years and a Boy of 4 Years old, were delivered to her Sister whose Husband gave a Note of Hand for £10, to Willing and Morris—By which Means She paid for the Freight of her Family £100—That nevertheless she being near 46 years of Age has been sold to John Brown for £22 and 6 shillings to serve him and his Assigns[3] for 5 Years—In which Account she and her poor Orphans are greatly overcharged and prays the advice and assistance of the German Society.

RESOLVED that Mr. Christopher Ludwick wait upon Messrs Willing & Morris, with a Copy of this entry, and that to desire to know of them whether the Facts alleged by the said Woman are true, And whether the Gentlemen would be pleased to favor us with a Copy of the Account of that Woman as it stands in their Books.

A true Copy
Ludwick Weiss & Michael Shubart
[After the GSP's representatives met several times with the ship owners, they apparently agreed that Martin had paid the full freight, and she was freed.]

From German Society of Pennsylvania Minutes, German American Collection, German Society of Pennsylvania Collections, Philadelphia, Pennsylvania.

Discussion Questions

1. What was Mary Christina Martin's claim?
2. Why did Willing and Morris think that they could sell an extra five years of her indenture?
3. Why did Martin go to the German Society of Pennsylvania?
4. What does this case tell you about the position of women in eighteenth-century Philadelphia?

Notes

1. A city in the Netherlands.
2. A gold coin worth twenty-one shillings (£1 is twenty shillings).
3. Heirs.

Spiritual and Temporal Guidelines for a Texas Mission, Late 1700s

---

*T*HESE INSTRUCTIONS WERE WRITTEN BY A FRANCISCAN *priest in Mexico for a priest new to mission work who was being sent to the Immaculate Conception Mission in San Antonio, Texas. He would have been the only priest at the mission, so he would probably have read these instructions often and anxiously. The missionary would also have had a* fiscal, *a secular official to help him with running the mission. By the time these instructions were written, probably in the 1780s, Immaculate Conception Mission was home to over one hundred Texas Indians. Besides the mission, San Antonio's population included the Spanish governor of Texas, soldiers staffing the presidio, and several hundred settlers.*

1. On all feast days, whether two-cross days, obligatory for Indians, or one-cross days, mass is said and all should gather to hear it. The feasts are distinguished in that for two-cross feast days bells peal at noon and at night on the previous day and right before mass on the feast day, whereas for one-cross feast days they do not peal at noon on the previous day but only on the night before and immediately before the mass.

[Instructions 2 through 23 deal with when to say mass and conduct other liturgies. Then the instructions for running the mission begin.]

24. Saturday, after mass, the women must sweep the monastery patios, and the Fiscal designates two women to sweep the church and the sacristy. When the sweeping is done, all the women come for their ration of soap, which the Fiscal distributes to each woman according to her family and the amount of clothes that need to be washed.

25. Every Sunday, after mass, the Priest gives the Fiscal two handfuls of tobacco to distribute among all the adults, both men and women. This should be done at the church door or some other place where the Priest can watch. Leftover tobacco should be given back to him in the tray so that he can provide for those who come to ask for more in the middle of the week. The Priest should be careful to wait until Wednesday before giving any more, because if he gives it to them before Wednesday, the Indians, knowing that they still have some even while asking for more, will despise what is given to them on Sunday and trade it for any trifle at the presidio; but when he gives it to them in the middle of the week, it should be only two or three leaves to last them till Sunday.

26. Every Monday the Fiscal gets the key to the granary from where it hangs in the Priest's cell, and all the women come for their ration of corn. The amount of corn portioned out differs according to the seasons. When the crop is so plentiful that it looks like there will be a surplus, married women are given half a bushel of ears of corn each; and widows, about three-eighths of a bushel, but when there is little corn, only three-eighths of a bushel to the married women, and a quarter bushel to the widows. . . .

27. Every week the Fiscal designates a woman to make tortillas for the Priest and decides whether to give her corn every day or every third day, whichever seems best.

28. In some missions it is the custom for the priests to give out a weekly ration of salt. Not in this mission. Instead, whenever someone asks for salt, the Priest gives it, according to the need of the person asking for it and how often some people ask for it. To keep supplied with salt, he should find out when people go to the presidio to get it, and should arrange to get it from the mule team driver in exchange for corn, money, or other things, whatever gets the best exchange.

29. The Indian women often pester and importune the Priest for candy, lard, beans, chilies, and a thousand other things, and if the Priest is soft-hearted and gives them everything they ask for, there will not be one cent left in the house. He should therefore adjust his gifts according to the seasons and the circumstances.

30. On Fridays during every Lent, the Priest orders a large kettle of beans to be prepared, and the Fiscal has them cooked for people to eat at noon so they will not have meat in their houses. And if there are pumpkins, he gives them out, too. When there seem to be enough beans to give out every day of Lent, it should be done, although it is rare for enough beans to be grown to last through all of Lent if they are eaten every day, and the Priest should plan ahead to provide them on every day of abstinence[1] throughout the year. On Christmas Eve as well, a kettle of beans is put out, and another kettle of cooked

pumpkin, and a third of sweet potatoes, which, if they don't grow in the Mission, he will be sure to buy in the presidio. Also, he has fritters prepared regularly and distributes them with candies.

[Items 31 through 81 give more instructions on handing out food, clothing, and other supplies, and overseeing the mission's agriculture.]

82. The authority of the Superior over those inferior to him, and of the Prelate over his subjects, is so necessary in the religious communities and villages that without it no government can exist and everything would be chaos. The Missionary must bear himself with the Indians in such manner that they will all be subject to him and respect him; he should punish the disobedient, rebellious and unruly, never wavering from the affable humility and prudence needed for governing.

83. Some of the women are used to going out in the afternoon to eat prickly pears, blackberries, wild onions, agritos,[2] nuts, sweet potatoes, and other fruits and field roots. The Priest permits all these walks according to what seems best to him. If there is no inconvenience or danger from enemies, they often go walking to other missions or to the presidio, and for that they must ask permission from the Priest, who permits or refuses as seems best to him.

Translated by John DuVal from *Guidelines for a Texas Mission: Instructions for the Missionary of Mission Concepción in San Antonio: Transcript of the Spanish Original and English Translation*, ed. Benedict Leutenegger (San Antonio, 1976), 3–49, original at College of Our Lady of Guadalupe, Zacatecas, Mexico.

Discussion Questions

1. To what extent does the author's advice balance prudence and calculating manipulation against charity? Do you approve?

2. What can you tell about the lives of women in the missions?

3. What advice might they have given an Indian woman thinking of moving to the mission?

4. Most Indians in Texas did not convert to Catholicism or settle in missions. What do you think they thought of the missions?

Notes

1. As in the forty days of Lent, Catholics were supposed to eat no meat on days of abstinence, which included every Friday. The instructions take into account all non-meat food necessary to cover all of these days.

2. A plant with berries, native to Texas.

V

SLAVERY

T HIS SECTION EXPLORES FORCED LABOR IN COLONIAL NORTH AMERICA, mostly of Africans and their descendants. For the documents written by masters, reflect on the following questions: How did they imagine slaves should act? What slave actions might they have been reacting to? Why did they think they had the right to enslave other human beings? For the documents written by slaves and former slaves: How did they make sense of being enslaved? What did they do to make their lives livable? How did colonial-era slaves' lives differ from those of nineteenth-century plantation slaves?

Los Negros Fugitivos a le Rey de España

Excerpt

Señor,

*T*ODOS LOS NEGROS FUGITIVOS DE LOS PLANTAGES DE LOS YNGLESES, *obbedientes y fieles esclavos de V. M. [Vuestra Majestad], desimos que V. M. nos hizo la real charidad de mandar que nos diesen livertad por haver venido nosotros a este país a ser Cristianos y seguir la religión verdadera en que nos salvamos.*

*Y sin obedeser tan alta y sagrada orden nos han tenido hechos esclavos muchos años, pasando muchas miserias y hambres en la esclavitud. Y obedeciendo los leales mandatos de V. M., el Gobernador presente, Don Manuel de Montiano, nos ha puesto en livertad, de que damos a V. M. muchas gracias y agradesimos por este tan real beneficio, y así mismo nos ha ofrecido y asegurado el dicho Gobernador que nos hará formar un lugar que se llame Gracia Real, donde podamos servir a Dios y a V. M., cultivando la tierra para que aya frutos en este país.**

*From original letter in the Audiencia de Santo Domingo 844, fol. 607, reel 15, P. K. Yonge Library, University of Florida, Gainesville. Translation begins on p. 179.

François Froger's Plan of
Ft. St. Jacques, Gambia, 1695

*F*T. ST. JACQUES WAS A SLAVE-TRADING FORT *on an island in the Gambia River, on the coast of West Africa. European rivalries among the Dutch, English, and French forced it to change hands repeatedly after its founding in the 1650s. Froger was able to sketch it in detail because he was with French admiral de Gennes, who seized the fort from the English in 1695. Africans on the coast gave Europeans this bit of land and brought captured enemies to sell as slaves. Tens of thousands of West Africans passed through this fort, bound for slavery in North America.*

Discussion Questions

1. What kinds of buildings did the fort include?
2. Why were there two kinds of lodging for "the Negroes"?
3. What sights and sounds might Europeans and Africans have seen and heard in the fort?
4. Why was the fort on a fortified island? Whom were the builders afraid of?

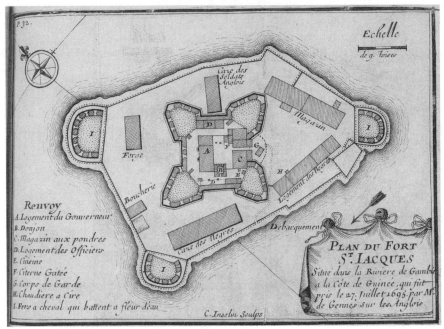

François Froger, *Relation d'un voyage fait en 1695, 1696, & 1697, aux Côtes d'Afrique, détroit de Magellen, Brésil, Cayenne et Isles Antilles* (Paris, 1698), facing 32. Courtesy John Carter Brown Library at Brown University.

Map of Fort St. Jacques, situated in the Gambia River on the Guinea Coast, which was taken July 27, 1695, by M. de Gennes from the English:

A.	Logement du gouverneur	Governor's house
B.	Donjon	Brig
C.	Magazin aux poudres	Magazine
D.	Logement des officiers	Officers' barracks
E.	Cuisine	Kitchen
F.	Citerne gâtée	Polluted cistern
H.	Chaudière a cire	Boiler for melting wax[1]
I.	Fers a cheval qui battent a fleur d'eau	Horseshoe-shaped battery, near the water

Cases des nègres	Huts for the Negroes
Logement des nègres	Barracks for the Negroes
Case des soldats Anglois	Hut for the English soldiers
Forge	Forge
Boucherie	Butchery
Magazin	Magazine
Débarquement	Dock

Note

1. "Boiler for melting wax" was probably for candle making.

New Netherland Act Emancipating Certain Slaves, 1644

<hr>

*T*HE DUTCH BROUGHT THE FIRST SLAVES TO THEIR COLONY *of New Netherland in 1626. The West India Company, which ran the colony, bought most of them. In 1640, a dispute with the Raritan Indians escalated into a full-blown Indian war, which came to be known as Kieft's War, named for Willem Kieft, the director general of New Netherland. In wartime, Dutch colonists needed the loyalty and service of their slaves, so when eleven men who had served in the war petitioned in 1644 for freedom, the company found it hard to say no.*

We, Willem Kieft, Director, and the Council of New Netherlands, having considered the petition for freedom and liberty from servitude of the following Negroes who have served Company A for 19 years: Paulo Angola, Big Manuel, Little Manuel, Manuel de Gerrit de Reus, Simon Congo, Anthony Portugis, Gracia, Peter Santomee, Jan Francisco, Little Anthony, and Jan Fort Orange; especially because they have served the Honorable West India Company for many years and have been promised their freedom for a long time and also because they are burdened with many children and if they continue in the servitude of the Company cannot support their wives and children as they have been accustomed to doing; we the Director and Council do release for the term of their natural lives the above-named men and their wives from slavery, setting them free and at liberty on the same footing as other free people here in New Netherlands, where they shall be able to earn their livelihood by farming the land manifested and granted to them,[1] on condition that they, the above-named Negroes, shall be bound to pay to the West India Company or its Deputy here, for the freedom they have received, each man for himself every year as long as he lives, 30 skepels[2] of corn, wheat, peas, or beans, and one fat hog valued at 20 guilders. And every Negro, each and of himself, promises to pay every year from this date on said 30 skepels and said hog to said Company, on pain of forfeiture of his freedom and remission into the slavery of that Company should he fail to pay the yearly tribute, with the additional condition that his present children and his children yet to be born be bound and obliged to serve the West India Company as slaves.[3]

It is likewise required that the above-named men serve the Honorable West India Company here, whether by water or by land, where called upon to serve, receiving fair wages from the Company.

Act of 23 February 1644, Fort Amsterdam, New Netherlands.

[Other slaves subsequently made the same deal, and some achieved full freedom for themselves and their families in 1664, although they still had to pay an annual tribute in exchange for their land. When the English took New Netherland from the Dutch the following decade, the colony initially retained the same rules regarding slavery. But the New York Slave Revolt of 1712 scared the English into passing harsher laws, including prohibiting any slaves freed after 1712 from owning property.]

Translated by E. B. O'Callaghan in *Laws and Ordinances of New Netherland, 1638–1674* (Albany, 1868), 36–37, and revised by John DuVal from Dutch Colonial Council Minutes, February 25, 1644, series A1809, box 1, vol. 4, 183–84, New York Colonial Manuscripts, New York State Archives, Albany.

Discussion Questions

1. What do the names of the slaves who petitioned the council tell you about their backgrounds?

2. What did the emancipated slaves gain from their emancipation?

3. What about the deal has led some to label it "half-freedom"?

4. What did the West India Company gain and lose from emancipating these slaves?

Notes

1. The land that they received was on the edges of the settled areas of Manhattan Island. All of these men did take possession of their land.

2. A *skepel* was a Dutch measurement of a little less than a bushel.

3. These terms of freedom, which have sometimes been called "half-freedom," are similar to those that the company often gave to aging slaves or slaves whose labor was needed for only part of the year. Half-freedom was not automatically extended to the slave's children.

Virginia Codes Regulating Servitude and Slavery, 1642–1705

*S*EVENTEENTH-CENTURY VIRGINIA USED BOTH *white and black unfree laborers, and their circumstances were more similar than you might think. Some English people bought passage on a ship to Virginia in exchange for signing an indenture, committing them to work without pay for a certain number of years. Many English children were kidnapped and forced to work in Virginia. Slave traders brought African laborers against their will and sold them as unfree laborers. In Virginia, these white and black men and women worked under fairly similar conditions. Many black servants gained freedom, and some even acquired land and bought their own servants. But over time, English Virginians came to see permanent race-based slavery as the best way to farm tobacco. Below are acts that the Virginia General Assembly passed to regulate servitude, in chronological order.*

1642 Whereas many great abuses and much detriment have been found to arise both against the law of God and likewise to the service of many masters of families in the colony occasioned through secret marriages of servants, their masters and mistresses being not any ways made privy thereto, as also by committing of fornication, for preventing the like abuses hereafter: Be it enacted and confirmed by this Grand Assembly that what manservant soever hath since January 1640 or hereafter shall secretly marry with any maid or woman servant without the consent of her master or mistress if she [the mistress] be a widow, he or they so offending shall in the first place serve out his or their time or times with his or their masters or mistresses, and after shall serve his or their master or mistress one complete year more for such offence committed, and the maid or woman servant so marrying without consent as aforesaid shall for such her offence double the time of service with her master and mistress, and a freeman so offending shall give satisfaction to the master or mistress by doubling the value of the service[1] and pay a fine of five hundred pounds of tobacco to the parish where such offence shall be committed, and it is also further enacted and confirmed by the authority of this Grand Assembly that if any manservant shall commit the act of fornication with any maid or woman servant, he shall for his offence, besides the punishment by the law appointed in like cases,[2] give satisfaction for the loss of her service, by one whole year's service, when he shall be free from his master according to his indentures, and if it so fall out that a freeman offend as formerly he shall be compelled to make satisfaction to the master or mistress of the woman servant by his service for one complete year, or otherwise give forthwith such valuable consideration as the commissioners in their discretion shall think fit.

Whereas complaints are at every quarter court exhibited against divers[3] persons who entertain and enter into covenants with runaway servants and freemen who have formerly hired themselves to others to the great prejudice if not the utter undoing of divers poor men, thereby also encouraging servants to run from their masters and obscure themselves in some remote plantations, upon consideration had for the future preventing of the like injurious and unjust dealings: Be it enacted and confirmed that what person or persons soever shall entertain any person as hireling, or sharer or upon any other conditions for one whole year without certificate from the commander or any one commissioner of the place, that he or she is free from any engagement of service, the person so hiring without such certificate as aforesaid, shall for every night that he or she entertain any servant either as hireling or otherwise, forfeit to the master or mistress of the servant twenty pounds of tobacco. . . .

Whereas there are divers loitering runaways in the colony who very often absent themselves from their masters' service, and sometimes in two or three months cannot be found, whereby their masters are at great charge in finding them, and many times even to the loss of their year's labor before they be had: Be it therefore enacted and confirmed that all runaways that shall absent themselves from their masters' service shall be liable to make satisfaction by service at the end of their times by indenture double the time of service so neglected, and in some cases more if the commissioners for the place appointed shall find it requisite and convenient. And if such runaways shall be found to transgress the second time or oftener (if it shall be duly proved against them) that then they shall be branded in the cheek with the letter R and pass under the statute of incorrigible rogues, provided notwithstanding that where any servants shall have just cause of complaint against their masters or mistresses by harsh or unchristianlike usage or otherwise for want of diet, or convenient necessaries that then it shall be lawful for any such servant or servants to repair to the next commissioner to make his or their complaint.

1661 Whereas there are divers loitering runaways in this country who very often absent themselves from their masters' service and sometimes in a long time cannot be found, the loss of the time and the charge in the seeking them often exceeding the value of their labor: Be it therefore enacted that all runaways that shall absent themselves from their masters' service, shall be liable to make satisfaction by service after the times by custom or indenture is expired, viz. double their times of service so neglected, and if the time of their running away was in the crop[4] or the charge of recovering them extraordinary the court shall limit a longer time of service proportional to the damage the master shall make appear he hath sustained. . . . and in case any English servant shall run away in company of any negroes who are incapable of making satisfaction by addition of time, it is enacted that the English so running away in the company with them shall at the time of service to their own masters expired, serve the masters of the negroes for their absence so long as they should have done by this act if they had not been slaves, every christian in company serving his proportion; and if the negroes be lost or die in such time of their being run away, the christian servants in company with them shall by proportion among them, either pay four thousand five hundred pounds of tobacco and cask or four years' service for every negro so lost or dead.

1662 Whereas some doubts have arisen whether children got by any Englishman upon a negro woman should be slave or free: Be it therefore enacted . . . that all children born in this country shall be held bond or free only according to the condition of the mother. . . .

1667 Whereas some doubts have arisen whether children that are slaves by birth, and by the charity and piety of their owners made partakers of the blessed sacrament of baptism, should by virtue of their baptism be made free: It is enacted . . . that the conferring of baptism doth not alter the condition of the person as to his bondage or freedom; that divers masters, freed from this doubt, may more carefully endeavor the propagation of christianity by permitting [slaves] to be admitted to the sacrament.

1669 Whereas the only law[5] in force for the punishment of refractory servants resisting their master, mistress or overseer cannot be inflicted upon negroes, nor the obstinacy of many of them by other than violent means suppressed: Be it enacted [that] if any slave resist his master (or others by his master's order correcting him) and by the extremity of the correction should chance to die, that his death shall not be accounted felony, but the master (or that other person appointed by the master to punish him) be acquit from molestation, since it cannot be presumed that prepensed malice (which alone makes murder felony) should induce any man to destroy his own estate.

1680[6]   Whereas the frequent meeting of considerable numbers of negro slaves under pretence of feasts and burials is judged of dangerous consequence; for prevention whereof for the future: Be it enacted . . . that from and after the publication of this law, it shall not be lawful for any negro or other slave to carry or arm himself with any club, staff, gun, sword or any other weapon of defense or offence, nor to go or depart from off his master's ground without a certificate from his master, mistress or overseer, and such permission not to be granted but upon particular and necessary occasions; and every negro or slave so offending not having a certificate as aforesaid shall be sent to the next constable, who is hereby enjoined and required to give the negro twenty lashes on his bare back well laid on, and . . . if any negro or other slave shall presume to lift up his hand in opposition against any christian, shall for every such offence, upon due proof made thereof by the oath of the party before a magistrate, have and receive thirty lashes on his bare back well laid on. And it is hereby further enacted . . . that if any negro or other slave shall absent himself from his master's service and lie hid and lurking in obscure places, committing injuries to the inhabitants, and shall resist any person or persons that shall by any lawful authority be employed to apprehend and take the negro, that then in case of such resistance, it shall be lawful for such person or persons to kill the negro or slave.

1691   For the prevention of that abominable mixture and spurious issue which hereafter may increase in this dominion, as well by negroes, mulattoes, and Indians intermarrying with English, or other white women, as by their unlawful accompanying with one another: Be it enacted . . . that for the time to come, whatsoever English or other white man or woman being free shall intermarry with a negro, mulatto, or Indian man or woman bond or free shall within three months after such marriage be banished and removed from this dominion forever. . . . And be it further enacted . . . that if any English woman being free shall have a bastard child by any negro or mulatto, she pay the sum of fifteen pounds sterling, within one month after such bastard child shall be born, to the Church wardens of the parish where she shall be delivered of such a child, and in default of such payment she shall be taken into the possession of the Church wardens and disposed of for five years, and the fine of fifteen pounds, or whatever the woman shall be disposed of for,[7] shall be paid, one third part to their majesties for and towards the support of the government and the contingent charges thereof, and one other third part to the use of the parish where the offense is committed, and the other third part to the informer, and that such bastard child be bound out as a servant by the Church wardens until he or she shall attain the age of thirty years, and in case such English woman that shall have such a bastard child be a servant, she shall be sold by the Church wardens (after her time is expired that she ought by law to serve her master) for five years, and the money she shall be sold for divided as is before appointed, and the child to serve as aforesaid.

And forasmuch as great inconveniences may happen to this country by the setting of negroes and mulattoes free, by their either entertaining negro slaves from their masters' service, or receiving stolen goods, or being grown old bring a charge upon the country; for prevention thereof: Be it enacted . . . that no negro or mulatto be after the end of this present session of assembly set free by any person or persons whatsoever, unless such person or persons, their heirs, executors or administrators pay for the transportation of such negro or negroes out of the country.

1705 Be it enacted . . . that all servants imported and brought into this country, by sea or land, who were not christians in their native country, (except turks and moors in amity with her majesty, and others that can make due proof of their being free in England, or any other christian country, before they were shipped, in order to transportation hither) shall be accounted and be slaves, and as such be here bought and sold notwithstanding a conversion to christianity afterwards. . . .

And also be it enacted . . . that all masters and owners of servants, shall find and provide for their servants, wholesome and competent diet, clothing, and lodging, by the discretion of the county court; and shall not, at any time, give immoderate correction; neither shall, at any time, whip a christian white servant naked, without an order from a justice of the peace. . . .

And for a further christian care and usage of all christian servants: Be it also enacted . . . that no negroes, mulattoes, or Indians, although christians, or Jews, Moors, Mohammedans, or other infidels, shall, at any time, purchase any christian servant. . . .

And for a further prevention of that abominable mixture and spurious issue, which hereafter may increase in this her majesty's colony and dominion, as well as by English, and other white men and women intermarrying with negros and mulattos, as by their unlawful coition with them: Be it enacted . . . that whatsoever English, or other white man or woman, being free, shall intermarry with a negro or mulatto man or woman, bond or free, shall, by judgment of the county court, be committed to prison, and there remain during the space of six months, without bail or mainprize; and shall forfeit and pay ten pounds current money of Virginia. . . .

And be it further enacted, that no minister of the Church of England, or other minister, or person whatsoever, within this colony and dominion, shall hereafter wittingly presume to marry a white man with a negro or mulatto woman; or to marry a white woman with a negro or mulatto man.

From William Waller Hening, *The Statutes at Large: Being a Collection of All the Laws of Virginia* (Richmond, 1809), 1: 252–55; 2: 116–17, 170, 260, 270, 481–82; 3: 86–88, 447–49, 453–54.

Discussion Questions

1. What were the early restrictions on black and white servitude in Virginia?
2. What regulations did the assembly add over time? Pay attention to the changing vocabulary used to describe types of servants.
3. What do laws tell us about what was going on?
4. Why do you think English Virginians eventually decided that race-based slavery was the best way to farm tobacco? Might they have chosen a different path?

Notes

1. That is, paying twice what the service was worth.
2. The fine usually charged for fornication.
3. Many.
4. Harvest time.
5. The "only law" added time onto the servant's indenture.
6. In 1676, Nathaniel Bacon had led a rebellion against the government of Virginia, and the assembly was determined to prevent future insurrections, particularly ones that brought disgruntled whites and blacks together.
7. The price paid for her indenture.

Louisiana's Code Noir, 1724

*F*RENCH INVOLVEMENT IN THE AFRICAN SLAVE TRADE *began in the early 1500s. In the 1600s the French established plantation colonies in the West Indies, including Martinique, Guadeloupe, and Saint Domingue (now Haiti), first growing tobacco and later sugar and coffee. The original Code Noir was issued by French king Louis XIV in 1685 to govern slavery in these islands. This 1724 version is the similar code that Louis XV issued for French Louisiana as it began importing African slaves to work tobacco, indigo, and cotton plantations.*

Louis, King of France and Navarre by the grace of God: to all people now and to come, greetings.

The Directors of the Company of the Indies having informed us that the Province and Colony of Louisiana has been firmly established by a great number of our subjects who make use of Black slaves to cultivate their lands, we have judged that to conserve that colony it is in our authority and jurisdiction to establish there a law and certain rules to maintain the teaching of the Roman Catholic Apostolic Church and to regulate matters concerning the state and quality of slaves in those same islands. And we do desire to make known to our subjects who have settled there and who will in the future set up residence there that although they live in climates infinitely far away, we are always present to them by the reach of our power and our diligence in succoring them.

For these reasons and for others which do move us, on the advice of our Council, acting with our certain knowledge, full power, and royal authority, we . . . do speak, decree, ordain, desire, and be pleased that:

Article 1. We do desire and understand that the edict of 23 April 1615, enacted by the late King of glorious memory, our very honored lord and father, be executed in our islands.[1] Therefore, we do enjoin all our officers to expel from our islands all Jews who have established residence there, and we do command them, as being enemies to the name of Christian, to depart from them within three months from the publication of this edict on pain of confiscation of their bodies and their goods.

Article 2. All slaves who shall be within this same province of ours shall be instructed in the Roman Catholic Apostolic religion and baptized. We do order the inhabitants who buy newly arrived Negroes to have them instructed and baptized within a reasonable time on pain of a set fine. . . .

Article 3. We prohibit all public practice of any religion other than Catholic, Apostolic, and Roman. It is our will that all offenders be punished as rebellious and disobedient to our commands. We do forbid all gatherings to that effect and declare them to be unlawful and seditious cabals. This article pertains likewise to all masters who permit or tolerate such gatherings.

Article 4. No overseers who do not profess the Catholic, Apostolic, Roman religion shall be given charge over Negroes on pain of confiscation of said Negroes from their masters and arbitrary punishment assigned to those overseers who accept such charge.

Article 5. We do enjoin all our subjects of every rank and quality whatsoever to observe strictly all Sundays and Feast Days. We forbid them to work or put their slaves to work on those days, from midnight to midnight, in the fields or at any other kind of work, on pain of fines and arbitrary punishment for the masters as well as confiscation of any slaves caught by our officers in the act of working. They may nevertheless send their slaves to market.[2]

Article 6. We do forbid our White subjects of either sex to enter into marriage with Black people, on pain of punishment and arbitrary fines; we forbid all priest and curates, all lay and ordained missionaries, and even chaplains aboard ships, to marry them. We do forbid our White subjects and even our freed Black subjects and those who are born free to live in concubinage with slaves. It is our will that every person who has had one or more children from such a union, as well as every master who tolerates such a union, be each condemned to pay a fine of three hundred pounds. And if they are the masters of the very slaves by whom they have had said children, it is our will that in addition to the fine they be deprived of the slave and of the children of the slave, and that the slaves be assigned to the local hospital with no possibility of being freed. We do not, however, intend for this article to apply when the Black man, freed or born free, who was not married to his slave during their concubinage, marries, according to the rituals prescribed by the Church, that slave; that slave will be freed accordingly, and her children rendered free and legitimate.

Article 7. The solemnities prescribed for wedlock by the Ordinance of Blois and by the Declaration of November, 1639,[3] shall be observed for slaves as well as for free people, without, however, the consent of the father and mother being required for slaves, but only the consent of the master.

Article 8. We do expressly forbid priests to marry slaves without explicit consent of their masters. We also forbid masters to use any constraints to compel their slaves to marry against their will.

Article 9. Children born of marriages between slaves shall belong to the masters of the women slaves and not to the masters of the men slaves if the husband and wife have different masters.

Article 10. It is our will that if the male slave has married a free wife, the children, male as well as female, shall follow the condition of their mother and be free notwithstanding the servitude of their father; and if the father is free and the mother slave, the children shall be likewise slave.

Article 11. Masters shall be obliged to have their baptized slaves buried in holy ground in graveyards for that purpose. As for slaves who die without the benefit of baptism, they shall be buried at night in some field near to the place where they died.

Article 12. We do forbid slaves to bear weapons or large sticks, on pain of whipping and confiscation of the weapons for the profit of whoever takes the weapons from them; the only exceptions being those whom their masters send out hunting and those who carry recognizable permits.

Article 13. We do likewise forbid slaves belonging to different masters to assemble at day or at night, on pretext of weddings or any other pretext, on their masters' lands or anywhere else, or worse yet on the highways or the byways, on pain of corporal punishment which shall be no less harsh than whipping or branding with the fleur-de-lis; in case of frequent recidivism or other aggravating circumstances, the penalty may be death, which decision we leave to the consideration of the judges. We do enjoin all our subjects to accost those who transgress against this law, arrest them, and carry them off to jail, even if those subjects are not officers and have no warrant to arrest.

Article 14. Masters who are convicted of having permitted or tolerated assemblages including other slaves than their own will themselves be condemned to pay for all damages to their neighbors as a result of said assemblages, in addition to a fine of thirty pounds, and double that amount for repeated offenses.

Article 15. We do forbid slaves to put up for sale, either at market or in private homes, any kind of produce, be it fruit or vegetables, firewood, plants, or any kind of grain, or any other merchandise, or clothes new or old, without the express permission of their masters on a note or some other recognizable sign, on pain of confiscation of all goods without compensation by the masters and an additional fine of six pounds leveled against those who buy the fruits, vegetables, firewood, plants, fodder, and grain. We do also will that those who offend by buying merchandise or clothes, new or old, be fined fifteen hundred pounds as well as all costs, damages, and interests and be prosecuted to the full extent of the law as thieves and receivers of stolen goods.[4]

Article 18. We do desire that the Officers of our Supreme Council of Louisiana send information regarding the quantity of victuals and the quality of apparel that masters should be required to provide for their slaves. Such information shall pertain to the victuals provided per week and the apparel provided per year so that we may regulate and decree accordingly. In the meantime, however, we do permit said Officers to regulate said victuals and apparel. We forbid the masters of said slaves to give them any kind of alcoholic spirits in place of said sustenance or said apparel. . . .

Article 21. Slaves sick from old age, disease, or any other malady, incurable or not, shall be nourished and sustained by their masters. . . .

Article 22. We do declare that slaves may have nothing that does not belong to their master and that everything that comes to them whether through their own labors or the generosity of other people or by any other means, becomes the sole property of their master and that neither the slaves' children, nor their parents, nor their relatives nor any other free person or slave may have claim to that property by right of succession, or arrangement between living persons, or because of death. We do declare all such arrangements null and void, together with all promises they might have made or obligations they might have entered into, considering them as people incapable of arranging or entering into contracts on their own behalf. . . .

Article 24. Slaves shall be neither assigned to public office nor granted public commissions, nor assigned to anyone other than their masters as agents for managing or administering any business; nor shall they be arbitrators, experts, or witnesses in civil or criminal hearings. In cases where they are heard to give witness, their dispositions shall only serve as reminders to aid the judges in clarifying matters, with no derivation of presumptive evidence, conjecture, or the least supporting evidence. Nor may slaves be witnesses in either civil or criminal suits, unless they must be witnesses of necessity and only when White witnesses are lacking, but in no case may they serve as witnesses for or against their masters.

Article 27. The slave who strikes his master, his mistress, or the husband of his mistress,[5] or their children with contusion or loss of blood, or on the face, shall be punished by death. . . .

Article 32. A slave who is fugitive for a month from the day on which his master denounced him to the law shall have his ears cut off and shall be branded with the fleur-de-lis on his shoulder. In case of second offense, for the same amount of time, counting from the day of denunciation, he shall have the ligament behind his knee cut and be branded with the fleur-de-lis on the other shoulder. A third offense shall be punished by death. . . .

Article 38. We do also forbid the subjects of these territories, of whatever rank or condition, to apply or to order to be applied, on their own independent authority, torture upon their slaves while questioning them or for any pretext whatsoever, or to mutilate their bodies or cause their bodies to be mutilated, on pain of confiscation of said slaves and extreme prosecution of the law. We allow only, when they believe that the slaves have deserved it, for masters to chain and beat their slaves with rods or ropes.

Article 39. We do require that our officers criminally prosecute masters or military commanders who have killed or mutilated the bodily members of slaves in their power or under their supervision and to punish according to the atrociousness of the circumstances; if there are grounds for pardon, we do allow our officers to pardon and release the masters and commanders without having to obtain letters of absolution.

Article 43. The husband, wife, and pre-adolescent children may not be seized and sold separately if they are all under the control of the same master. We do declare null and void seizures and sales which thus separate. We do desire in cases of willful separation that a master who effects such transfers of property be deprived of the slave or slaves whom he has held back and that they be delivered over to the buyer at no additional charge.

Translated by John DuVal from Louis Sala-Molins, *Le Code Noir, ou le calvaire de Canaan* (Paris, 1987), 91–185.

Discussion Questions

1. Which articles would you categorize as granting rights to slaves? Which articles restrict their rights? Which articles affect the rights of masters? What other kinds of rules are there?

2. What is similar to the Virginia codes regulating slavery? What is different?

3. The king's claim that "although they live in climates infinitely far away, we are always present to them by the reach of our power and our diligence in succoring them" is probably a bluff—Paris really was a long way off. How effective do you think the code was?

4. There was a loophole in the 1685 Code Noir's version of Article 6 for a master who had a child by a slave: if he married the woman in the church, he did not have to pay a fine, and she and the child were free. What changes in this code? Why might it have changed?

5. Do you think that many slaves needed the provisions of Article 21?

Notes

1. On April 23, 1615, Louis XIII (actually Louis XV's great-great-grandfather) issued an edict banishing Jews from France and forbidding French Christians from protecting or even associating with them. Subsequent kings, partly out of fear that religious violence that plagued France would spread to the colonies, generally tried to prevent Jews (and Protestants) from settling in them. The reference to *islands* is a remnant of the 1685 version of the code.

2. Slaves were often sent to do the shopping in the market, which was not necessarily closed for Sundays and Feast Days.

3. The Ordinance of Blois and the Declaration of 1639 regulated marriage in France.

4. Presumably, the higher fine was for goods that were more valuable and more likely to have been acquired illegally.

5. French women could own their own property (including slaves, whom Europeans defined as property) during marriage, so it was possible for a man to be the husband of the mistress of slaves whom he didn't own himself. This was not the case in the British colonies, in which married women, under the legal system of coverture, could not own their own property.

Venture Smith's Account of
Slavery and Freedom, 1700s

VENTURE SMITH WAS BORN IN WEST AFRICA and stolen into slavery as a boy. He was a slave in New York and Connecticut until he succeeded in buying his freedom in around 1765. Although illiterate, Smith related his life story and published it in 1798. By then he was a successful entrepreneur and substantial property owner in Connecticut. His narrative gives insights into a kind of slavery that is notably different from plantation slavery and into the determination that some slaves had to be free and the means they used to gain freedom. The story begins when Smith was a young boy named Broteer.

I was born at Dukandarra, in Guinea, about the year 1729. My father's name was Saungm Furro, Prince of the Tribe of Dukandarra. My father had three wives. Polygamy was not uncommon in that country, especially among the rich, as every man was allowed to keep as many wives as he could maintain. By his first wife he had three children. The eldest of them was myself, named by my father, Broteer. The other two were named Cundazo and Soozaduka. My father had two children by his second wife, and one by his third. I descended from a very large, tall and stout race of beings, much larger than the generality of people in other parts of the globe, being commonly considerable above six feet in height, and every way well proportioned.

[One day, a rumor spreads of an invasion by an army equipped by "some white nation," and Prince Furro decides to retreat rather than try to defend against an attack that his people are not prepared for.]

The same night which was fixed upon to retreat, my father and his family set off about break of day. The king and his two younger wives went in one company, and my mother and her children in another. We left our dwellings in succession, and my father's company went on first. We directed our course for a large shrub plain, some distance off, where we intended to conceal ourselves from the approaching enemy, until we could refresh and rest ourselves a little. But we presently found that our retreat was not secure. For having struck up a little fire for the purpose of cooking victuals, the enemy who happened to be encamped a little distance off, had sent out a scouting party who discovered us by the smoke of the fire, just as we were extinguishing it, and about to eat. As soon as we had finished eating, my father discovered the party, and immediately began to discharge arrows at them. This was what I first saw, and it alarmed both me and the women, who being unable to make any resistance, immediately betook ourselves to the tall thick reeds not far off, and left the old king to fight alone. For some time I beheld him from the reeds defending himself with great courage and firmness, till at last he was obliged to surrender himself into their hands.

They then came to us in the reeds, and the very first salute I had from them was a violent blow on the head with the fore part of a gun, and at the same time a grasp round the neck. I then had a rope put about my neck, as had all the women in the thicket with me, and were immediately led to my father, who was likewise pinioned and haltered for leading. In this condition we were all led to the camp. The women and myself being pretty submissive, had tolerable treatment from the enemy, while my father was closely interrogated respecting his money which they knew he must have. But as he gave them no account of it, he was instantly cut and pounded on his body with great inhumanity, that he might be induced by the torture he suffered to make the discovery. All this availed not in the least to make him give up his money, but he despised all the tortures which they inflicted, until the continued exercise and increase of torment, obliged him to sink and expire. He thus died without informing his enemies of the place where his money lay. I saw him while he was thus tortured to death. The shocking scene is to this day fresh in my mind, and I have often been overcome while thinking on it. He was a man of remarkable stature. I should judge as much as six feet and six or seven inches high, two feet across his shoulders, and every way well proportioned. He was a man of remarkable strength and resolution, affable, kind and gentle, ruling with equity and moderation.

[Smith has to walk some four hundred miles to the coast.]

I and other prisoners were put on board a canoe, under our master, and rowed away to a vessel belonging to Rhode-Island, commanded by Capt. Collingwood, and the mate Thomas Mumford. While we were going to the vessel, our master told us all to appear to the best possible advantage for sale. I was bought on board by one Robertson Mumford, steward of said vessel, for four gallons of rum, and a piece of calico, and called VENTURE, on account of his having purchased me with his own private venture. Thus I came by my name. All the slaves that were bought for that vessel's cargo, were two hundred and sixty.

After all the business was ended on the coast of Africa, the ship sailed from thence to Barbados. After an ordinary passage, except great mortality by the smallpox, which broke out on board, we arrived at the island of Barbados: but when we reached it, there were found out of the two hundred and sixty that sailed from Africa, not more than two hundred alive. These were all sold, except myself and three more, to the planters there.

The vessel then sailed for Rhode-Island, and arrived there after a comfortable passage. Here my master sent me to live with one of his sisters, until he could carry me to Fisher's Island, the place of his residence. I had then completed my eighth year. After staying with his sister some time I was taken to my master's place to live. . . .

The first of the time of living at my master's own place, I was pretty much employed in the house at carding wool and other household business. In this situation I continued for some years, after which my master put me to work out of doors. After many proofs of my faithfulness and honesty, my master began to put great confidence in me. My behavior to him had as yet been submissive and obedient. I then began to have hard tasks imposed on me. Some of these were to pound four bushels of ears of corn every night in a barrel for the poultry, or be rigorously punished. At other seasons of the year I had to card wool until a very late hour. These tasks I had to perform when I was about nine years old. . . .

After I had lived with my master thirteen years, being then about twenty-two years old, I married Meg, a slave of his who was about my age. My master owned a certain Irishman, named Heddy, who about that time formed a plan of secretly leaving his master. After he had long had this plan in meditation he suggested it to me. At first I cast a deaf ear to it, and rebuked Heddy for harboring in his mind such a rash undertaking. But after he had persuaded and much enchanted me with the prospect of gaining my freedom by such a method, I at length agreed to accompany him. Heddy next inveigled two of his fellow servants to accompany us. The place to which we designed to go was the Mississippi. Our next business was to lay in a sufficient store of provisions for our voyage. We privately collected out of our master's store, six great old cheeses, two firkins of butter, and one whole batch of new bread. When we had gathered all our own clothes and some more, we took them all about midnight, and went to the waterside. We stole our master's boat, embarked, and then directed our course for the Mississippi river.[1]

We mutually confederated not to betray or desert one another on pain of death. We first steered our course for Montauk point, the east end of Long-Island. After our arrival there we landed, and Heddy and I made an incursion into the island after fresh water, while our two comrades were left at a little distance from the boat, employed at cooking. When Heddy and I had sought some time for water, he returned to our companions, and I continued on looking for my object. When Heddy had performed his business with our companions who were engaged in cooking, he went directly to the boat, stole all the clothes in it, and then traveled away for East-Hampton, as I was informed. I returned to my fellows not long after. They informed me that our clothes were stolen, but could not determine who was the thief, yet they suspected Heddy as he was missing. After reproving my two comrades for not taking care of our things which were in the boat, I advertised Heddy and sent two men in search of him. They pursued and overtook him at Southampton and returned him to the boat. I then thought it might afford some chance for my freedom, or at least a palliation for my running away, to return Heddy immediately to his master, and inform him that I was induced to go away by Heddy's address. Accordingly I set off with him and the rest of my companions for our master's, and arrived there without any difficulty. I informed my master that Heddy was the ringleader of our revolt, and that he had used us ill. He immediately put Heddy into custody, and myself and companions were well received and went to work as usual. Not a long time passed after that, before Heddy was sent by my master to New-London jail.

At the close of that year I was sold to a Thomas Stanton, and had to be separated from my wife and one daughter, who was about one month old. He resided at Stonington-point. To this place I brought with me from my late master's, two johannes,[2] three old Spanish dollars, and two thousand of coppers, besides five pounds of my wife's money. This money I got by cleaning gentlemen's shoes and drawing boots, by catching muskrats and minks, raising potatoes and carrots, etc., and by fishing in the night, and at odd spells. . . .

About one year and a half after that time, my master purchased my wife and her child, for seven hundred pounds old tenor. One time my master sent me two miles after a barrel of molasses, and ordered me to carry it on my shoulders. I made out to carry it all the way to my master's house. When I lived with Captain George Mumford, only to try my strength, I took up on my knees a tierce of salt containing seven bushels, and carried it two or three rods.[3] Of this fact there are several eyewitnesses now living.

Towards the close of the time that I resided with this master, I had a falling out with my mistress. This happened one time when my master was gone to Long-Island a gunning. At first the quarrel began between my wife and her mistress. I was then at work in the barn, and hearing a racket in the house, induced me to run there and see what had broken out. When I entered the house, I found my mistress in a violent passion with my wife, for what she informed me was a mere trifle; such a small affair that I forbear to put my mistress to the shame of having it known. I earnestly requested my wife to beg pardon of her mistress for the sake of peace, even if she had given no just occasion for offence. But whilst I was thus saying my mistress turned the blows which she was repeating on my wife to me. She took down her horse-whip, and while she was glutting her fury with it, I reached out my great black hand, raised it up and received the blows of the whip on it which were designed for my head. Then I immediately committed the whip to the devouring fire.

When my master returned from the island, his wife told him of the affair, but for the present he seemed to take no notice of it, and mentioned not a word about it to me. Some days after his return, in the morning as I was putting on a log in the fire-place, not suspecting harm from any one, I received a most violent stroke on the crown of my head with a club two feet long and as large round as a chair-post. This blow very badly wounded my head, and the scar of it remains to this day. The first blow made me have my wits about me you may suppose, for as soon as he went to renew it, I snatched the club out of his hands and dragged him out of the door. He then sent for his brother to come and assist him, but I presently left my master, took the club he wounded me with, carried it to a neighboring Justice of the Peace, and complained of my master. He finally advised me to return to my master, and live contented with him till he abused me again, and then complain. I consented to do accordingly. But before I set out for my master's, up he come and his brother Robert after me. The Justice improved this convenient opportunity to caution my master. He asked him for what he treated his slave thus hastily and unjustly, and told him what would be the consequence if he continued the same treatment towards me. After the Justice had ended his discourse with my master, he and his brother set out with me for home, one before and the other behind me. When they had come to a bye place, they both dismounted their respective horses, and fell to beating me with great violence. I became enraged at this and immediately turned them both under me, laid one of them across the other, and stamped both with my feet what I would.

This occasioned my master's brother to advise him to put me off. A short time after this I was taken by a constable and two men. They carried me to a blacksmith's shop and had me hand-cuffed. When I returned home my mistress enquired much of her waiters, whether Venture was hand-cuffed. When she was informed that I was, she appeared to be very contented and was much transported with the news. In the midst of this content and joy, I presented myself before my mistress, showed her my hand-cuffs, and gave her thanks for my gold rings. For this my master commanded a negro of his to fetch him a large ox chain. This my master locked on my legs with two padlocks. I continued to wear the chain peaceably for two or three days, when my master asked me with contemptuous hard names whether I had not better be freed from my chains and go to work. I answered him, No. Well then, said he, I will send you to the West-Indies or banish you, for I am resolved not to keep you. I answered him I crossed the waters to come here, and I am willing to cross them to return.

For a day or two after this not any one said much to me, until one Hempsted Miner, of Stonington, asked me if I would live with him. I answered him that I would. He then requested me to make myself discontented and to appear as un-reconciled to my master as I could before that he bargained with him for me; and that in return he would give me a good chance to gain my freedom when I came to live with him. I did as he requested me. Not long after Hempsted Miner purchased me of my master for fifty-six pounds lawful. He took the chain and padlocks from off me immediately after.

[For safekeeping, Smith buries the money that he has saved up. Miner breaks his promise and sells Smith to another master, Col. Oliver Smith.]

This was the third time of my being sold, and I was then thirty-one years old. As I never had an opportunity of redeeming myself whilst I was owned by Miner, though he promised to give me a chance, I was then very ambitious of obtaining it. I asked my master one time if he would consent to have me purchase my freedom. He replied that he would. I was then very happy, knowing that I was at that time able to pay part of the purchase money, by means of the money which I some time since buried. This I took out of the earth and tendered to my master, having previously engaged a free negro man to take his security for it, as I was the property of my master, and therefore could not safely take his obligation myself. What was wanting in redeeming myself, my master agreed to wait on me for, until I could procure it for him. I still continued to work for Col. Smith. There was continually some interest accruing on my master's note to my friend the free negro man above named, which I received, and with some besides which I got by fishing, I laid out in land adjoining my old master Stanton's. By cultivating this land with the greatest diligence and economy, at times when my master did not require my labor, in two years I laid up ten pounds. This my friend tendered my master for myself, and received his note for it.

Being encouraged by the success which I had met in redeeming myself, I again solicited my master for a further chance of completing it. The chance for which I solicited him was that of going out to work the ensuing winter. He agreed to this on condition that I would give him one quarter of my earnings. On these terms I worked the following winter, and earned four pounds sixteen shillings, one quarter of which went to my master for the privilege, and the rest was paid him on my own account. This added to the other payments made up forty-four pounds, eight shillings, which I had paid on my own account. I was then about thirty-five years old.

The next summer I again desired he would give me a chance of going out to work. But he refused and answered that he must have my labor this summer, as he did not have it the past winter. I replied that I considered it as hard that I could not have a chance to work out when the season became advantageous, and that I must only be permitted to hire myself out in the poorest season of the year. He asked me after this what I would give him for the privilege per month. I replied that I would leave it wholly with his own generosity to determine what I should return him a month. Well then, said he, if so two pounds a month. I answered him that if that was the least he would take I would be contented.

Accordingly I hired myself out at Fisher's Island, and earned twenty pounds; thirteen pounds six shillings of which my master drew for the privilege, and the remainder I paid him for my freedom. This made fifty-one pounds two shillings which I paid him. In October following I went and wrought six months at Long Island. In that six month's time I cut and corded four hundred cords of wood, besides threshing out seventy-five bushels of grain, and received of my wages down only twenty pounds, which left remaining a larger sum. Whilst I was out that time, I took up on my wages only one pair of shoes. At night I lay on the hearth, with one coverlet over and another under me. I returned to my master and gave him what I received of my six months labor. This left only thirteen pounds eighteen shillings to make up the full sum for my redemption. My master liberated me, saying that I might pay what was behind if I could ever make it convenient, otherwise it would be well. The amount of the money which I had paid my master towards redeeming my time, was seventy-one pounds two shillings. The reason of my master for asking such an unreasonable price, was he said, to secure himself in case I should ever come to want. Being thirty-six years old, I left Col. Smith once for all. I had already been sold three different times, made considerable money with seemingly nothing to derive it from, been cheated out of a large sum of money, lost much by misfortunes, and paid an enormous sum for my freedom.

[Smith later buys his wife, daughter Hannah, son Solomon (who dies soon thereafter, leading Venture and Meg to name a subsequent son Solomon in his memory), son Cuff (who serves in the Continental Army during the American Revolution), and two other men.]

I am now sixty-nine years old. Though once straight and tall, measuring without shoes six feet one inch and an half, and every way well proportioned, I am now bowed down with age and hardship. My strength which was once equal if not superior to any man whom I have ever seen, is now enfeebled so that life is a burden, and it is with fatigue that I can walk a couple of miles, stooping over my staff. Other griefs are still behind, on account of which some aged people, at least, will pity me. My eye-sight has gradually failed, till I am almost blind, and whenever I go abroad one of my grandchildren must direct my way; besides for many years I have been much pained and troubled with an ulcer on one of my legs. But amidst all my griefs and pains, I have many consolations; Meg, the wife of my youth, whom I married for love, and bought with my money, is still alive. My freedom is a privilege which nothing else can equal. Notwithstanding all the losses I have suffered by fire, by the injustice of knaves, by the cruelty and oppression of false hearted friends, and the perfidy of my own countrymen whom I have assisted and redeemed from bondage, I am now possessed of more than one hundred acres of land, and three habitable dwelling houses. It gives me joy to think that I *have* and that I *deserve* so good a character, especially for *truth* and *integrity*. While I am now looking to the grave as my home, my joy for this world would be full—if my children, Cuff for whom I paid two hundred dollars when a boy, and Solomon who was born soon after I purchased his mother—If Cuff and Solomon—O! that they had walked in the way of their father. But a father's lips are closed in silence and in grief!—Vanity of vanities, all is vanity!

From Venture Smith, *A Narrative of the Life and Adventures of Venture, a Native of Africa: But Resident above Sixty Years in the United States of America, Related by Himself* (New London, CT, 1798), 5–31.

Discussion Questions

1. What did Venture Smith remember about Africa? Is his memory reliable?
2. How did he react to enslavement? What angered him the most?
3. From what Smith chose to discuss, can you tell what was important to him?
4. Compare Smith's autobiography with Equiano's as to their effectiveness in the cause of abolition.

Notes

1. This trip would have been over one thousand miles.
2. A Portuguese coin.
3. A tierce is a cask capable of holding 159 liters, and a rod is 16.5 feet.

Afro-Floridians to the Spanish King, 1738

IN 1693, SPANISH KING CARLOS II DECREED THAT SLAVES WHO FLED Carolina were free in Florida, if they became Catholic. The king's motives were humanitarian and practical—he wanted to weaken the English colonies. Many Carolina slaves took up the offer. After some Spanish Floridians ignored the decree and reenslaved runaways, Francisco Menéndez, a captain of the free black militia who could write in Spanish, wrote petitions asking for the fugitives' freedom and warning that the Afro-Floridians might join the English or Indians against the Spanish. The petitions succeeded when a new governor of Florida, Manuel de Montiano, in 1738 acknowledged the freedom of all Carolina runaways. In gratitude, the former slaves wrote this letter to the king.

My lord,

All the Black people who escaped from the English plantations, obedient and loyal slaves to Your Majesty, declare that Your Majesty has done us true charity in ordering us to be given freedom for having come to this country and for being Christian and following the true religion[1] that saves us.

Disobeying a very high and sacred law, they[2] bound us and made us slaves for many years, putting us through many miseries and much hunger. But obeying laws which Your Majesty decreed, the present Governor, Don Manuel de Montiano, has set us free, for which we greatly appreciate Your Majesty and thank him for this most royal kindness.

Likewise, the Governor has offered and assured us that he will establish a place for us, which is called Gracia Reál,[3] where we may serve God and Your Majesty, cultivating the land so that there may be fruit in this country.

We promise Your Majesty that, whenever the opportunity arises, we will be the cruelest enemies to the English and will risk our lives in the service of Your Majesty, even to spilling the last drop of blood, in defense of the great crown of Spain and our holy faith.

Thus Your Majesty may order any amount of service from us because we are his faithful slaves all of our life and we will always pray Our Lord to guard Your Majesty's life and the life of all the Royal Family throughout the slow years that we poor people need.

Saint Augustine, Florida, 10 June 1738.

Translated by John DuVal from Audiencia de Santo Domingo 844, fol. 607, reel 15, P. K. Yonge Library, University of Florida, Gainesville.

Discussion Questions

1. Why did the freed slaves name their settlement Gracia Reál (Royal Grace)?

2. Do you think they wanted to live in a settlement separate from the Spaniards at St. Augustine?

3. Why would people who had worked so hard to escape slavery declare themselves the king's "faithful slaves"? Why did they promise to be "the cruelest enemies to the English"?

4. How does this letter compare to what the Dutch agreed to give Paulo Angola and others in the 1644 New Netherland Act, printed earlier in this section?

Notes

1. Catholicism.

2. Spaniards in Florida disobeying the king's decree.

3. Gracia Reál (Royal Grace) de Santa Teresa de Mose was the settlement the freed slaves built in 1738 outside St. Augustine. Francisco Menéndez led this community, which lasted until 1763, when Florida became a British colony.

George Whitefield Admonishes Southern Slaveholders, 1740

*G*EORGE *W*HITEFIELD (PRONOUNCED *W*HITFIELD) WAS AN *E*NGLISH PREACHER *and one of the founders of Methodism. He was said to have a voice like a trumpet, calling people to change their ways. In 1738, Whitefield began to preach in Georgia. His rousing sermons in Georgia and throughout the British colonies helped to spark a religious revival movement that some scholars have called the "Great Awakening." After Whitefield wrote this letter, newspapers around the British colonies reprinted it, and Benjamin Franklin published a pamphlet that included it and two other of Whitefield's letters.*

To the Inhabitants of Maryland, Virginia, North and South Carolina,

As I recently passed through your provinces in my way hither, I was sensible touched with a fellow-feeling of the miseries of the poor Negroes. Could I have preached more frequently amongst you, I should have delivered my thoughts in my public discourses; but as my business here required me to stop as little as possible on the road, I have no other way to discharge the concern which at present lies upon my heart, than by sending you this letter. How you will receive it I know not. Whether you will accept it in love, or be offended with me, as the master of the damsel was with Paul, for casting the evil spirit out of her, when he saw the hope of his gain was gone, I am uncertain.[1] Whatever be the event, I must inform you in the meekness and gentleness of Christ, that I think God has a quarrel with you for your abuse of and cruelty to the poor Negroes. Whether it be lawful for Christians to buy slaves, and thereby encourage the nations from whom they are bought to be at perpetual war with each other, I shall not take upon me to determine. Sure I am, it is sinful, when bought, to use them as bad, nay worse, than as though they were brutes; and whatever particular exceptions there may be (as I would charitably hope there are some) I fear the generality of you that own Negroes, are liable to such a charge; for your slaves, I believe, work as hard if not harder than the horses whereon you ride. These, after they have done their work, are fed and taken proper care of. But many Negroes when wearied with labor in your planta-tions, have been obliged to grind their own corn after they return home.

Your dogs are caressed and fondled at your tables. But your slaves, who are frequently styled dogs or beasts, have not an equal privilege. They are scarce per-mitted to pick up the crumbs which fall from their masters' tables.[2] Nay, some, as I have been informed by an eye-witness, have been, upon the most trifling provocation, cut with knives, and had forks thrown into their flesh—not to mention what numbers have been given up to the inhuman usage of cruel task masters, who by their unrelenting scourges have ploughed upon their backs, and made long furrows, and at length brought them even to death itself.

It's true, I hope there are but few such monsters of barbarity suffered to sub-sist amongst you. Some, I hear, have been lately executed in Virginia for killing slaves, and the laws are very severe against such who at any time murder them.

And perhaps it might be better for the poor creatures themselves, to be hur-ried out of life, than to be made so miserable, as they generally are in it. And indeed, considering what usage they commonly meet with, I have wondered, that we have not more instances of self-murder among the Negroes, or that they have not more frequently rose up in arms against their owners. Virginia has once, and Charlestown more than once been threatened in this way.

And though I heartily pray God they may never be permitted to get the upper hand, yet should such a thing be permitted by Providence, all good men must acknowledge the judgment would be just. For is it not the highest ingratitude, as well as cruelty, not to let your poor slaves enjoy some fruits of their labor?

When, passing along, I have viewed your plantations cleared and cultivated, many spacious houses built, and the owners of them faring sumptuously every day, my blood has frequently almost run cold within me, to consider how many of your slaves had neither convenient food to eat or proper raiment to put on, notwithstanding most of the comforts you enjoy were solely owing to their indefatigable labors. The Scripture says, "Thou shalt not muzzle the ox that treadeth out the corn."[3] Does God take care of oxen? And will he not take care of the Negroes also? Undoubtedly he will. Go to now, ye rich men, weep and howl for your miseries that shall come upon you! Behold the provision of the poor Negroes, which have reaped down your fields, which is by you denied them, crieth; and the cries of them which reaped, are entered into the ears of the Lord of Sabaoth![4] We have a remarkable instance of God's taking cog-nizance of, and avenging the quarrel of poor slaves, 2 Samuel 21:1. "Then there was a famine in the days of David, three years, year after year; and David enquired of the Lord. And the Lord answered, it is for Saul and his bloody house, because he slew the Gibeonites." Two things are here very remarkable. First, that these Gibeonites were only hewers of wood and drawers of water, or in other words, slaves like yours. Secondly, that this plague was sent by God many years after the injury, the cause of the plague, was committed. And for what end was this and such like examples recorded in Holy Scripture? Without doubt, for our learning, upon whom the ends of the world are come. For God is the same today as he was yesterday, and will continue the same forever. He does not reject the prayer of the poor and destitute, nor disregard the cry of the meanest Negroes! The blood of them spilt for these many years in your respective provinces will ascend up to Heaven against you. I wish I could say it would speak better things than the blood of Abel.[5]

But this is not all. Enslaving or misusing their bodies would, comparatively speaking, be an inconsiderable evil, was proper care taken of their souls. But I have great reason to believe that most of you, on purpose, keep your Negroes ignorant of Christianity; or otherwise, why are they permitted through your provinces, openly to profane the Lord's Day, by their dancing, piping, and such like? I know the general pretense for this neglect of their souls is that teaching them Christianity would make them proud, and consequently unwilling to submit to slavery. But what a dreadful reflection is this on your Holy Religion? What blasphemous notions must those that make such an objection have of the precepts of Christianity? Do you find any one command in the gospel that has the least tendency to make people forget their relative duties? Do you not read that servants, and as many as are under the yoke of bondage, are required to be subject, in all lawful things, to their masters; and that not only to the good and gentle, but also to the froward?[6] Nay, may I not only appeal to your own hearts, whether deviating from the laws of Jesus Christ is not the cause of all the evils and miseries mankind now universally groan under, and of all the vices we find both in ourselves and others? Certainly it is. And therefore, the reason why servants generally prove so bad is because so little care is taken to breed them up in the nurture and admonition of the Lord. But some will be so bold perhaps as to reply that a few of the Negroes have been taught Christianity, and, notwithstanding, have been remarkably worse than others. But what Christianity were they taught? They were baptized and taught to read and write: and this they may do, and much more, and yet be far from the Kingdom of God; for there is a vast difference between civilizing and Christianizing a Negro. A black as well as a white man may be civilized by outward restraints, and afterwards break through those restraints again. But I challenge the whole world to produce a single instance of a Negro's being made a thorough Christian, and thereby made a worse servant. It cannot be.

But farther, if teaching slaves Christianity has such a bad influence upon their lives, why are you generally desirous of having your children taught? Think you they are any way better by nature than the poor Negroes? No, in no wise. Blacks are just as much, and no more, conceived and born in sin, as white men are. Both, if born and bred up here, I am persuaded, are naturally capable of the same improvement. And as for the grown Negroes, I am apt to think whenever the Gospel is preached with power amongst them, that many will be brought effectually home to God. Your present and past bad usage of them, however ill-designed, may thus far do them good, as to break their wills, increase the sense of their natural misery, and consequently better dispose their minds to accept the redemption wrought out for them, by the death and obedience of Jesus Christ. God has, not long since, been pleased to make some of the Negroes in New England vessels of mercy; and some of them, I hear, have been brought to cry out, "What shall we do to be saved?" in the province of Pennsylvania. Doubtless there is a time, when the fullness of the Gentiles will come in.[7] And then I believe, if not before, these despised slaves will find the Gospel of Christ to be the power of God to their salvation, as well as we. But I know all arguments to prove the necessity of taking care of your Negroes' souls, though never so conclusive, will prove ineffectual, till you are convinced of the necessity of securing the salvation of your own. That you yourselves are not effectually convinced of this, I think is too notorious to want evidence. A general deadness as to divine things, and not to say a general profaneness, is discernible both in pastors and people.

Most of you are without any teaching priest. And whatever quantity of rum there may be, yet I fear but very few Bibles are annually imported into your different provinces. God has already begun to visit for this as well as other wicked things. For near this two years past, he has been in a remarkable manner contending with the people of South Carolina. Their houses have been depopulated with the smallpox and fever, and their own slaves have rose up in arms against them.[8] These judgments are undoubtedly sent abroad, not only that the inhabitants of that, but of other provinces, should learn righteousness. And unless you all repent, you all must in like manner expect to perish. God first generally corrects us with whips; if that will not do, he must chastise us with scorpions. A foreign enemy[9] is now threatening to invade you, and nothing will more provoke God, to give you up as a prey into their teeth, than impenitence and unbelief—let these be removed, and the sons of violence shall not be able to hurt you. No, your oxen shall be strong to labor; there shall be no decay of your people by epidemical sickness; no leading away into captivity from abroad, and no complaining in your streets at home. Your sons shall grow up as young plants, and your daughters be as the polished corners of the temple;

and to sum up all blessings in one, then shall the Lord be your God.[10] That you may be the people who are in such a happy case, is the earnest prayer of

Your sincere well-wisher and servant in Christ,
G. Whitefield
Savannah, January 23, 1740

From George Whitefield, *Three Letters from the Reverend Mr. G. Whitefield* (Philadelphia, 1740), 13–16.

Discussion Questions

1. What does this letter tell you about Whitefield's beliefs about the Christian God and the duties of Christians?

2. What do you think slaveholders' response to this letter might have been? What might slaves have agreed with in this letter? What might they have disagreed with?

3. What does Whitefield mean when he says that Christians, by buying slaves, "thereby encourage the nations from whom they are bought to be at perpetual war with each other"?

4. Does it surprise you to learn that, within a few years of writing this letter, Whitefield had acquired a South Carolina plantation worked by slaves, whose profits he used to fund an orphanage, and was supporting the legalization of slavery (as well as religious instruction) in Georgia, a colony that had initially outlawed slavery?

Notes

1. When the Christian apostle Paul cast a demon out of a slave girl, her master was angry because she could no longer tell fortunes. Acts 16:16–24.

2. Matthew 15:22–28.

3. Deuteronomy 25:4.

4. Whitefield paraphrases James 5:4, substituting "Negroes" for "laborers." *Sabaoth* means armies in Hebrew.

5. Hebrews 13:8; 12:24.

6. 1 Peter 2:18. Froward means inappropriate or bad.

7. Acts 16:25–33; Romans 11:25–26.

8. Whitefield refers here to South Carolina's 1738 smallpox epidemic and 1739 Stono Rebellion.

9. Spain.

10. Psalm 144:12–15.

Advertisement for a Slave Sale, Charleston, c. 1770s

*T*HIS ADVERTISEMENT IN A CHARLESTON NEWSPAPER INFORMED *readers of an up-coming auction of slaves newly arrived from Africa. Newspapers in many colonies regularly featured ads for slave sales, particularly when a slave ship arrived, as well as for the return of runaways. The pictures were standard plates that a printer could use in an auction ad.*

Discussion Questions

1. What information does the advertisement give?
2. From reading it, what concerns do you think slave buyers might have had?
3. What kind of work do you think the Africans were bound for?
4. What might they have thought if they could read the ad?

TO BE SOLD, on board the Ship *Bance-Island*, on tuesday the 6th of *May* next, at *Ashley-Ferry*; a choice cargo of about 250 fine healthy

NEGROES,

just arrived from the Windward & Rice Coast. ——The utmost care has already been taken, and shall be continued, to keep them free from the least danger of being infected with the SMALL-POX, no boat having been on board, and all other communication with people from *Charles-Town* prevented.

Austin, Laurens, & Appleby.

N. B. Full one Half of the above Negroes have had the SMALL-POX in their own Country.

Source: *Library of Congress.*

VI

WOMEN AND COLONIALISM

W OMEN APPEAR IN MANY OF THIS BOOK'S DOCUMENTS, but this section particularly asks you to explore the relationship between women and the
goals and experiences of their peoples during the colonial era. How did the
colonizing of North America affect different women? What kinds of women
were there, and how did their positions differ? How did women interpret their
place in relation to men of their own society, to people of other societies, and
to colonialism and slavery?

Lettre du Père Jacques Gravier

Excerpt

*T*OUT LE MONDE PARTIT POUR L'HYVERNEMENT LE 26 SEPTEMBRE *à la réserve de quelques vieilles qui restèrent dans 14 ou 15 cabanes et d'un assez bon nombre de Kaskaskia. Quelque diligence que j'aye faite pour que l'on n'embarquasse pas les petits enfants malades sans avoir reçu le baptesme, il m'en est échappé quelques-uns que les parens n'ont pas voulu me permettre de baptiser, j'en ai poursuivi d'autres jusqu'à l'embarquement afin de tacher de leur donner leur viatique pour l'éternité, bien m'en prit de ne mettre pas rebuté des railleries que les parens et toutes les femmes qui étoient presqu'à s'embarquer firent de mes inquiétudes, car Dieu récompensa mes peines par le salut de plusieurs de ces petits innocens. Le chef des Peouareoua étonné de me voir au bord de l'eau, demanda ce que je faisois là et si j'attendois la mère d'un enfant malade: [je] lui répondis en raillant que je voulois baptiser son enfant, sur quoi il se mit à faire quelques plaisanteries: ne vous étonnez pas, lui dis je, et à ceux qui étoient présent, s'il y a si longtems que je me tiens ici debout; je m'étonne bien plus de ce qu'on n'a pas pitié des enfans qui sont et seront esclaves du démon s'ils meurent sans baptesme. Quoique cette raison ne leur soit pas évidente pour se defaire de mes importunités on a souffert que j'en ai ondoyé plusieurs.**

*From "Lettre du Père Jacques Gravier en forme de Journal de la Mission de l'Immaculée Conception de Notre Dame aux Ilinois," February 15, 1694, in *The Jesuit Relations and Allied Documents: Travels and Explorations of the Jesuit Missionaries in New France, 1610–1791*, ed. Reuben Gold Thwaites (New York, 1959), 64: 188–214. Translation begins on p. 206.

Anne Bradstreet's Prologue to
The Tenth Muse, 1650

*T*HIS POET WAS BORN ANNE DUDLEY AROUND 1612 IN ENGLAND. *She married Simon Bradstreet in 1628. Two years later, Anne Bradstreet moved with her husband and parents to the young colony of New England. This poem was the prologue to her book of poems written in New England and published in London in 1650. Other collections of her work were published after her death in 1672. Bradstreet was the first published poet living in North America. In this poem, she justifies writing poetry.*

To sing of Wars, of Captains, and of Kings,
Of Cities founded, Commonwealths begun,
For my mean Pen are too superior things,
And how they all, or each, their dates have run:
Let Poets and Historians set these forth,
My obscure verse, shall not so dim their worth.

But when my wondering eyes, and envious heart,
Great Bartas' sugared lines[1] do but read o'er;
Fool, I do grudge, the Muses did not part
'Twixt him and me, that over-fluent store;
A Bartas can do what a Bartas will,
But simple I, according to my skill.

From Schoolboy's tongue, no rhetoric we expect,
Nor yet a sweet Consort, from broken strings,
Nor perfect beauty, where's a main defect,
My foolish, broken, blemished Muse so sings;

And this to mend, alas, no Art is able,
'Cause nature made it so irreparable.

Nor can I, like that fluent sweet-tongued Greek
Who lisped at first, speak afterwards more plain;[2]
By Art, he gladly found what he did seek,
A full requital of his striving pain;
Art can do much, but this maxim's most sure,
A weak or wounded brain admits no cure.

I am obnoxious to each carping tongue,
Who says my hand a needle better fits,
A Poet's Pen, all scorn, I should thus wrong;
For such despite[3] they cast on female wits:
If what I do prove well, it won't advance,
They'll say it's stolen, or else, it was by chance.

But sure the antique Greeks were far more mild,
Else of our Sex why feigned they those nine,[4]
And Poesy made, Calliope's own child,
So 'mongst the rest, they placed the Arts divine;
But this weak knot they will full soon untie,
The Greeks did naught, but play the fools and lie.

Let Greeks be Greeks, and Women what they are,
Men have precedency, and still excel,
It is but vain, unjustly to wage war,
Men can do best, and Women know it well;
Preeminence in each and all is yours,
Yet grant some small acknowledgment of ours.

And oh, ye high-flown quills, that soar the skies,
And ever with your prey, still catch your praise,
If e'er you deign these lowly lines your eyes
Give wholesome Parsley wreath, I ask no bays;[5]
This mean and unrefined stuff of mine,
Will make your glistering gold but more to shine.

From Anne Bradstreet, *The Tenth Muse, Lately Sprung Up in America; Or Several Poems Compiled with Great Variety of Wit and Learning, Full of Delight* (London, 1650), 3–4.

Discussion Questions

1. What did Bradstreet claim that her poems were *not* doing? What place did she claim for women?

2. New Englanders did not punish Bradstreet for writing poetry, and there is no evidence that they objected to her writing. Why not?

3. Bradstreet had a busy life, running a colonial home and raising eight children. Why do you think she wrote poetry too? Do you think she was happy that it was published?

4. Does she protest too much?

Notes

1. Guillaume du Bartas, a sixteenth-century Protestant French poet, popular in Bradstreet's time through Joshua Sylvestre's translations into English.

2. Overcoming a lisp was part of the mythology of several Greek orators. Bradstreet probably refers to Demosthenes (c. 384–322 BC), who overcame a speech impediment by practicing with pebbles in his mouth.

3. Spite.

4. The nine Greek muses were female goddesses who inspired the arts: Calliope for epic poetry, Euterpe for lyric poetry, Erato for love poetry, Polyhymnia for sacred poetry and prose, Clio for history, Melpomene for tragedy, Thalia for comedy, Terpsichore for dance, and Urania for astronomy. Whoever gave Bradstreet's book its title (presumably not her) honored her by calling her the tenth muse.

5. A bay (laurel) wreath was an ancient way to crown a victory. A parsley wreath would have been considerably more humble and domestic.

Marie de L'Incarnation to Her Son, 1667

*M*ARIE GUYART WAS BORN IN *1599* IN TOURS, *a French town in the Loire Val-ley. She took the name Marie de L'Incarnation when she became a nun in the Ursuline order, a teaching order called to instruct Catholic girls. A few years later, she dreamed of a distant and foggy land and read the call of Father Paul Le Jeune, a Jesuit whose account of the Montagnais is in this volume, for women to come to New France to assist the Jesuit mission. Although Ursulines were clois-tered and rarely left their convents, the forty-year-old Marie de L'Incarnation and two other nuns crossed the Atlantic and started a school for French and Indian girls in Quebec. She wrote the following letter when she was sixty-eight years old.*

My dear son,[1]

In an earlier letter I told you what happened this year with the Iroquois and how because of the wise policies of Monsieur de Tracy they came to us after their defeat to ask for peace.[2] Two of the proudest and cruelest of these na-tions,[3] living at a distance of sixty leagues from each other, were the first to do so. They and all the others were so terrified by the defeat of the Mohawks and the courage of the French (whom they had previously regarded as so many chickens) that they imagined a French army following at their heels every-where they went. In their terror they were glad to be able to come asking for peace and agreeing to every condition offered them, that is to say, to bring back all of our people they had taken prisoner and to bring members of their own families, too, as hostages for the priests and other French people getting ready to venture into their territory.[4]

All this was carried out to the letter. The priests left with some Frenchmen and some Iroquois who had been instructed during their captivity and were now good Christians. We are instructing their families who are living here as hostages, and many of them are to be baptized on the feast of the Conception of the Holy Virgin, which is the feast for all these regions.[5]

An Iroquois woman has given us her daughter on the condition that she become French like us. She is a very bright child and is so completely taken with the mysteries of the faith and French ways that she doesn't want to go back to her parents. She has the disposition of the women of her nation, who are the sweetest, most docile creatures in the world.

Monsieur de Tracy has demonstrated his zeal and charity in effecting these transmigrations. In addition to the Iroquois women, he has seen to the return of other Indian wives and girls who had been captive and had forgotten our language and religion during their captivity.[6] He has dressed them and generously paid pensions[7] for them. As for us, we haven't wasted the time and effort we have spent on them, because with the help of divine grace, we have reawakened their first memories and rekindled their faith, which had almost gone out in their souls. We have married one to a Frenchman with a good house and another, an Algonquin woman, to an Iroquois, on condition that he become Christian. This man had kept her in his country as his wife, although she was his captive, and was so much in love with her that he was constantly in our sitting-room, for fear the Algonquins would take her back. At last we had to give her to him for the sake of peace, on the conditions I just mentioned. I never thought a savage could have such love for a foreigner. We could see him mourning, stuttering, lifting his eyes, stamping his feet, pacing back and forth like a madman. The young woman just laughed at him, and it didn't offend him in the least.

The ones who have made peace are the Mohawks and Oneidas. That leaves the Onondagas, Cayugas, and Senecas, none of whom have shown up yet. They claim it's because they are making preparations for peace, and they make excuses, saying that they have already sent eleven delegations without getting any satisfaction from us. The truth is, these peoples are proud by nature and jealous because other nations have preceded them. Besides, they're in the midst of a big war against the Susquehannas[8] of New Sweden. Nevertheless, they give hopes for next spring. And that's where we are with the Iroquois.

If New Netherland, now occupied by the English,[9] belonged to the King of France, we would be master of all these peoples, and we would build an admirable French colony. The forts that have been constructed along the Iroquois route are still in place with their garrisons. People are clearing a lot of land, especially at the Chamblay and Soret forts. These gentlemen,[10] who are very reliable, are here with the King's permission to establish French colonies.

They have families and keep oxen, cows, and fowl. They have beautiful lakes with plenty of fish in winter as well as summer, and the hunting is good in all weather. All of them live as good Christians. The priests and the other ecclesiastics are going there to set up missions. And Monsieur the Abbot de Carignan, chaplain of the regiment, is going to live either at the Chamblay fort or at Fort Sainte Thérèse. They have built paths to communicate with one another, because they have beautiful houses and the success of their businesses depends on alliances with other families of the country.

This year ninety-two girls came from France. By now they have all been married, mostly to soldiers, but also to workmen who are given places to live and provisions for eight months while they clear land to support themselves on. Many men have also come funded directly by the King, who wants to populate this country. His Majesty has also sent horses, mares, goats, and sheep to stock the country with herds and flocks and domestic animals. For our part, we've been given a horse and two beautiful mares, for the plow as well as for the wagon. They say that the troops are going back next year, but it looks as if most of them will be staying here as settlers, having acquired lands—which they probably don't have in their own country.

As for the missions, the priests are very zealous. Father Dalois,[11] who had left to be among the Ottawas[12] for two years, during which time we had no news from him, came back last August with some people from that nation who came to trade. This good priest says that when he couldn't win the hearts of the Ottawas to the faith, he resolved to go in search of some other people more susceptible to grace. With this purpose he traveled fourteen or fifteen hundred leagues and found many who were tractable and accepted unresistingly the sowing of the Gospel. He baptized three hundred forty, of whom three hundred died after being baptized.[13] These were old people and children, because the sacrament isn't given to other people until after much preparation and many signs of perseverance. See what grace God has given to those who otherwise would now be lost in Hell forever.

The priest suffered great hardships on his mission. For two years he lived on almost nothing but sour limes and acorns scraped on rocks. I asked him how he could live on such bad food and what taste he could find in them. "Everything seems good," he told me, "to someone who's hungry." To eat this awful food he boiled the acorns in lye to get some of the bitterness out and then mixed in his sour lime to come up with a sagamité black as ink and sticky as pitch.[14] That's what this worker in the fields of missions feasted on, not to mention the bread of sorrow—I mean his other work on his mission. He came here looking for people to help him when he went back to that great nation.

He found some priests who were willing and left again with them, after staying only three days. First they went to Montreal to make the voyage with some Ottawas, who gave them a lot of trouble. After loading their baggage onto the canoes, those barbarians got some kind of whim into their heads, threw it all back onto the land, and made the priests and the Frenchmen get off too, no matter how much they were promising to pay them. The priests were upset and discouraged to find themselves powerless to go on, but two of them, Father Dalois and Father Nicolas, stole around and threw themselves into two other canoes that were off to the side. They departed with no other provisions or baggage than their notes on Indian languages; so if God doesn't send down a miracle to soften the hearts of those barbarians, the priests will die of hunger and hardship. Three hundred leagues they have to travel among them! If they do reach that country, they will be living on those acorns and sour limes and covering themselves with a few skins when their clothes wear out. That's the only way they'll get past the Ottawas. Nevertheless, the Reverend Father Superior has made up his mind to send them help next summer, if any French decide to go there for trade.[15] Pray for all these good fathers who are scattered hither and yon for the glory of God, and pray for the salvation of souls. Pray for the salvation of mine, too.

Quebec, 18 October 1667.

Translated by John DuVal from Marie de L'Incarnation, *Correspondance*, ed. Dom Guy Oury (Solesmes, 1971), 786–89.

Discussion Questions

1. According to Marie de L'Incarnation, what made a good colony? What kinds of colonists did she mention?

2. What was her opinion of Indians? What do you think Indians thought of her and the rest of the French?

3. Why didn't she go out and found a mission as Father Dalois and Father Nicholas did?

4. The translator uses the English word "nation" to translate the French word *nation*. Should he use the word "tribe" instead when the word refers to an Indian people? Why or why not?

Notes

1. Marie Guyart had felt called to the life of a nun since childhood, but her parents persuaded her to marry when she was seventeen. From that marriage, she had a son, Claude Martin. When her husband died two years into their marriage, she worked for

several years to support her son, then joined the Ursuline convent when he was eleven, having to ignore him when he stood outside the convent and cried for his mama. In adulthood, he seems to have forgiven her, and he joined the Benedictine order. After Marie's death, Claude published a biography of her, which included some of her writing. The first complete edition of her surviving letters was published in 1884.

2. The Iroquois Confederacy made peace with the French in the summer of 1667. Lt. Gen. Alexandre de Prouville de Tracy had led French troops, along with Hurons and Algonquians, against the Mohawks of the Iroquois Confederacy. Knowing of the coming attack, the Mohawks evacuated their towns and thus avoided a battle, but they lost their crops and homes.

3. The Mohawks and the Oneidas.

4. The Iroquois family members were left at the French post as insurance that the French people would not be harmed on Iroquois lands.

5. The feast of the Immaculate Conception is December 8.

6. These were Algonquian Indians, who had learned the French language and religion in their youth but then had been captured by the Iroquois.

7. He paid for their maintenance, including board for students at L'Incarnation's school.

8. The Susquehannas lived in present-day Delaware, Maryland, and Pennsylvania.

9. The English seized New Netherland in 1664. The Dutch would recapture it and lose it again in the 1670s. Under the English, the region became the colonies of New York and New Jersey and parts of Connecticut and Delaware.

10. Jacques de Chamblay and Pierre de Soret, who established Ft. St. Louis and Ft. Ste. Thérèse along the route to Iroquois country in 1665, in anticipation of Tracy's attack on the Mohawks.

11. This was Father Claude-Jean Allouez, one of the most renowned Jesuit missionaries in seventeenth-century Canada.

12. The Ottawas lived in the Great Lakes region, west of Quebec and Montreal. In the preceding decades, they had been pushed westward by the Iroquois Confederacy.

13. European diseases were spreading across North America.

14. Sagamité was a corn porridge common throughout North America.

15. In the fall of 1668, Father Nicolas returned to Quebec with the news that he and Father Dalois (Allouez) had survived and made it past the Ottawas to find new people to convert.

Deodat Lawson Describes
Events at Salem, 1692

*D*EODAT *L*AWSON WAS AN *E*NGLISH *P*URITAN MINISTER. *From 1684 to 1688, he served as the pastor in Salem Village, the rural area near Salem Town, Massachusetts. In 1692, rumors reached Boston, where he was living by then, that the niece of Salem Village's new minister, Samuel Parris (whom Lawson refers to as Mr. P), had been afflicted by a witch. Lawson was worried about his successor and his former parishioners, but the next piece of news hit closer to home. There were rumors that witches had played a role in the death of Lawson's own wife and daughter, who had died while he was the minister in Salem Village. Wanting to discover the truth, Lawson set out for Salem Village in March 1692.*

On the nineteenth day of March last I went to Salem Village, and lodged at Nathaniel Ingersol's near to the Minister Mr. P[arris]'s house, and presently after I came into my lodging Capt. Walcut's daughter Mary came to Lieut. Ingersol's and spoke to me, but, suddenly after as she stood by the door, was bitten, so that she cried out of her wrist, and looking on it with a candle, we saw apparently the marks of teeth both upper and lower set, on each side of her wrist.

In the beginning of the evening, I went to give Mr. P a visit. When I was there, his kinswoman, Abigail Williams (about 12 years of age),[1] had a grievous fit; she was at first hurried with violence to and fro in the room (though Mrs. Ingersol endeavored to hold her), sometimes making as if she would fly, stretching up her arms as high as she could, and crying "Whish, Whish, Whish!" several times. Presently after, she said there was Goodwife N [Rebecca Nurse][2] and said, "Do you not see her? Why there she stands!" And the said

Goodwife N offered her The Book,[3] but she was resolved she would not take it, saying often, "I won't, I won't, I won't take it, I do not know what Book it is: I am sure it is none of God's Book, it is the Devil's Book, for ought I know." After that, she ran to the fire, and began to throw firebrands about the house; and ran against the back, as if she would run up chimney, and, as they said, she had attempted to go into the fire in other fits.

On Lord's Day, the twentieth of March, there were sundry of the afflicted persons at meeting, as Mrs. Pope, and Goodwife Bibber, Abigail Williams, Mary Walcut, Mercy Lewis, and Doctor Griggs' maid. There was also at meeting Goodwife C [Martha Corey] (who was afterward examined on suspicion of being a witch).[4] They had several sore fits, in the time of public worship, which did something interrupt me in my first prayer, being so unusual. After Psalm was sung, Abigail Williams said to me, "Now stand up, and name your text." And after it was read, she said, "It is a long text." In the beginning of sermon, Mrs. Pope, a woman afflicted, said to me, "Now there is enough of that." And in the afternoon, Abigail Williams upon my referring to my doctrine said to me, "I know no doctrine you had. If you did name one, I have forgot it."

In sermon time when Goodwife C was present in the meetinghouse Abigail W called out, "Look where Goodwife C sits on the beam suckling her yellow bird betwixt her fingers!" Anne Putnam, another girl afflicted, said there was a yellow bird sat on my hat as it hung on the pin in the pulpit, but those that were [near]by restrained her from speaking loud about it.

On Monday the 21st of March, the magistrates of Salem appointed to come to examination of Goodwife C. And about twelve of the clock, they went into the meetinghouse, which was thronged with spectators. Mr. Noyes[5] began with a very pertinent and pathetic prayer,[6] and Goodwife C being called to answer to what was alleged against her, she desired to go to prayer, which was much wondered at, in the presence of so many hundred people. The magistrates told her they would not admit it; they came not there to hear her pray, but to examine her, in what was alleged against her. The worshipful Mr. Hathorne asked her, why she afflicted those children? She said, she did not afflict them. He asked her, who did then? She said, "I do not know. How should I know?"

The number of afflicted persons were about that time ten, *viz.* four married women, Mrs. Pope, Mrs. Putnam, Goodwife Bibber, and an ancient woman named Goodall; three maids, Mary Walcut, Mercy Lewis at Thomas Putnam's, and a maid at Dr. Griggs's; there were three girls from 9 to 12 years of age, each of them, or thereabouts, *viz.* Elizabeth Parris, Abigail Williams and Ann Putnam. These were most of them at Goodwife C's examination, and did vehemently accuse her in the assembly of afflicting them, by biting, pinching, strangling, etc. And that they did in their fit see her likeness coming to them, and bringing a Book to them. She said, she had no Book. They affirmed, she had a yellow bird that used to suck betwixt her fingers, and being asked about it, if she had any familiar spirit that attended her, she said she had no familiarity with any such thing. She was a Gospel Woman, which title she called herself by; and the afflicted persons told her, ah! she was a Gospel Witch. Ann Putnam did there affirm that one day when Lieutenant Fuller was at prayer at her father's house, she saw the shape of Goodwife C and she thought Goodwife N praying at the same time to the Devil. She was not sure it was Goodwife N; she thought it was, but very sure she saw the shape of Goodwife C. The said C said, they were poor, distracted children, and no heed [should] be given to what they said. Mr. Hathorne and Mr. Noyes replied, it was the judgment of all that were present, they were bewitched, and only she, the accused person, said they were distracted. It was observed several times that if she did but bite her under-lip in time of examination the persons afflicted were bitten on their arms and wrists and produced the marks before the magistrates, ministers and others. And being watched for that, if she did but pinch her fingers, or grasp one hand hard in another, they were pinched and produced the marks before the magistrates and spectators. After that, it was observed, that if she did but lean her breast against the seat in the meetinghouse (being the bar at which she stood), they were afflicted. Particularly Mrs. Pope complained of grievous torment in her bowels as if they were torn out. She vehemently accused said C as the instrument, and first threw her muff at her; but that flying not home, she got off her shoe, and hit Goodwife C on the head with it. After these postures were watched, if said C did but stir her feet, they were afflicted in the feet, and stamped fearfully. The afflicted persons asked her why she did not go to the company of witches which were before the meetinghouse mustering? Did she not hear the drum beat? They accused her of having familiarity with the devil, in the time of examination, in the shape of a black man whispering in her ear. . . .

They told her she had covenanted with the Devil for ten years, six of them were gone, and four more to come. She was required by the magistrates to answer that question in the Catechism, "How many persons be there in the God-Head?"[7] She answered it but oddly, yet was there no great thing to be gathered from it. She denied all that was charged upon her, and said, they could not prove [her] a witch. She was that afternoon committed to Salem Prison, and after she was in custody, she did not so appear to them and afflict them as before.

On Wednesday the 23 of March, I went to Thomas Putnam's, on purpose to see his wife. I found her lying on the bed, having had a sore fit a little before. She spoke to me, and said she was glad to see me. Her husband and she both desired me to pray with her while she was sensible, which I did, though the apparition [according to Mrs. Putnam] said I should not go to prayer. At the first beginning she attended, but after a little time was taken with a fit, yet continued silent, and seemed to be asleep. When prayer was done, her husband going to her, found her in a fit. He took her off the bed, to set her on his knees, but at first she was so stiff, she could not be bended; but she afterwards set down, but quickly began to strive violently with her arms and legs. She then began to complain of, and as it were to converse personally with, Goodwife N, saying, "Goodwife N. Be gone! Be gone! Be gone! Are you not ashamed, a woman of your profession, to afflict a poor creature so? What hurt did I ever do you in my life! You have but two years to live, and then the Devil will torment your soul, for this your name is blotted out of God's Book, and it shall never be put in God's Book again. Be gone for shame. Are you not afraid of that which is coming upon you? I know, I know, what will make you afraid; the wrath of an angry God, I am sure that will make you afraid; be gone, do not torment me, I know what you would have (we judged she meant her soul) but it is out of your reach; it is clothed with the white robes of Christ's righteousness." After this, she seemed to dispute with the apparition about a particular text of Scripture. The apparition seemed to deny it (the woman's eyes being fast closed all this time). She said, she was sure there was such a text, and she would tell it, and then the shape would be gone, for said she, "I am sure you cannot stand before that text!" Then she was sorely afflicted. Her mouth drawn on one side, and her body strained for about a minute, and then said, "I will tell, I will tell; it is, it is, it is!" three or four times, and then was afflicted to hinder her from telling. At last she broke forth and said, "It is the third Chapter of the Revelations." I did something scruple the reading it, and did let my scruple appear, lest Satan should make any superstitious lie to improve the Word of the Eternal God. However, though not versed in these things, I judged I might do it this once for an experiment. I began to read, and before I had near read through the first verse, she opened her eyes, and was well. This fit continued near half an hour. Her husband and the spectators told me, she had often been so relieved by reading texts that she named, something pertinent to her case, as Isaiah 40:1, Isaiah 49:1, Isaiah 50:1, and several others.

On Thursday the twenty-fourth of March (being in course the Lecture Day at the Village), Goodwife N was brought before the magistrates Mr. Hathorne and Mr. Corwin, about ten of the clock, in the forenoon, to be examined in the meetinghouse. The Reverend Mr. Hale began with prayer, and the warrant being read, she was required to give answer, Why she afflicted those persons? She pleaded her own innocence with earnestness. Thomas Putnam's wife, Abigail Williams and Thomas Putnam's daughter accused her that she appeared to them and afflicted them in their fits, but some of the others said, that they had seen her, but knew not that ever she had hurt them; amongst which was Mary Walcut, who was presently after she had so declared bitten, and cried out . . .

producing the marks of teeth on her wrist. It was so disposed, that I had not leisure to attend the whole time of examination, but both magistrates and ministers told me that the things alleged by the afflicted, and defenses made by her, were much after the same manner, as the former was. . . . There was once such a hideous screech and noise (which I heard as I walked, at a little distance from the meetinghouse), as did amaze me, and some that were within told me the whole assembly was struck with consternation, and they were afraid that those that sat next to them, were under the influence of witchcraft. This woman also was that day committed to Salem Prison. The magistrates and ministers also did inform me that they apprehended a child of Sara G⁸ and examined it, being between 4 and 5 years of age, and as to matter of fact, they did unanimously affirm that when this child did but cast its eye upon the afflicted persons, they were tormented, and they held her head, and yet so many as her eye could fix upon were afflicted, which they did several times make careful observation of. The afflicted complained they had often been bitten by this child, and produced the marks of a small set of teeth. Accordingly, this [girl] was also committed to Salem Prison; the child looked hail, and well as other children. I saw it at Lieut. Ingersol's. After the commitment of Goodwife N, Thomas Putnam's wife was much better, and had no violent fits at all from that 24th of March to the 5th of April. Some others also said they had not seen her so frequently appear to them to hurt them.

On the 25th of March (as Capt. Stephen Sewall, of Salem, did afterwards inform me) Elizabeth Parris had sore fits, at his house, which much troubled himself, and his wife, so as he told me they were almost discouraged. She related, that the great black man came to her, and told her, if she would be ruled by him, she should have whatsoever she desired, and go to a Golden City. She relating this to Mrs. Sewall, she told the child, it was the Devil, and he was a liar from the beginning, and bid her tell him so, if he came again, which she did accordingly, at the next coming to her, in her fits.

On the 26th of March, Mr. Hathorne, Mr. Corwin, and Mr. Higginson were at the prison-keeper's house, to examine the child [Dorcas Good], and it told them there, it had a little snake that used to suck on the lowest joint of its forefinger; and when they inquired where, pointing to other places, it told them, not there, but there, pointing on the lowest point of forefinger; where they observed a deep red spot, about the bigness of a flea-bite, they asked who gave it that snake whether the great black man. It said no, its mother gave it.

The 31 of March there was a public fast kept at Salem on account of these afflicted persons. And Abigail Williams said, that the witches had a sacrament that day at a house in the Village, and that they had red bread and red drink. The first of April, Mercy Lewis, Thomas Putnam's maid, in her fit, said they did eat red bread like man's flesh, and would have had her eat some, but she would not, but turned away her head, and spit at them, and said, "I will not eat, I will not drink, it is blood," etc. She said, "That is not the Bread of Life, that is not the Water of Life; Christ gives the Bread of Life, I will have none of it!" This first of April also Mercy Lewis aforesaid saw in her fit a white man and was with him in a glorious place, which had no candles nor sun, yet was full of light and brightness, where was a great multitude in white glittering robes, and they sung the song in the fifth of Revelation the ninth verse, and the 110 Psalm, and the 149 Psalm, and said with herself, "How long shall I stay here? Let me be along with you." She was loath to leave this place, and grieved that she could tarry no longer. This white man hath appeared several times to some of them, and given them notice how long it should be before they had another fit, which was sometimes a day, or day and half, or more or less. It hath fallen out accordingly.

The third of April, the Lord's Day, being Sacrament Day, at the Village, Goodwife C [Sarah Cloyse] upon Mr. Parris's naming his text, John 6:70, "One of them is a Devil,"⁹ the said Goodwife C[loyse] went immediately out of the meetinghouse, and flung the door after her violently, to the amazement of the congregation. She was afterward seen by some in their fits, who said, "O Goodwife C[loyse], I did not think to see you here!" (and being at their red bread and drink) said to her, "Is this a time to receive the Sacrament, you ran away on the Lord's Day, and scorned to receive it in the meetinghouse, and, Is this a time to receive it? I wonder at you!" This is the sum of what I either saw myself, or did receive information from persons of undoubted reputation and credit.

From Deodat Lawson, "A Brief and True Narrative of Witchcraft at Salem Village, 1692," in *Narratives of the Witchcraft Cases, 1648–1706,* ed. George Lincoln Burr (New York, 1914), 152–62.

Discussion Questions

1. Historians have proposed various theories for the 1692 events in Massachusetts: religious, political, or land disputes between neighbors; fear of older women who seemed outside normal society; trauma resulting from Indian raids; teenaged girls' desire for attention; hallucinogens. What do you think was going on?

2. How might an accused witch defend herself?

3. Why do you think this episode ended up in the executions of twenty accused witches (thirteen women and seven men), including a minister (plus several others who died in prison)?

Notes

1. Parris's niece (Abigail Williams) and daughter (Elizabeth Parris) were the first girls who had fits and seemed to be "afflicted" by a witch.

2. Rebecca Nurse (Goodwife N) was a local woman in her early seventies. She was subsequently hanged as a witch.

3. Lawson and his contemporaries believed that the devil and his witches (here, Rebecca Nurse) tried to persuade people to sign their names in the devil's book, which would commit them to his service.

4. Those whom Lawson lists here as afflicted by witches included Bathshua Pope, Sarah Bibber, and Mercy Lewis (a maid to the Putnams, two of whom were also afflicted). Martha Corey (Goodwife C) was a woman in her late sixties or early seventies. She and her husband were subsequently executed as witches.

5. Mr. Noyes was Salem Town's minister, Nicholas Noyes.

6. A pathetic prayer is one that is moving or emotional.

7. The answer to this question in the Christian catechism is three—the Father, the Son, and the Holy Ghost, who together make one God.

8. Sarah Good was one of the first women accused and imprisoned, before Lawson's visit, and hanged on July 19. Her young daughter was Dorcas (Dorothy) Good, who was imprisoned for several months. Her father later stated that the child's time in prison had left her emotionally scarred.

9. "One of them is a Devil" is part of John 6:70, in which Jesus hints of his future betrayal by Judas. Sarah Cloyse (this Goodwife C) was the sister of Rebecca Nurse.

Father Jacques Gravier Describes Indian Conversions at the Illinois Mission, 1694

JACQUES GRAVIER WAS A FRENCH JESUIT MISSIONARY assigned to the mission founded by Jacques Marquette at Starved Rock on the Illinois River. In 1693, Gravier moved the mission down the Illinois River near present-day Peoria. Gravier worked to learn the local languages and to convert Indians to Catholicism. Most of his potential converts belonged to the Illinois culture group and were divided into separate nations, including Peorias and Kaskaskias. In this account, Gravier describes his efforts, including attempted baptisms and the story of a seventeen-year-old Kaskaskia convert named Marie Rouensa, or Aramepinchieve.

Everybody left for winter quarters on the twenty-sixth of September, except for some old women who stayed in fourteen or fifteen cabins and a good number of Kaskaskias. Despite all my efforts to keep them from taking along the little sick children unbaptized,[1] some of them slipped past me because their parents did not want me baptizing them. I followed after others all the way to the boats to try to give the babies their passport to eternity, and was determined not to be daunted by the parents and all the women about to leave, who were making fun of me because of my worry—and God recompensed me for my troubles with the salvation of several of these little innocents. The Chief of the Peorias was surprised to see me at the water's edge and asked me what I was doing there and if I was waiting for the mother of some sick child. I answered jokingly that I was wanting to baptize *his* child, at which he laughed and made some jokes. "Don't be surprised," I said to him and the people there, "that I've been standing here so long. What surprises me much more is that no one takes pity on the children, who are and will be slaves to the devil if they die unbaptized." Although this argument did not convince them, to rid themselves of my nagging, they did let me splash several of the babies.

I admit that this year I didn't let any scruples keep me from baptizing the little sick children: I did it behind their parents' backs, believing I wasn't obliged always to wait for their permission just because the eternal joy or sorrow of their sick children meant less to them than their mistaken fears that baptism might kill the children, which is what the enemies of the faith try to persuade them: that baptism kills children. This is what they reproach me with in most of the cabins when I talk to them about the need for salvation. I often have trouble persuading a mother whose first child died to have the second baptized, or the third.

It's good not to get discouraged, and there are many women who, to avoid having me always in their homes asking about the health of their children, have brought them to the church to be baptized. Although I have had more resistance against baptizing newborns from most of the parents this year than previous years, I have still baptized many more than last year, and many of these are among the blessed, praying now for the conversion of their parents.

. . . There is nothing *savage* about the devotion of the woman who married Monsieur Ako.[2] She is full of the spirit of God and expresses her thoughts and noble sentiments to me with such open simplicity that I cannot thank God enough for revealing Himself so abundantly to a young savage in the midst of an infidel and corrupted nation.

They had to wage a long struggle with her to get her to agree to the marriage, because she meant never to marry, so as to belong completely to Jesus Christ. She answered her father and her mother, who had brought her to me along with the Frenchman they wanted for a son-in-law, that she did not want to marry and that she had given all her "heart to God and did not want anyone else to share it." These are her own words, which had not been heard before in this barbarous place and which were not welcome when they were heard. I sincerely believe that she could have been inspired only by God, but since there was nothing savage in her sentiments, her father, her mother, and especially the Frenchman who wanted to marry her were convinced it was I who was making her talk that way. I told them that God did not order her to marry, and that no one could force her to marry, lest he offend God, because she was mistress of her own will to marry or not to marry. She did not reply to me, nor to all the nagging and threats of her father and her mother, who, as they left in disappointment, had no other thought than to unleash their fury on me, imagining that I was the one who forbade their daughter to give her consent.

As I was calling the people to prayer throughout the town and walking past the father's cabin, he stopped me and told me since I was keeping his daughter from obeying him, he, in turn, would keep people from going to the chapel.

Then he came outside, screaming and raging against me and blocking the passage of those who were following me, which did not prevent the Peorias and some of the Kaskaskias from coming to the chapel anyway by taking the long way around so he wouldn't see them.

He had just thrown his daughter out of his house and stripped her of her jerkin, her socks and shoes, and her trinkets of jewelry, and she had not said a word or shed a single tear. But when he tried to take the clothes that covered her, "Ah, Father, what are you trying to do?" she asked him. "Leave me alone. Enough! I won't give you what I have left. You can take my life, but you can't tear these from me." Her father stopped short and without another word thrust her out of doors.

Not daring to appear before people in this state, she went and hid herself among the reeds along the water, where an old catechumen[3] on his way to the chapel found her and threw his own jerkin to her. She put it on, went straight to the chapel, and joined the others in prayers and singing as if nothing had happened to her.

She waited for me after the service. I encouraged her to take heart, do exactly what God inspired her to do, and fear nothing. I had someone escort her secretly to the house of the man who had clothed her with his jerkin.

That night the father summoned the Chiefs of the villages and told them that since I was keeping the French from forming an alliance with them (adding a hundred lies to that one), he enjoined them to keep the women and children from going to the chapel. It wasn't hard for him to convince people who themselves weren't carried away by Christianity.

Despite their threats and interdictions, on the next day fifty people from the Peoria village and a few Kaskaskias showed up at the chapel, as well as the daughter, who was risking all sorts of abuse if her father found her there.

He had sent a spy to see if anyone went, and, shocked to learn so many had gone, had it proclaimed throughout the village that it was a strange thing when people disobeyed their Chiefs, which is exactly what the many people who had gone to the chapel had done, so no one should be surprised if he punished those who persisted in trying to go.

The women who presided over the young married women and the grown girls among the Peorias told me they would come in the evening and advised me not to issue the call to chapel throughout the town.[4] I told them that if I didn't, people would think the decrees and threats frightened me; I realized that those who had the courage would obey me.

They did come of their own accord that evening to the chapel, but I still issued my call as usual. From several of the cabins people responded by telling me to stop and saying no one was going to the chapel to pray to God because the Chiefs forbade it. "Don't anybody leave your house," one person said; "you are forbidden to pray." "Call out loud and clear," another told me, "there are some who will obey you."

As it turned out, nobody left the cabins except a few little girls who went the long way around to avoid the men blocking the streets, and they joined up with the women who were waiting for me at the chapel. The daughter of the Kaskaskia Chief came too, and there were only thirty people in all.

I had barely begun to sing the *Veni Creator* when a man of about forty-five came into the chapel with a club in his hand and menaced us: "Didn't you hear the Chiefs' decree? Obey and get out. Quick!"

He tried to grab one of the women by the arm, but she held fast. I rushed up to him: "Get out yourself, and respect the house of God!"

"The Chiefs forbid them to pray," he answered.

"And God commands them to," I said. "Be quiet, and get out." (I hadn't expected him to give me time to say even that.) Then I turned back to the foot of the altar and continued the prayer.

He grabbed another by the arm to make her leave. "You're not obeying," he told them.

"Be careful not to anger the Master we serve here," I shouted at him. "Go away and let us pray to God. And all of you who honor the Lord of Heaven and Earth, don't be afraid. He is with you. He protects you."

He stayed a little longer without speaking. Then, seeing he wasn't getting anywhere, he left with an old man who had followed him. I praised the congregation because they had held out and made the emissaries of the Devil lose heart. The Devil, I said, "is jealous because people are beginning to call to God in this country, and he has stirred up this little persecution." . . .

I decided that I could not keep silent after such an insult against God and sought out the Commander of the fort,[5] who was glorying in it. He answered me with insults, saying I had brought it all on myself with my stubborn refusal to allow the girl to marry the Frenchman (who was with him), and that if the man wanted to marry her he would do it anyway. . . .

God gave me the grace to accept these humiliations with, I believe, a tranquil spirit. To keep the Indians from perceiving that we were quarreling, I answered almost none of this abuse, and the only times I raised my voice, a little, were when I felt I had to uphold God's religion and His glory. Since I kept reminding the Commander of the insult in the chapel, demanding some sort of satisfaction and some action against the Chiefs to make sure no one else behaved like that, or worse, again, he replied coldly that he would speak to the Chiefs, but instead of assembling them right away would wait until the afternoon of the next day. The only satisfaction he was willing to give me was to send me word that the Chiefs assured him they had not told the man to commit the insult in the chapel.

It was no thanks to him that the same savage did not commit the same insult, because when we gathered for mass, a great rainstorm broke out and he thought no one would come to the chapel, and when he realized he was wrong he didn't have time to get there, his club poorly concealed beneath his clothes, until people were leaving.

During these same two days, the Kaskaskia Chief was doing everything he could, from flattery to threats, to persuade his daughter to give in. On top of the threats he promised that if she didn't obey him she would go through all kinds of anguish, that nobody would get to pray to God anymore, that he would go to war, and that she would never see him again.

She came to me and assured me that God was keeping her strong and she was still determined to offer her virginity to God. She said she had wept two days over this conspiracy against prayer, which her father himself had organized, and she was afraid he would be swept by even greater fury into some extreme act. "All the threats against me don't bother me at all," she said; "I am happy in my heart, but I am afraid for the word of God, because I know my father and my mother."

"Don't be afraid," I said. "Prayer is homage to God."

"My father has shown me mercy," she said, "and I have an idea. I don't know whether it's a good one. I think that if I agree to the marriage, he will listen to you, really, and he will bring everybody with him. I want to please God," she said, "and that is why I determined to be always as I am and to please Jesus Christ alone; but I've thought about agreeing—against my inclination and for the love of Him—to the marriage. Is that reasonable?" These were her words. All I do is change them from Illinois into French.

"My daughter," I said, "God does not forbid you to marry. I am not telling you, 'Marry,' or 'Don't marry.' If the only reason you agree is for the love of God and because you believe that by marrying you will win your family to God, it is a good idea. But you have to make it clear to your parents that their threats aren't forcing you into the marriage."

And that is what she did do: when they kept pressing her, she told her mother, "I feel sorry for my father. I don't resent the way he has treated me. I'm not afraid of his threats. But I believe I will agree to what he's asking because I believe that you and he will agree to what I will ask of you."

Finally, after she did tell her father that she would consent to the marriage, the father, the mother, and the Frenchman came to me when she was in the chapel so that they could learn from her whether her priestly father was telling the truth. She answered in a clear voice, pointing to the Frenchman, "I hate this man because he is always speaking evil of my Black-Robe father.[6] He lies when he claims the Father is what has kept me from marrying." Then she said to me in a low voice, "No fear of my father is making me marry. You know why I'm agreeing. . . ."

After the Kaskaskia Chief was sure of his daughter's consent to marry the Frenchman, he announced to all the village Chiefs, with a great show of gifts, that he was allying himself with a Frenchman. To better reconcile herself, the daughter received her first holy communion on the feast of the Assumption of Our Lady.[7] She had been preparing for it for the previous three months with such fervor that she seemed infused with the great mystery of it. . . . For her patron saints she took the Christian ladies most sanctified in marriage, St. Paula, St. Frances, St. Marguerite, St. Elizabeth, and St. Bridget. She calls upon them several times a day and tells them things you would never expect in a young savage.

Her first conquest for God was her husband, who had been famous in the land of the Illinois for his debauchery. He was completely changed. He confessed to me that he didn't even recognize himself anymore. And the only explanations he could give for his conversion were the prayers of his wife, her exhortations, and the example she set him. "How could I resist," he kept repeating to me, "everything she said to me. I'm ashamed that a savage child, just recently instructed in the faith, knows more than I who was born and raised a Christian, and that she speaks to me with such sweetness and tenderness that she would make a man with no feeling weep. And my own experience tells me that there is no joy except for those who do what is right. Up until now I have never been happy, always had a conscience thrashing about with remorse," he continued, "and I'm so horrified by my past life that I hope that with the help of God nobody will ever budge me from the resolution I've made to live well in the future."

So that the husband might expiate his past faults, God has allowed certain people who used to encourage him in his wickedness to be displeased and to make him despised by everybody. His wife is all his consolation as she speaks with him. "What does it matter," she tells him, "if the whole world is against us. If we love God and He loves us, it is better to pay while we are living for the evil we have done so that after our death God will show us mercy."

Translated by John DuVal from "Lettre du Père Jacques Gravier en forme de Journal de la Mission de l'Immaculée Conception de Notre Dame aux Ilinois," February 15, 1694, in *The Jesuit Relations and Allied Documents: Travels and Explorations of the Jesuit Missionaries in New France, 1610–1791*, ed. Reuben Gold Thwaites (New York, 1959), 64:188–214.

Discussion Questions

1. At the beginning of this document, Father Gravier gives his account of attempts to baptize Peoria and Kaskaskia children. How do you think the parents would have told the story?

2. Why did Marie Rouensa's parents want her to marry Michel Ako? Why did Ako want the marriage? Why did Marie Rouensa resist? What were Father Gravier's motivations? Why did Marie Rouensa change her mind?

3. What disagreements emerged within the Kaskaskia population and within the French population over Marie Rouensa's refusal? What do those disagreements tell us about each population?

4. Whereas the Spanish used the word *Indios* for Native Americans, the French used the word *sauvages*. Your translator generally uses the English word "Indians" to translate both words; however, in translating this French narration, he sometimes uses the English word "savages." Would it be better to always translate *sauvages* as "Indians"? Would it be better to always translate *sauvages* as "savages"? While you are answering this question, look up the etymology of the word "savage" in your dictionary.

Notes

1. There were many children dying of European diseases, and Gravier believed they would not go to heaven if unbaptized.

2. The young woman was Marie Rouensa, or Aramepinchieve, daughter of the Kaskaskia chief Rouensa. The groom was Michel Ako, or Accault, a French trader.

3. Someone being trained in the doctrines of Christianity.

4. This was the call for Vespers, the evening prayers. The missionary called the people to the church multiple times during the day.

5. La Salle and Henri de Tonti built French Ft. St. Louis during La Salle's first voyage in 1682, near the Jesuit mission at Starved Rock. It moved to the Peoria site in 1691. (It should not be confused with St. Louis, Missouri, founded in 1764 on the western side of the Mississippi.)

6. Black Robe was the name for Jesuit priests, who wore long black robes.

7. Catholic holy day commemorating the acceptance of Mary, the mother of Jesus, into heaven.

María de Jesús de Agreda and Catherine Tekakwitha, 1600s

IN 1630, PLAINS INDIANS TOLD FRANCISCANS IN NEW MEXICO that a "Lady in Blue" had appeared to them and told them, in their own languages, to seek Christian instruction. A young nun in a convent in Agreda, Spain, named María de Jesús claimed responsibility. Although her body had never left Spain, she said that she had made hundreds of spiritual flights to New Mexico and Texas. In Iroquois country, in 1660, smallpox killed the parents and scarred the face of a Mohawk Indian girl named Tekakwitha. As a young woman, she was baptized Catherine (Kateri). She joined a Jesuit mission near Montreal, where she inspired other Indian women who dedicated their lives to Christianity. Currently, there are movements within the Catholic Church to make both women saints. These engravings are from the 1700s.

Discussion Questions

1. What do the two images have in common?
2. How do they differ?
3. What was different about the role of women versus men in seventeenth- and eighteenth-century Catholicism?
4. A large percentage of the famous women from the colonial era were known for their religious deeds and devotion. Why is this so?

María de Jesús de Agreda preaching to the Chichimecos of New Mexico. Source: *Courtesy of Catholic Archives of Texas.*

Catherine tekakoüita Iroquoise du Saut
S. Louis de Montreal en Canada morte
en odeur de Sainteté.

Catherine Tekakwitha, Iroquois woman of Saut St. Louis of
Montreal in Canada, who died in the odor of sanctity. Note:
Catholics believed that bodies that did not smell of decay
and that smelled sweet after death were marked as holy.
Source: *Claude-Charles Bacqueville de La Potherie,* Histoire
de l'Amerique septentrionale *(Paris, 1722). Courtesy John
Carter Brown Library at Brown University.*

Susannah Johnson Recalls
Her Captivity, 1754–1757

SUSANNAH WILLARD WAS BORN IN MASSACHUSETTS *in 1730. Because land was becoming scarce in the parts of New England settled by the English, she and her husband, James Johnson, moved to Charlestown, on the Connecticut River in western New Hampshire. English colonists' presence this far northwest caused tension with Indians and the French, who both claimed jurisdiction over the area. As her account begins, in 1754, the first skirmishes of the Seven Years' War are breaking out between the English and their enemies, including the Abenaki Indians, an Algonquian nation indigenous to New England.*

The commencement of the year 1754 began to threaten another rupture between the French and English; and, as the dividing line between Canada and the English colonies was the object of contention, it was readily seen that the frontier towns would be in imminent danger. . . . [Mr. Johnson] made preparations to remove to Northfield,[1] as soon as our stock of hay was consumed, and our dozen of swine had demolished our ample stores of grain, which would secure his family and property from the miseries and ravages of war. . . . The neighbors made frequent parties at our house, . . . and time passed merrily off, by the aid of spirit and a ripe yard of melons. As I was in the last days of pregnancy, I could not join so heartily in their good cheer as I otherwise might. Yet, in a new country, pleasure is often derived from sources unknown to those less accustomed to the woods. . . .

On the evening of the 29th of August our house was visited by a party of neighbors, who spent the time very cheerfully with watermelons and flip,[2] till midnight. . . . We then went to bed with feelings well tuned for sleep, and rested with fine composure, till midway between daybreak and sunrise, when we were roused by neighbor [Peter] Labarree's knocking at the door, who had shouldered his ax to do a day's work for my husband. Mr. Johnson slipped on his jacket and trousers, and stepped to the door to let him in. But by opening the door he opened a scene—terrible to describe!—"Indians! Indians!" were the first words I heard; he sprang to his guns, but Labarree, heedless of danger, instead of closing the door to keep them out, began to rally our hired men upstairs for not rising earlier. But in an instant a crowd of savages, fixed horribly for war, rushed furiously in. I screamed, and begged my friends to ask for quarters.[3]

By this time they were all over the house, some upstairs, some hauling my sister out of bed, another had hold of me, and one was approaching Mr. Johnson, who stood in the middle of the floor to deliver himself up; but the Indian supposing that he would make resistance, and be more than his match, went to the door and brought three of his comrades, and the four bound him. I was led to the door, fainting and trembling; there stood my friend Labarree bound; Ebenezer Farnsworth, whom they found up in his chamber, they were putting in the same situation; and, to complete the shocking scene, my three little children were driven naked to the place where I stood. On viewing myself, I found that I too was naked. An Indian had purloined three gowns, who, on seeing my situation, gave me the whole. I asked another for a petticoat, but he refused it. After what little plunder their hurry would allow them to get was confusedly bundled up, we were ordered to march. . . .

Two savages laid hold of each of my arms, and hurried me through thorny thickets in a most unmerciful manner. I lost a shoe, and suffered exceedingly. We heard the alarm guns from the fort. This added new speed to the flight of the savages. They were apprehensive that soldiers might be sent for our relief. When we got a mile and a half, my faintness obliged me to sit down. This being observed by an Indian, he drew his knife, as I supposed, to put an end to my existence; but he only cut some bands with which my gown was tied, and then pushed me on. My little children were crying, my husband and the other two were bound, and my sister and myself were obliged to make the best of our way, with all our might. The loss of my shoe rendered traveling extremely painful. At the distance of three miles there was a general halt; the savages supposing that we, as well as themselves, might have an appetite for breakfast, gave us a loaf of bread, some raisins and apples, which they had taken from the house. While we were forcing down our scanty breakfast, a horse came in sight, known to us all by the name of Scoggin, belonging to Phineas Stevens, Esq. One of the Indians attempted to shoot him, but was prevented by Mr. Johnson. They then expressed a wish to catch him, saying, by pointing to me, for squaw to ride. My husband had previously been unbound to assist the children, and he, with two Indians, caught the horse. By this time my legs and feet were covered with blood, which being noticed by Mr. Labarree, he, with that humanity which never forsook him, took his stockings and presented them to me, and the Indians gave me a pair of moccasins. Bags and blankets were thrown over Scoggin, and I mounted on the top of them, and on we jogged. . . .

I had time to reflect on our miserable situation. Captives, in the power of unmerciful savages, without provision, and almost without clothes, in a wilderness where we must sojourn as long as the children of Israel did, for ought we knew; and, what added to our distress, not one of our savage masters could understand a word of English. Here, after being hurried from home with such rapidity, I have leisure to inform the reader respecting our Indians as masters. They were eleven in number, men of middle age, except one, a youth of sixteen, who, in our journey, discovered a very mischievous and troublesome disposition. According to their national practice, he who first laid hands on a prisoner considered him as his property. My master, who was the one that took my hand when I sat on the bed, was as clever an Indian as ever I saw; he even evinced, at numerous times, a disposition that showed he was by no means void of compassion. The four who took my husband, claimed him as their property; and my sister, three children, Labarree, and Farnsworth, had each a master. When the time came for us to prepare to march, I almost expired at the thought. To leave my aged parents, brothers, sisters, and friends, and travel with savages, through a dismal forest, to unknown regions, in the alarming situation I then was in, with three small children, the eldest, Sylvanus, only six years old. My eldest daughter, Susanna, was four, and Polly, the other, two. My sister Miriam was fourteen. My husband was barefoot and otherwise thinly clothed; his master had taken his jacket, and nothing but his shirt and trousers remained. My two daughters had nothing but their shifts, and I only the gown that was handed me by the savages. In addition to the sufferings which arose from my own deplorable condition, I could not but feel for my friend Labarree; he had left a wife and four small children behind, to lament his loss, and render his situation extremely unhappy.

With all these misfortunes lying heavily upon me, the reader may imagine my situation. The Indians pronounced the dreadful word "munch" (march) and on we must go. I was put on the horse, Mr. Johnson took one daughter, and Labarree, being unbound, the other. We went six or eight miles, and stopped for the night. The men were made secure, by having their legs put in split sticks, somewhat like stocks, and tied with cords, which were tied to the limbs of trees too high to be reached. My sister, much to her mortification, must lie between two Indians, with a cord thrown over her, and passing under each of them; the little children had blankets, and I was allowed one for my use. Thus we took lodging for the night, with the sky for a covering, and the ground for a pillow. The fatigues of the preceding day obliged me to sleep several hours, in spite of the horrors which surrounded me. The Indians observed great silence, and never spoke, but when really necessary, and the prisoners were disposed to say but little: my children were much more peaceable than could be imagined—gloomy fear imposed a dead silence.

In the morning we were roused before sunrise, the Indians struck up a fire, hung on their stolen kettles, and made us some water-gruel for breakfast. After a few sips of this meager fare, I was again put on the horse, with my husband by my side to hold me on. My two fellow prisoners took the little girls, and we marched sorrowfully on for an hour or two, when a keener distress was added to my multiplied afflictions—I was taken with pangs of childbirth. The Indians signified to us that we must go on to a brook. When we got there, they showed some humanity, by making a booth for me. Here the compassionate reader will drop a tear for my inexpressible distress! Fifteen or twenty miles from the abode of any civilized being, in the open wilderness, rendered cold by a rainy day—in one of the most perilous hours,[4] and unsupplied with the least necessary that could yield convenience at the hazardous moment! My children were crying at a distance, where they were held by their masters, and only my husband and sister to attend me! None but mothers can figure to themselves my unhappy fortune! The Indians kept aloof the whole time.[5] About ten o'clock a daughter was born.[6] They then brought me some articles of clothing for the child, which they had taken from the house. My master looked into the booth, and clapped his hands with joy, and cried, "Two monies for me, two monies for me!"

I was permitted to rest the remainder of the day. The Indians were employed in making a bier for the prisoners to carry me on, and another booth for my lodging during night. They brought a needle and two pins, and some bark, to tie the child's clothes, which they gave my sister, and a large wooden spoon to feed it with. At dusk they made some porridge, and brought a cup to steep some roots in which Mr. Labarree had provided. In the evening I was removed to the new booth. For supper, they made more porridge and some Johnny cakes. My portion was brought me in a little bark. I slept that night beyond expectation.

In the morning we were summoned for the journey, after the usual breakfast of meal and water. I, with my infant in my arms, was laid on the litter, which was supported alternately by Mr. Johnson, Labarree, and Farnsworth. My sister and son were put upon Scoggin, and the two little girls rode on their masters' backs. Thus we proceeded two miles, when my carriers grew too faint to proceed any further. This being observed by our sable masters, a general halt was called, and they embodied themselves for council. My master soon made signs to Mr. Johnson, that, if I could ride on the horse, I might proceed, otherwise I must be left behind. Here I observed marks of pity in his countenance, but this might arise from the fear of losing his "two monies." I preferred an attempt to ride on the horse, rather than to perish miserably alone. Mr. Labarree took the infant, and every step of the horse almost deprived me of life. My weak and helpless condition rendered me, in a degree, insensible to everything; my poor child could have no subsistence from my breast, and was supported entirely by water-gruel. My other little children, rendered peevish by an uneasy mode of riding, often burst into cries, but a surly check of their masters soon silenced them. We proceeded on with a slow, mournful pace.

[As the party travels on, the Indians have trouble getting provisions, so there is little to eat. Finally, they eat the horse, depriving Johnson of her mode of transportation. She tries to walk, but eventually her master helps her husband to build a packsaddle to carry her.]

Six days had now almost elapsed since the fatal morn in which we were taken, and by the blessing of the Providence whose smiles give life to the creation, we were still in existence. My wearied husband, naked children, and helpless infant, formed a scene that conveyed severer pangs to my heart than all the sufferings I endured myself. . . . Despair would have robbed me of life, had I not put my whole confidence in that Being who has power to save. Our masters began to ford the stream. I swallowed most of my broth, and was taken up by my husband. The river was very rapid, and passing dangerous. Mr. Labarree, when half over with my child, was tripped up by its rapidity, and lost the babe in the water; little did I expect to see the poor thing again, but he fortunately reached a corner of its blanket, and saved its life. The rest got safe to the other shore—another fire was built, and my sister dried the infant and its clothes. Here we found a proof of Indian sagacity, which might justly be supposed not to belong to a band of rambling barbarians. In their journey over to Connecticut river, they had in this place, killed a bear; the entrails were cleansed; and filled with the fat of the animal, and suspended from the limb of a tree; by it was deposited a bag of flour, and some tobacco: all which was designed for future stores, when traveling that way. Nothing could have been offered more acceptable, than these tokens of Indian economy and prudence. The flour was made into pudding, and the bear's grease sauce was not unrelishing. Broth was made, well seasoned with snakeroot, and those who were fond of tobacco had each their share. The whole formed quite a sumptuous entertainment.

But these savage dainties made no sensible addition to our quota of happiness. My weakness increased, my children were very unwell, and Mr. Johnson's situation was truly distressing. By traveling barefoot over such a length of forest, and supporting me on his shoulders, his feet were rendered sore beyond description. I cannot express too much gratitude for Mr. Labarree's goodness. My infant was his sole charge, and he supported it by pieces of the horseflesh, which he kept for its use, which, by being chewed in his own mouth, and then put into the child's, afforded it the necessary nutriment. After supper, my booth was made, the evening yell sounded, and we encamped for the night. By this time the savages had relaxed part of their watchfulness, and begun to be careless of our escaping. Labarree and Farnsworth were slightly bound, and my husband had all his liberty. My sister could sleep without her two Indian companions, and the whole company appeared less like prisoners. . . .

The Indians signified to us, that we should arrive, before night [of the ninth day], at East Bay, on Lake Champlain.[7] This was a cordial to our drooping spirits, and caused an immediate transition from despair to joy; the idea of arriving at a place of water carriage translated us to new life. Those who languished with sickness, fatigue, or despair, now marched forward with nervous alacrity. Two Indians were sent on a hunting scout, who were to meet us at the Bay with canoes. . . . The life, which nine days painful suffering in the wilderness had brought to its last moment of duration, now started into new existence, and rendered the hour I sat on the shore of Lake Champlain the happiest I ever experienced. Here we were to take passage in boats, and find relief from the thorny hills and miry swamps of the damp desert. My husband could now be relieved from the burden which had brought him as nigh to eternity as myself. My little children would soon find clothing, and all my fellow sufferers would be in a condition to attain some of life's conveniences; twelve hours sailing would waft us to the settlements of civilized Frenchmen. Considering how much we had endured, few will deem it less than a miracle that we were still among the living. . . . The Indians had been surprisingly patient, and often discovered tokens of humanity. At every meal, we all shared equal with them, whether a horse or a duck composed the bill of fare, and more than once they gave me a blanket to shelter me from a thunder storm.

I will only detain the reader a few moments longer in this place, while I eat the leg of a woodcock, and then request him to take a night's sailing in the canoe with me across the Lake, though I sincerely wish him a better passage than I had. No sooner was our repast finished, than the party were divided into four equal parties for passage. In my boat were two savages, besides my son and infant. I was ordered to lie flat on the bottom of the canoe, and when pain obliged me to move for relief, I had a rap from a paddle. At daybreak, we arrived at a great rock on the west side of the Lake, where we stopped and built a fire. The Indians went to a French house, not far distant, and got some meat, bread, and green corn. Although we were not allowed to take the meat yet, by the grateful effluvia of the broiling steak we were finely regaled, and the bread and roasted corn were a luxury. Here the savages, for the first time, gave loud tokens of joy, by hallooing and yelling in a tremendous manner.

The prisoners were now introduced to a new school. Little did we expect the accomplishment of dancing would ever be taught us by the savages. But the war-dance must now be held, and every prisoner that could move, must take his awkward steps. The figure consisted of circular motion round the fire; each sung his own music, and the best dancer was the one most violent in motion. The prisoners were taught each a song; mine was, "Danna witchee natchep-ung"; my son's was, "Narwiscumpton"; the rest I cannot recollect. Whether this task was imposed on us for their diversion, or a religious ceremony, I cannot say, but it was very painful and offensive. In the forenoon, seven Indians came to us, who were received with great joy by our masters, who took great pleasure in introducing their prisoners. The war-dance was again held; we were obliged to join, and sing our songs, while the Indians rent the air with infernal yelling. We then embarked, and arrived at Crown Point[8] about noon. Each prisoner was then led by their masters to the residence of the French Commander. The Indians kept up their infernal yelling the whole time. We were ordered to his apartment, and used with that hospitability which characterizes the best part of the nation. We had brandy in profusion, a good dinner, and a change of linen. This was luxury indeed, after what we had suffered for the want of these things. None but ourselves could prize their value. After dinner we paraded before Mr. Commander, and underwent examination; after which we were shown a convenient apartment, where we resided four days, not subject to the jurisdiction of our savage masters. Here we received great civilities, and many presents. I had a nurse, who, in a great measure, restored my exhausted strength. My children were all decently clothed, and my infant in particular. The first day, while I was taking a nap, they dressed it so fantastically, à la France, that I refused to own[9] it when brought to my bedside, not guessing that I was the mother of such a strange thing.

On the fourth day, to our grief and mortification, we were again delivered to the Indians, who led us to the waterside, where we all embarked in one vessel for St. John's. The wind shifted after a short sail, and we dropped anchor. In a short time a canoe came alongside of us, in which was a white woman, who was bound for Albany. Mr. Johnson begged her to stop for a few minutes, while he wrote to Col. Lydius of Albany, to inform him of our situation, and to request him to put the same in the Boston newspapers, that our friends might learn that we were alive. The woman delivered the letter, and the contents were published, which conveyed the agreeable tidings to our friends, that, although prisoners, we were then alive.

[The party canoes up the St. Lawrence River, meeting more French at other settlements along the way, but continuing on to the home of their captors—St. Francis,

on the St. Lawrence north of Montreal and south of Trois-Rivières. At St. Francis,
they make a triumphal entrance.]

No sooner had we landed, than the yelling in the town was redoubled, and
a cloud of savages of all sizes and sexes soon appeared running towards us;
when they reached the boats, they formed themselves into a long parade, leaving a small space, through which we must pass. Each Indian took his prisoner
by the hand, and after ordering him to sing the war-song, began to march
through the gauntlet. We expected a severe beating before we got through, but
were agreeably disappointed, when we found that each Indian only gave us a
tap on the shoulder.[10] We were led directly to the houses, each taking his prisoner to his own wigwam. When I entered my master's door, his brother
saluted me with a large belt of wampum,[11] and my master presented me with
another: both were put over my shoulders, and crossed behind and before. My
new home was not the most agreeable; a large wigwam without a floor, with a
fire in the center, and only a few water vessels and dishes to eat from, made of
birch bark, and tools for cookery, made clumsily of wood, for furniture, will
not be thought a pleasing residence for one accustomed to civilized life.

[Johnson tries to settle into life at St. Francis, assuming that this might be her
home for years. Soon after her arrival, her master trades her and her infant
daughter to a different Abenaki in exchange for her son, Sylvanus.]

I was taken to the house of my new master, and found myself allied to the
first family; my master was son-in-law to the grand sachem,[12] was accounted
rich, had a store of goods, and lived in a style far above the majority of his
tribe. Soon after my arrival at his house, the interpreter came to inform me,
that I was adopted into his family. I was then introduced to the family, and was
told to call them brothers and sisters. I made a short reply, expressive of gratitude, for being introduced to a house of high blood, and requested their patience while I should learn the customs of the nation.[13] This was scarce over,
when the attention of the village was called to the grand parade, to attend a
rejoicing, occasioned by the arrival of some warriors, who had brought some
scalps. They were carried in triumph on a pole. Savage butchery upon murdered countrymen! The sight was horrid. As I retired to my new residence, I
could hear the savage yells that accompany the war-dance. I spent the night in
sad reflection.

My time was now solitary beyond description; my new sisters and brothers
treated me with the same attention that they did their natural kindred, but it
was an unnatural situation to me. I was a novice at making canoes, bunks, and
tumplines,[14] which was the only occupation of the squaws; of course idleness
was among my calamities. . . . Mr. Johnson tarried but a few days with me, before he was carried to Montreal to be sold. My two daughters, sister, and Labarree, were soon after carried to the same place, at different times. Farnsworth

was carried by his master on a hunting scout, but not proving so active in the chase and ambush as they could have wished, he was returned, and sent to Montreal. I now found an increase to my trouble, with only my son and infant in this strange land, without a prospect of relief. . . . In this dilemma, who can imagine my distress, when my little son came running to me one morning, swollen with tears, exclaiming, that the Indians were going to carry him into the woods to hunt! He had scarcely told the piteous story, before his master came to pull him away; he threw his little arms around me, begging, in the agony of grief, that I would keep him. The inexorable savage unclenched his hands, and forced him away: the last words I heard, intermingled with his cries, were, "Ma'am, I shall never see you again!" The keenness of my pangs almost obliged me to wish that I never had been a mother. "Farewell, Sylvanus!" said I, "God will preserve you."

It was now the 15th day of October. Forty-five days had passed since my captivity, and no prospect, but what was darkened with clouds of misfortune. The uneasiness occasioned by indolence was in some measure relieved by the privilege of making shirts for my brother. At night and morn, I was allowed to milk the cows. The rest of the time I strolled gloomily about, looking sometimes into an unsociable wigwam, at others sauntering into the bushes, and walking on the banks of brooks. Once I went to a French house three miles distant, to visit some friends of my brother's family, where I was entertained politely a week. At another time I went with a party to fish, accompanied by a number of squaws. My weakness obliged me to rest often, which gave my companions a poor opinion of me; but they showed no other resentment, than calling me "no good squaw," which was the only reproach my sister ever gave me when I displeased her. All the French inhabitants I formed an acquaintance with treated me with that civility which distinguishes the nation. . . .

St. Francis contained about thirty wigwams, which were thrown into a clump. There was a church, in which mass was held every night and morning, and every Sunday: the hearers were summoned by a bell; and attendance was pretty general. Ceremonies were performed by a French friar, who lived in the midst of them, for the salvation of their souls. He appeared to be in that place what the legislative branch is in civil government, and the grand sachem the executive. The inhabitants lived in perfect harmony, holding most of their property in common. They were prone to indolence when at home, and not remarkable for neatness. They were extremely modest, and apparently averse to airs of courtship. Necessity was the only thing that called them to action; this induced them to plant their corn, and to undergo the fatigues of hunting. Perhaps I am wrong in calling necessity the only motive; revenge, which prompts them to war, has great power. I had a numerous retinue of relations, which I visited daily; but my brother's house being one of the most decent in the village, I fared full as well at home. Among my connections was a little brother Sabaties, who brought the cows for me, and took particular notice of my child. He was a sprightly little fellow, and often amused me with feats performed with his bow and arrow.

In the early part of November, Mr. Johnson wrote from Montreal, requesting me to prevail on the Indians to carry me to Montreal for sale, as he had made provision for that purpose. I disclosed the matter, which was agreed to by my brother and sister, and, on the 7th, we set sail in a little bark canoe.[15] . . . On the 11th, we arrived at Montreal, where I had the supreme satisfaction of meeting my husband, children, and friends. Here I had the happiness to find, that all my fellow prisoners had been purchased, by gentlemen of respectability, by whom they were treated with great humanity. Mr. Du Quesne[16] bought my sister, my eldest daughter was owned by three affluent old maids of the name of Jaisson, and the other was owned by the mayor of the city. . . . I was received into Mr. Du Quesne's family. My joy at being delivered from savage captivity was unbounded. . . .

In justice to the Indians, I ought to remark, that they never treated us with cruelty to a wanton degree: few people have survived a situation like mine, and few have fallen into the hands of savages disposed to more lenity and patience. Modesty has ever been a characteristic of every savage tribe; a truth which the whole of my family will join to corroborate to the extent of their knowledge. As they are aptly called the children of nature, those who have profited by refinement and education ought to abate part of the prejudice which prompts them to look with an eye of censure on this untutored race. Can it be said of civilized conquerors, that they in the main are willing to share with their prisoners the last ration of food when famine stares them in the face? Do they ever adopt an enemy, and salute him by the tender name of brother? And I am justified in doubting, whether, if I had fallen into the hands of French soldiery, so much assiduity would have been shown to preserve my life.

[After more difficulties, the Johnsons eventually got their freedom, including young Sylvanus, who by then had learned the Abenaki language and mode of hunting. The family made their way back to Charlestown by January 1758. In the meantime, Johnson had birthed another child, who died in Canada, and was pregnant with another, who died two months after his birth in New Hampshire. James died the following summer at the Battle of Ticonderoga. In 1759, Robert Rogers and his "Rangers," a British colonial militia unit, destroyed St. Francis. Susannah Johnson lived another fifty years, remarrying, caring for her family, and writing her book.]

From Susannah Johnson, *A Narrative of the Captivity of Mrs. Johnson: Containing an Account of Her Sufferings during Four Years with the Indians and French* (Walpole, NH, 1796), 8–40.

Discussion Questions

1. Can you tell from the beginning of Johnson's story what her life was like under normal conditions?

2. What kinds of difficulties do all of the captives face? What particular difficulties does Johnson face? Why does she repeatedly note the Abenakis' "modesty"?

3. Compare the treatment of Susannah Johnson by her captors with the treatment of Venture Smith and Olaudah Equiano by their captors.

4. What can you infer from Johnson's experience about the lives and emotions of enslaved women more generally?

5. What can you tell about life for the Abenaki townspeople in St. Francis? What were women's roles? How did the fact that St. Francis was at war affect people's tasks?

Notes

1. Northfield, Massachusetts, farther south and thus farther from the dangerous Canadian border.

2. A mixed drink of alcohol, sugar, egg, and cream.

3. Clemency.

4. Women in colonial America rightly considered childbirth some of their "most perilous hours." About one in one hundred births in 1750s New England ended in the death of the mother.

5. Like European men, Indian men knew little of childbirth, and Johnson's captors were all men. Considering that her sister was only fourteen, Johnson was probably the only person there who had witnessed a childbirth.

6. Johnson named her daughter Elizabeth Captive Johnson.

7. They had reached present-day western Vermont, having walked some eighty miles.

8. Crown Point was the site of the French fort St. Frederic, present-day Essex County, New York.

9. "Own" means both recognize and claim.

10. As Johnson realized, she was being adopted into Abenaki society. The captivity narrative was a popular genre, and she had either read earlier captivity narratives or had heard tales of Iroquois gauntlets, in which beatings were intended to beat the old

identity out of adoptees, clearing the way for them to become Iroquois. The Abenakis were employing a mild version of the gauntlet ceremony.

11. A woven belt of beads. For other examples of wampum use, see the Great Law of the Iroquois League in Section 3 and Ohio Indians talking to the British in Section 7.

12. The community's political and spiritual leader.

13. This family is officially adopting Johnson, which her first master never did. From here on, she refers to them as her brothers and sisters.

14. An Abenaki (Algonquian) word meaning a sling for carrying a load on the back, supported by a strap that goes around the chest or across the forehead.

15. They may have agreed to part with their "sister" because she had not fully accepted adoption and because the French promised them other captives in exchange.

16. The Marquis Duquesne (pronounced "doo-kain"), the governor of New France.

Phillis Wheatley's "On Being Brought from Africa to America," 1773

*P*HILLIS WHEATLEY WAS BORN IN WEST AFRICA, *where slave traders captured her as a child. She arrived in Boston in 1761 and was bought by John and Susannah Wheatley. During her time as their slave, she converted to Christianity and received a classical education. She published her first poem in 1767. After a failed effort to publish a book in Boston, she sailed to England with one of the Wheatley sons, where she published* Poems on Various Subjects. *The book included a statement by Boston notables, including John Hancock, that a young black woman really had written the poems. Back in Boston, the Wheatleys freed her. She continued to publish her poems in magazines until her death in 1784, although she never made a living from them.*

On Being Brought from Africa to America

'Twas mercy brought me from my *Pagan* land,
Taught my benighted soul to understand
That there's a God, that there's a *Savior* too:
Once I redemption neither sought nor knew.
Some view our sable race with scornful eye,
"Their color is a diabolic die."
Remember, *Christians: Negros*, black as *Cain*,[1]
May be refin'd, and join th'angelic train.

From Phillis Wheatley, *Poems on Various Subjects, Religious and Moral. By Phillis Wheatley, Negro Servant to Mr. John Wheatley, of Boston, in New England* (London, 1773), 18.

Discussion Questions

1. How did Wheatley describe Africa?

2. How did she interpret being brought into slavery? Can you understand why she might make this interpretation?

3. What is her advice to Christians who might think that blackness is "diabolic"?

4. Thomas Jefferson, who believed that African Americans were incapable of sophisticated thought, said of Wheatley's poetry, "The compositions published under her name are below the dignity of criticism." What do you make of his judgment?

Note

1. In the Bible, God punished Cain for killing his brother by putting a "mark" on him. Some early modern Christians believed that this mark was black skin and that black skin was a sign of being cursed.

VII

VIOLENT CONFLICT

PEOPLE WHO ESTABLISHED COLONIES OR EXPANDED EXISTING ONES needed to persuade others to do what was in the interest of the colony—to work hard, to trade, to give land, to acknowledge the colony's land claims. Unsurprisingly, this pressure sometimes led to violence. In these documents, what kinds of violence do we observe? What led men to kill one another? How did they justify killing? Why couldn't they all just get along?

Antonio de Otermín a Francisco de Ayeta

Excerpt

M UY REVERENDO MI PADRE SEÑOR Y AMIGO *amantísimo Fray Francisco de Ayeta. Llegada la hora que con lágrimas en los ojos y con arto dolor de mi corazón, empecé a referir parte de la lamentable tragedia y nunca tal sucedida en el Mundo, que ha pasado por este miserable Reino y Santa Custodia, permitiéndolo así su Divina Magestad por mis enormes pecados; y antes que empieze mi narración, quiero, como obligado y agradecido, darle a Vuestra Paternidad Reverenda las gracias debidas por las demostraciones de amor y fineza con que obrao en la solicitud de saber y inquirir las noticias ciertas tanto de mi vida como de las demás de este Reino, entre las voces ciertas de mi muerte, y de las demás que se habían dibulgado, y a no perdonando ni a toda suerte de diligencia, ni a la magnificencia del gasto. Premio que solo el Cielo se lo puede pagar, a Vuestra Paternidad Reverenda, aunque no dudo lo hará también Su Majestad que Dios guarde.** *

*From Antonio de Otermín to Francisco de Ayeta, September 8, 1680, "Testimonio de autos tocantes al alzamiento general de los Indios de la Provincia de la Nueva Mexico," packet 2, folder 420, carton 29, part 1, MSS C-B 840, Bancroft Library, Berkeley, California; original in Section V, Group A, Series 4, Audiencia de Guadalajara 138 (67-3-32), Archivo General de Indias, Seville, Spain. Ayeta was a Franciscan coming from Mexico City with a caravan of supplies. Translation begins on p. 252.

Francisco López de Mendoza Grájales's Account of the Conquest of Florida, 1565

*I*N THE 1500S, SOME FRENCH HUGUENOTS *(Protestants) proposed an American colony. To the young French king Charles IX and his regent, his mother Catherine de Medici, a joint Huguenot and Catholic colony in Florida seemed to support their efforts to appease Huguenots and avoid civil war. After a failed attempt at Parris Island, South Carolina, the colonists in 1564 built Ft. Caroline on the St. John's River (present-day Jacksonville, Florida). The Spanish were appalled to learn of these attempts. Not only had the French founded a colony on land that Spain claimed, but many were Protestants. Plus, the Spanish feared that the fort would be a base for attacking Spanish ships. In response, the Spanish crown sent Gen. Pedro Menéndez de Avilés with a division of soldiers to expel the French and establish a Spanish fort. Father Francisco López de Mendoza Grájales was the expedition's chaplain and kept a journal, which he saved for the king. This excerpt begins August 30, 1565, as the Spanish are looking for Ft. Caroline.*

My Lord General [Pedro Menéndez] realized that neither the pilots we had brought with us nor the French prisoners, who had actually been with the French forces at the harbor,[1] could find the harbor because the land was so low and flat there were no landmarks and there were no signals coming from it; so he sent fifty harquebusiers[2] and some company captains ashore. They lit several bonfires to arouse the Indians and make them come running. But the Indians were like dull beasts: they didn't care a bit about trading and didn't come running.

Our people therefore walked inland for four leagues and came upon a village of Indians[3] who received them well, fed them, and asked them for whatever they had brought with them. The soldiers were so highly honored that they gave them many of the things they had brought, and the Indians gave them two pieces of gold, not of many carats, but enough to reveal that there is some and that they do trade it. This corroborates what the Frenchmen we have with us say, having traded with the Indians for several days. . . . One of the Frenchmen understood the language, and they told him that we had passed the harbor about five leagues back—the same place where God brought us when we came in sight of land.

[The Spanish fleet finds Ft. Caroline at the mouth of the St. John's River, where several French ships are in the harbor. There is a skirmish, both fleets are scattered by a storm, and the Spanish forces manage to regather in a harbor some forty miles to the south.]

[On September 6], three companies came to shore, one commanded by the lord Captain Andrés López Patiño and another by the lord Captain Juan de San Vicente, a very important gentleman. The Indians received them well and gave them a chief's house, very large, by the banks of the river. Then Lord Captain Patiño and Captain San Vicente, with their good diligence and industry, ordered a ditch to be dug out all around the house, with large ramparts of dirt and mud, which are the only defense the land provides, there not being so much as a stone for a marker anywhere.[4]

We have kept inside the fort until this very day, with twenty-four bronze cannons, the least of which is twenty-five hundredweight. Our fort is about fifteen leagues from the enemy fort. Such was the industry and diligence of those two captains that with the soldiers' fingernails and no other tools they built a fort to defend themselves so that when the General disembarked he was amazed by what he had accomplished.

Saturday, the eighth of the month, feast of the birthday of Our Lady,[5] the Lord General disembarked with many banners flying, many trumpets blaring, much artillery going off, and other instruments of war. And since I had arrived the previous day, I took a cross, and we went out to greet him singing the psalm: "Te Deum laudamus." The General walked straight up to the Cross, as did all the people who came with him, and they bent their knees to the ground and kissed the cross. There were many Indians looking on at these ceremonies, and they did everything they saw our men do.

This same morning the General, my lord, took possession of this land for His Majesty, and all the captains swore oaths for now and from this time forward for the whole land. . . . Now we will be in this fort, some six hundred fighting men; and the French will be about as many, and somewhat more. I therefore believe that the lord General will not attack the enemy again this winter, but will reorganize his people and wait for help, which we expect at any hour, and he will destroy them. . . .

[General Menéndez decides to send a sloop ship out to unload the supplies and men from the galleon and another large ship, which are vulnerable because they cannot enter the harbor. As the sloop returns to shore with most of the supplies and men, the wind stops and the ship cannot sail. At daybreak, the men on the sloop see two ships approaching.]

When in the light of the new day, our people realized they were the French, they said a prayer to Our Lady of Comfort of Utrera, asking help from her, just a tiny bit of wind, because the French were coming down on them. Then it seemed that she herself boarded the ship, and with a little bit of wind that arose, the sloop came in over the sandbar and had just finished getting across it when the French reached it, and since the water was shallow over the bar and their ships were large, they could not enter.

Thus our men and supplies made it to safety. As the day got brighter, along with those two ships four more ships of the same enemy could be seen, somewhat farther off, the ones which we had come upon at night in their harbor earlier, as I told before. They were provided with people and artillery and approaching our galleon and our other ship where they were alone out at sea. At this point Our Lord granted us two remedies. The first is that that same night, now that the supplies and people had been unloaded, at about midnight without the enemy hearing them, the galleon and the ship that was with it hoisted sail and left, one for Spain and the other to return to Havana to bring back the fleet that was there. And thus the French were left without one prize or the other.[6] The other remedy and the one that made us happier was that the next day, after these things happened, such a furious hurricane blew in that most of the French could not have helped but be lost at sea, because it overtook them off the harshest shoreline I have ever seen,[7] very close to land, and if our people—I mean the galleon and its companion ship—were not lost, it was because they left in the middle of the night when the force of the storm had not arrived: they could not have failed to be more than twelve leagues out to sea and so have room to run until God brought other weather.

Having witnessed the events I have described, our good General, being so sharp in matters of war and such an enemy to the French, especially these French, since he pursues them so relentlessly, called his captains to council and told them that he had determined to go with five hundred men and attack the French. Although most of the captains and I and the other priest deputized to share in the councils disagreed, he said that he had decided that this was what must be done.

Monday, the sixteenth of September,[8] he left with five hundred men armed with harquebuses and pikes, each of the soldiers carrying a knapsack of bread weighing about twelve pounds and a skin of wine. They took two Indian chiefs, great enemies to the French, to show them the way. From the signs and signals they gave us, the way Indians do, we understood that we were five leagues from the enemy fort. Once they were on the way, it turned out to be fifteen leagues of the worst paths that the sun ever warmed. They have made the whole journey now, according to a letter we received from the Lord General today, the nineteenth of the month, in which he says the shallowest water they met with on the path came up to their knees, and the jungle was very thick. He writes he is planning to assault the enemy fort tomorrow. His heart and his enthusiasm are good. I only wish he could be a little more prudent, because it does seem to me that he needs prudence to attain his goals, and more to the point, His Royal Majesty's goals. . . . Pray God the Divine Majesty that He keep us company and give us aid, as He knows we need it!

Today, Wednesday afternoon, the nineteenth, we sent twenty men from this fort loaded with provisions: bread and wine and some cheeses, but so much rain has come storming down on them that I don't know how they could have gotten to where my lord the General and his army are. I pray to my God that he will do what needs to be done so that we may exalt His holy Catholic faith and destroy those heretics!

Today, Saturday, the twenty-second of the month, in the morning, as we finished celebrating the mass of Our Lord, at our request the lord Admiral ordered some sailors to go fishing because it was a meatless day and we priests could eat a little fish.[9] When we arrived at the beach where they intended to throw out the net, they saw a man coming onto the beach. They leapt back to dry land and ran after him. He lifted up a flag as a sign of peace. They went up to him and laid hold of him. He was French, one of our enemies. We dragged him prisoner to our camp. Afraid and believing we were going to hang him, he wept and trembled. I asked him if he was Christian. He said yes and said the prayers.[10]

Seeing this, I consoled him and told him he would have no punishment or fear if he answered the truth to every question he was asked, and he promised he would. To "Where did he come from and what was he looking for?" he answered that he was one of the Frenchmen from the fort and that his General had sent him out with fifteen others in a frigate eight days ago and that they came to scout out our harbor and they saw and heard what we were doing. When they had done that, they came down to the coast, and when they got to the mouth of the river where our harbor is, God Our Lord sent a ruinous storm and hurricane. To get away from it and from our harbor, they tried to put out to sea, but couldn't because the sea was so strong and the wind so wild that they were thrown back into the mouth of another river, five leagues from us on the south bank, where their frigate wrecked and five of them drowned.[11]

The next morning brought Indians down upon them. The Indians attacked and killed three more with spears. He and another fled to the jungle and escaped by hiding in a hole. The next day they agreed to go back to the ocean. They got down into the river and with only their heads out of water, arrived yesterday (Friday, the feast of St. Matthew) at the mouth of the river. His friend decided to throw himself into the ocean and head for the other bank, from where he could easily get to his harbor. But since the river is wide there and the current strong, I am sure he drowned. He also says he knows nothing about the rest of his companions; he didn't see them again.

Then we sent men out—soldiers and sailors—to look for the man's companions and bring back the frigate, which would be no small use to us. He says that in the fort there are about seven hundred men, a third of them Lutherans,[12] that they have two priests preaching the Lutheran sect, and that in their camp there are eight to ten Spaniards, and they found three of them among the Indians, dressed in skins and their bodies decorated like Indians'. They were from a ship that was wrecked on the coast, and after a long time, since no new ship came, they stayed among the Indians and married them. They say that they keep cattle and pigs for stock.

He says their fleet arrived no more than twenty days before ours did, and that they had not unloaded any artillery or munitions from the ship, or more than two hundred hundredweight of biscuit, three hundred twenty bushels of wheat, some meat, and other things. We were fairly happy to hear this, because if God Our Lord gives our General good success, as I believe He will, all will redound to our advantage. Best of all for us is that he says that more than two hundred men put out in four ships to come looking for us, and they haven't come back. They must have perished, because after they left, there came two of the biggest storms I have ever seen.

About noon of the same day, considering what the Frenchman had said and that the frigate had been grounded, the lord Admiral ordered ten men, fully equipped soldiers and sailors, to go in a boat to where the ship was, pull it out, and bring it back, and that is what they started to do. When our ten men approached the ship, a crowd of Indians appeared; and fearing that they would be cut down by arrows, our men thought it best to come back, especially since they could see the bodies of fifteen Frenchmen from the frigate, whom the Indians had killed.

Monday, the twenty-third[13] of the same month, angry because the ten men had come back without the frigate, the Admiral ordered a boat to be fitted out with a dozen men, and he went up river to find out what was up there and if there were some Indian villages. By good fortune he found a way to the mouth of the river where the frigate shipwrecked, and they went until they found it. As soon as the Indians realized they were Spanish, they received them very well and helped them pull out the frigate.

On Tuesday, about nine in the morning, they came into this harbor with it. When I saw and recognized that it was they, I ordered that the bells be rung and that there be great rejoicing throughout the camp. The frigate will be very advantageous for our plans, being a ship of fifteen anchors for every use.

News of Great Rejoicing, Worthy of Being Told

This same day, Monday, about an hour after the Admiral had come in with his prize frigate, we saw a man coming toward us and shouting loudly. The first man to go out to get news from him was I, and he embraced me with great joy, saying, "Victory! Victory! The French harbor is ours!" I promised a reward for him, and I gave him the best I could.

I told in the previous chapters how our General, against many contrary opinions, determined to attack the French by land with five hundred men. How he did it, and how this is the work of my Lord Jesus Christ and his Blessed Mother—the Holy Ghost enlightened the understanding of our good General so that it might be done for our salvation and with such a great victory! Just as my lord General, the first and the boldest, has always been so cunning and diligent in war and has given such a good account of himself in everything that His Majesty charged him to do, so he has given and will give no less in this enterprise which is so important to the royal crown. And he has done it with more eagerness and diligence than any prince in the world, not sparing his own body, an inspiration to the captains and the other soldiers, heartening them and driving them with such a brave spirit that his words alone, with no other reward, were provision enough to make any soldier fight like a Roman.

To better finish this so that you may taste the victory, I want to tell of some of the things that happened this day, because of course God and his Mother, and not the powers of men, brought this day about, against those enemies of their holy Catholic faith. . . . Thursday morning, our good General, with his son-in-law Pedro de Valdés and Captain Patiño at his side, attacked. They made straight for the enemy fort with such spirit that their charge seemed no labor at all. When the others saw, they took heart—all of them, not one exception—and did the same. It must be noted that the enemies never heard until our men were upon them. Since it was still morning, raining and storming, most of them hadn't gotten up out of their beds. Some came running out in buckskin and some in their shirts, saying, "I surrender, sir!" Nevertheless, there was a killing of one hundred forty-two. The rest, who added up to three hundred, fled across the walls of the fort, some for the jungle, and some took shelter in some ships they had on the river, with riches in them, so that within an hour the fort was ours without one of our men lost or even wounded.

There were six ships in the river. We took a brig and a galliot, although it wasn't in good shape, and another ship, which was beached and had had most of its merchandise unloaded. Of the other three, two were in the harbor mouth by the sandbar to defend the harbor entrance, assuming we had to come by sea. The third was just outside the harbor, loaded with wine and other supplies. It didn't want to surrender and hoisted its sails. Our people fired a shot from one of the cannons in the fort and sent it to the bottom, but it is where neither the frame nor what is in it will be lost. They found many things—and valuable—among the plunder: a hundred twenty very good corslets,[14] three hundred pikes, many harquebuses, many helmets, much and very good clothing, much linen, sailcloth, buckskin, and fine light wool, dozens of barrels of flour, many biscuits, much lard, cattle and pigs (but not many), three horses, four jackasses and two jennies,[15] three hundred twenty bushels of wheat, an oven and bakery, and many other things. . . . And the greatest prize, which I feel from this business, is the victory which Our Lord has given us so that his gospel may be planted and preached in these places where it is so needed for the healing of as many souls as are now lost here.

They found a great number of Lutheran books, and they found many decks of cards with pictures of the host and communion chalice on the backs, and many altars with crosses on them on the backs of other cards, mocking and sneering at the things of the Church. The Lutheran who had these things died among them and many other evil things that he had, a great cosmographer and necromancer who had formerly been a friar.

Thus, today, Monday, the twenty-fourth of the present month at about vespers, our good General came in accompanied by fifty soldiers, on foot, bruised, and weary, he and all who came with him. As soon as I heard the news, I ran to my house, got out a new robe—the best I had—and a surplice and took a crucifix in my hands and went out to receive them just before they arrived at the harbor. And he—gentleman and Christian!—got down on his knees with all the other men with him, giving thanks to Our Lord for the great kindnesses He had bestowed. Thus I and my companions came forward, singing and in procession, so that he was received in great joy by us, and we by him. He is so zealous in his Christianity that all these labors are relaxation for his soul, because it certainly does seem to me that no human strength could have endured what he must have endured. But the fire and desire to serve Our Lord in beating down and destroying this Lutheran sect, enemy to our holy Catholic faith, keep him from feeling the hardships. And if we begin to speak of his brother whom he brought with him, Captain Bartholomew Menéndez, no less zealous in exalting our holy Catholic faith and obeying the commands of his good brother and our General, we will never finish.

[There follows much praise for the general's brother and then for his son-in-law.]

After what I have told about up until now, last Friday, which would be the [twenty-]eighth of September of this year, as the lord General was resting with a brief siesta from all the work he had done, some Indians came to this camp and let us know by signs that along the coast to the south a French ship had been wrecked and sunk.

[General Menéndez, the admiral, Chaplain Mendoza, some sixty Spanish soldiers, and their Timucuan guides take off and spot the survivors of the French shipwreck across the river.]

We got there before dawn and hid ourselves along with the Indians who were with us in a little valley. When day broke, we saw many of the enemy going along the river hunting for shellfish. A little later, we saw them pull out a flag and extend it as if for war. Our good General, seeing all this and inspired by the Holy Ghost, said, "Gentlemen, I have decided to throw off these clothes, put on a sailor's uniform, take this Frenchman with me (one of the ones we had brought with us from Spain) and go speak with those Frenchmen. Maybe they'll be so beaten down they'll want to surrender without a fight."

He did just as he said he would do, and when he started shouting, one of the enemy threw himself into the water and swam across to speak with the General and made him understand how the ship had been wrecked on the sandbar and destroyed and what ruin they had endured and how for ten or twelve days they hadn't had a bite of bread. In addition, he admitted that all or most of them were Lutherans. The General sent him back to his companions to tell them, on his behalf, to surrender and hand in their weapons. If not, he would put all of them to the knife.

In reply to this, a French gentleman, a sergeant, came and brought a message from the enemy camp. They asked him to spare their lives and said they would surrender their bodies and hand over their weapons. After much discussion, our good General replied that he did not want to promise, but that they should bring their weapons and themselves so that he could do his will, because if he gave them life, he wanted them to thank him for it, and if death, he wanted no complaints that he had broken his promise.

Seeing that he could do nothing else, the messenger returned to his camp. A little later they all came with their weapons and flags and surrendered them to his Lordship and put their bodies in his power to do with them what he willed. Since they were all Lutherans, his Lordship decided to condemn them to death. And I, being a priest and having the stomach of a man, asked him to grant me a favor, which was that any Christians[16] we found not die, and he granted me that. When we picked through them, we found ten or a dozen and took them with us. All the rest died for being Lutherans and against our holy Catholic faith.

All this took place Saturday, the Feast of Saint Michael, the twenty-ninth of September, 1565. The number of Lutherans who died was a hundred and eleven men, not counting the fourteen or fifteen that we took prisoner.

I, Francisco López de Mendoza Grájales, his Lordship's Chaplain, give my word that everything recorded herein took place in reality and truth.

Translated by John DuVal from "Relación de la jornada de Pedro Menéndez en la Florida," in *Colección de documentos inéditos relativos al descubrimiento, conquista y colonización de las posesiones Españolas en América y Oceanía*, ed. Joaquin F. Pacheco, Francisco de Cárdenas, and Luis Torres de Mendoza (Madrid, 1865), 3: 441–79.

Discussion Questions

1. Are you surprised at the killings and the chaplain's responses to them? If so, what surprises you?
2. Why were the Spanish so opposed to the French settlement?
3. Why was the chaplain so certain that God was on the Spaniards' side?
4. What do you think the Timucuans thought of the French and the Spanish and their rivalry?

Notes

1. The French prisoners were pirates whom the Spanish had captured earlier.
2. A soldier armed with a harquebus, an early matchlock gun.
3. Timucuans, native to Florida.
4. This new Spanish fort was St. Augustine, the first permanent European settlement in the United States.
5. The birthday of Mary, the mother of Jesus, is celebrated on September 8.
6. Mendoza means that the French neither attacked the galleon and its companion ship nor succeeded in seizing the sloop.
7. Florida's eastern shoreline is harsh because of the reefs and shallows.
8. Monday was the seventeenth.
9. September 22, 1565, was one of the autumnal Ember Days, which required abstinence, including refraining from eating meat.
10. By "Christian," Mendoza means Catholic. The "prayers" would have been prayers particular to Catholics, probably the Ave Maria (Hail Mary) and the Creed.
11. This is one of the French ships mentioned earlier. The Florida coast is lined with thin islands that create multiple inlets and harbors. Thus, the Spanish and French (and modern-day readers) often find that the terms *upriver* and *downriver* don't quite work.
12. Protestants.
13. The twenty-third was a Sunday.
14. Body armor.
15. Female donkeys.
16. Catholics.

Henri Joutel's Account of the Murder of La Salle, 1687

---

*I*N 1683, FRENCHMAN RENÉ-ROBERT CAVELIER, *Sieur de La Salle, became the first European to lead a mission down the Mississippi to the Gulf of Mexico. Two years later he sailed from France with over two hundred men and women to found a colony at the Mississippi's mouth, named Louisiana for Louis XIV. But finding the river's mouth from the gulf was difficult, and he sailed past without spotting it, instead landing at Matagorda Bay in Spanish Texas. Supplies began to run out, disease struck, two ships wrecked, and the last one turned tail for France. In January 1687, La Salle led about seventeen men by foot in an attempt to find the Mississippi and the French Illinois settlements. We join this smaller party somewhere in East Texas two months after they set out from the main colony. Our narrator is La Salle's lieutenant Henri Joutel, who used the notes that he kept on the journey to write this narrative. It is March 15, food and tempers are short, and the men fear Spanish and Indian attack.*

When Monsieur de La Salle had come back from the Cenis,[1] he had had more Indian corn and beans than his horses could bear and had therefore decided to cache a portion of them. He had two reasons for this: first, he couldn't carry all this food anyway, and second, he realized there wasn't any hunting between there and the Ceni village except for a few turkeys—not hunting that could be depended on. Besides, we were running out of shot.

This is why, seeing that we didn't have enough provisions now to make it to the village, Monsieur de La Salle decided it was best to send people out to look for the cache of corn. So he gave orders to seven or eight men, including Monsieur [Pierre] Duhaut; his doctor [Liotot]; the Shawnee, his Indian;[2] Hiems;

Tessier; and Monsieur de La Salle's servant, Saget. Some of the [Ceni] Indians who had come with us accompanied them. But when they got there, all the corn was spoiled and rotten, either because the cache had been opened or because it hadn't been secured right, and water had seeped in. So they started back.

The Shawnee caught sight of two bison, went after them, and killed them. Then they chose a man to come to tell Monsieur de La Salle so that if he thought they ought to smoke the bison, he could send some horses to carry the meat. The one they chose was Monsieur de La Salle's servant, Saget, who arrived at the camp that evening with one of the Indians who had gone with them.

Monsieur de La Salle waited till the next morning to send someone, and then ordered his nephew Lord du Morenger to go, along with Monnier and Lord de Marle, as well as the servant to guide them back.[3] He ordered that as soon as they got there they should send meat back on one horse while they smoke-dried the rest.

They left on the seventeenth, but the day went by without any word back from them.

On the eighteenth Monsieur de La Salle looked very worried because no one had come back. He was afraid something might have happened to them, that Indians might have ambushed them or that they were lost. When evening fell, not knowing what to think, he determined to go see for himself. But since he wasn't familiar with the place and since the Indians who were camped near us had gone and come back with his servant Saget, Monsieur de La Salle told them that if they would guide him to the place he would give them a hatchet. One of them agreed to go. (These people are much better skilled than we are at finding the paths and places where they have been—they get used to it from the earliest years because hunting is one of their chief occupations.)

After the Indian promised to guide him, Monsieur de La Salle got ready to leave the next morning and ordered me to get ready to go with him, which was easy enough to do since we were always on the move. That night, as we talked together about what might have happened to those who had gone, he seemed to have a presentiment of what was about to happen. He asked me if I hadn't heard them scheming anything among themselves and if I hadn't noticed some plot among them. I answered that I hadn't heard anything except sometimes when there were disputes they complained that there was too much quarreling. I didn't know anything else. Besides, they thought of me as being close to him, and if they did have any plot in mind, they couldn't have told me. We spent the rest of the night very uneasily.

At last, when day broke, it was time to leave. It was the nineteenth. Despite the fact that he had decided I ought to go with him, he changed his mind in the morning, because otherwise there would have been no one left to oversee the camp. He told Father Anastase [Douay] to go with him instead. Then he told me to give him my rifle, because it was one of the most reliable ones we had. I gave it to him, and my pistol, too. Then they left, three of them: Monsieur de La Salle, Father Anastase, and the [Ceni] Indian who was guiding them. As he left, Monsieur ordered me to take care of everything and to make sure to send up smoke from time to time from a little hill near our camp so that if they got lost, it could set them right and they could walk toward the smoke.

So they left. There were just five of us who stayed—not much for defense considering that one was Tallon's little boy, and another one wasn't worth much. In short, the only ones left were Monsieur Cavelier, the priest; Lord [Colin] Cavelier, his nephew; and I.[4]

Following the orders Monsieur de La Salle gave me when he left, during the day I set fire to little batches of dry grass that would burn for a while; but toward evening, as I was going up the little hill I mentioned, I was amazed to see one of the men who had first gone to look for the corn. When he came close, he looked confused, or rather totally distracted. The first thing he said was he had much news and a terrible thing had happened. I asked him what. He answered that Monsieur de La Salle was dead, and so was his nephew Lord Morenger, and two others: the Shawnee Indian and La Salle's servant.

I stayed still, bewildered, not knowing what to say to this news that they were murdered. The man who had brought me the bad news added that the murderers had at first vowed to kill me, too. I could well believe it, having been always, as I had said, close to Monsieur de La Salle, and having had the command sometimes myself. It is hard to satisfy everybody, or to prevent there being a few malcontents. At this point I was very much at a loss as to what tack to take and if I shouldn't flee into the forest, wherever the providence of God might lead me. But, whether for good luck or bad, I didn't have a rifle. All I had brought with me was a pistol and I didn't even have any more powder or bullets than were in my horn. Everywhere I might turn, my life was in danger. True, this man who was warning me did assure me that on their way back they had changed their minds and agreed not to do any more killing, unless in self defense if we resisted. The man who brought me this news was named [Jean] l'Archevesque, born in the city of Bayonne. Monsieur Duhaut had recruited him in Petit-Goave, where he had enlisted. Although he told me no harm would come to me, it was a promise I didn't trust. But since I was in no condition to go far, with neither arms nor powder, I gave myself up to Providence and to whatever might happen. That is why I went back to camp. The wretched murderers had already taken all of Monsieur de La Salle's clothes and belongings and even my personal belongings. They had also seized all the weapons. When I got there, the first words Duhaut spoke—the one who had killed Monsieur de La Salle—were that each man should command in turn—to which I answered nothing. I could see Monsieur Cavelier praying to God in a corner, and, on the other side, Father Anastase, who did not dare speak to me; nor did I dare go toward him until I saw what the murderers were up to.

They were like mad men, but very worried, and embarrassed, too. I stayed for a long time without speaking and without moving, because, as I have already said, I didn't dare turn toward either Monsieur Cavelier or Father Anastase for fear of arousing our enemies' anger. Since they had cooked some meat when they arrived that evening, there was the matter of having supper. They portioned out the meat as seemed right to them, saying that other people had set the portions for them before, but from now on they would do it. They were obviously trying to force me to say something that would bring on a quarrel, but for my part I knew how to keep my mouth shut.

When night came, and there was the matter of sentry duty, they were at a loss because they couldn't do it all by themselves. For this reason, they told Monsieur Cavelier, Father Anastase, me, and the others who weren't in on their plot to do sentry duty as usual and that we must not think about what had happened, that it was a done deed and despair and desperation had driven them to it, that they had been angry but they no longer had any grudge against anybody. Monsieur Cavelier spoke up and told them they had killed themselves in killing Monsieur de La Salle, since he was the only one who could get us out of this country and that it did not look likely that we would be able to get ourselves out. Finally, after several opinions were set forth from one side or the other, they gave us our weapons. One of them had taken my rifle because it was better than the others. He had taken it from the hands of Monsieur de La Salle. He had also made away with my little bag of shot, my linens, knives, glass beads, necklaces, and things like that, but he gave them back to me, too.

So we did sentry duty, during which time Monsieur Cavelier told me how the plotters had arrived at camp and how they had stormed into Monsieur de La Salle's hut and grabbed everything. When Monsieur Cavelier learned of the death of Monsieur de La Salle, he told them that if they wanted to do the same to him, they should give him a little time to ask pardon of God. They answered that they would assist him as much as they were able, just as they had done up to that time, and that he should forget what was done, that they had been angry, but there was no help for it now, and that it was Monsieur de Morenger who was the root of all these troubles and who had forced them to do the wicked deed. Monsieur Cavelier told them he forgave them even though he had cause for resentment, having lost his brother and his nephew.

During the night we consulted together about what we could do. I told him I would never forsake him, not him nor Father Anastase, nor the young Lord

Cavelier, his other nephew. We promised to hold together to the death—which could come soon—or until we could reach some place of safety. We did not go so far as to plan some way to rid ourselves of those wretched murderers. However, we did agree not to say much to each other in front of them so as not to arouse their mistrust or suspicion. That's how we spent the night till morning, without being tempted by sleep, because I didn't put much trust in their promises after such a monstrous crime.

When day broke, they debated which route to take, that is, whether to go back to the village or push ahead. They decided to go straight to the Cenis. For this purpose, they asked the Indians if they would keep on with us for the forty leagues we still had to travel, promising them some knives in return for showing us the way. They accepted. We started out, but after we had gone about a league and a half, the Indians made a show of having forgotten something and went back the way we had come. They signaled to us that all we had to do was keep on going, and they would catch up.

Since the Indians saw that we were missing three men, in addition to Monsieur de La Salle, and since the one who had guided them had seen a dead body, and they knew very well how many we had been because they had walked for some time with us, and they saw that the Shawnee was missing, I believed that they were going back to find out what had happened, and no good could come of that. Even when I looked at the Indians' faces, it gave me a fear that they had some wicked design against us and that they meant to lag behind and wait for an opportunity to ambush us. However, since there was not a thing we could do about it, we kept going straight north in hopes of finding a little path to the village we were looking for, one that all the Indians in the region come and go on, whether a good one or not. We came upon lovely country with beautiful fields and with forests here and there. We made about five leagues and camped on the edge of a clump of woods. . . .

We spent the night sharing sentry duty again, and it was this night that l'Archevesque related the details of Monsieur de La Salle's death to me. Since I had not had time up until then to speak with anyone, I still didn't know what mean stratagem he had fallen prey to. I will record here the facts as l'Archevesque reported them to me.

Remember the two bison that I mentioned, which the Shawnee had killed, and the news of it that was sent to Monsieur de La Salle, who sent Lord Morenger and the others. The men worked smoking the meat so that when the horses arrived all they would have to do would be load the meat and carry it back on the horses. They cured all the meat, and they grilled the marrowbones and the organs, which don't keep, so that they could eat them then. But when Lord Morenger arrived, he seized the meat, including the organs, and told them he was in charge of the meat from now on and that they would not get to eat any, as they had previously done. He even grabbed up the food they had before them. This infuriated them. Besides, they already bore old grudges against the lord because he had mistreated some of them, even the doctor, even though he almost owed his life to the care that the doctor had devoted to him after he had been wounded on the coast. When the doctor found himself being mistreated after so many protestations of gratitude and friendship, he began to hate him. And there was something else: during the first voyage, Monsieur Duhaut had gotten lost, and he blamed Lord de Morenger, who hadn't wanted to wait for him, and he still resented it.[5] With this latest offense, the old grudges against Monsieur de Morenger rose to their gorge, and the evil spirit entered into their souls and urged them to do the evil deed. Monsieur Duhaut told them he could take no more and that they must have vengeance. They plotted together, five of them: Monsieur Duhaut; Doctor Liotot; Hiems; Tessier, who had been boatswain; and l'Archevesque, who later came to warn me.

Having talked it over, they resolved to murder Monsieur de Morenger. They even left room for suspicion in their choice of words, because that evening after supper (when Lord de Morenger had allotted them very little meat and reserved the rest for himself) they said they were going to go cut some *casse-têtes*, or *head-breakers*, that is, the kinds of clubs the Indians make for their ambushes, when they break the head of anyone unlucky enough to fall into their hands. Then the plotters went out to cut sticks for the clubs, just as they had plotted; and when Lord de Morenger was asleep, along with the Shawnee and Monsieur de La Salle's servant, Saget, these wretches, seeing their chance, thought of nothing but to execute their vile plot. Since all they had to do was wake them, they considered how they should act. But the doctor, more inhumane than the others, took a hatchet, got up, and started on Lord Morenger. He struck him several blows on the head, more than enough to kill a man. Then he fell upon Saget. And then on the poor Shawnee, who couldn't have had the least thing to do with all that had gone on between them. The wretch killed them all, all three in a few seconds, no time for them to say one word, except that Lord Morenger, not being completely dead, did pull himself to a sitting position, not saying a word, and those murderers forced Lord de Marle to finish him off, although he wasn't in on their plot.

As the doctor executed his plot, the others were on watch, weapons in their hands, lest someone wake and put up a defense. Once the murder was committed, that was not the end of it. They had accomplished nothing yet, because there was no way for them to approach Monsieur de La Salle. So they decided to get rid of him, too, seeing that there could be no excuse to cover their crime. Therefore, they concluded they would have to meet with him, and when they reached the camp, they would crack both our skulls, Monsieur de La Salle's and mine, and deal with the other men later. But it had rained the previous days, and the river that crossed their route was so swollen they couldn't ford it, much less carry their meat across, so they had to build a kind of raft, which caused a delay in their plans, and that was what caused Monsieur de La Salle to set out in search of them.

And the following is what Father Anastase told me about Monsieur de La Salle's murder: as I have already said, the two of them had left with an Indian to guide them. When they came close to the place and Monsieur de La Salle still didn't see anybody, he was worried, but then he saw eagles overhead, which made him think they couldn't be far. This is why he fired the rifle: so that if they were near, they could hear him and make some response. It was his bad luck, because the shot warned the murderers, and they got ready. When they heard the shot, they suspected it had to be their leader coming to meet them, and they got ready to surprise him. Duhaut had already crossed the river with l'Archevesque, and when Duhaut spied Monsieur de La Salle from a distance, coming straight toward them, he hid in the tall grass to wait for his leader, who suspected nothing and hadn't even reloaded his rifle after firing it.

Monsieur de La Salle first spotted l'Archevesque, who appeared a little farther off, and asked him where Monsieur de Morenger, his nephew, was. L'Archevesque answered that he was drifting. At the same time, a rifle shot went off, fired by Duhaut, who was close by hidden in the weeds. The bullet struck the lord in the head. He fell dead on the spot, without uttering a word, to the astonishment of Father Anastase, who was near and who thought he was about to receive the same. He didn't know what to do—keep walking or run away—that is what he told me later. But Duhaut appeared and cried out to him not to be afraid and that nobody had anything against him, that it was despair and desperation that had driven him to do it, that he had been wanting for a long time to wreak vengeance on Monsieur de Morenger who had tried to get him lost and who had been one of the reasons his brother had been lost and died, and many other things.[6] The priest said the look on his face was very troubling.

When the murderers were all together, they cruelly despoiled Monsieur de La Salle and stripped him down to his shirt. The doctor especially made fun of him, all naked as he was, calling him the "Great Pasha."[7] After that, they dragged him into the weeds and briars and left him to the discretion of wolves and other wild animals.

When they had satisfied their rage, they thought about continuing their journey back to us, where they were still planning to get rid of me in case they found me ready to defend myself. Since they wanted to bring the meat, too, they gave the Indians some knives so that they would help them carry it.

To get back to our long march: the twenty-first. We broke camp at about noon. The rain had delayed us for two days on the banks of a large river, where one of the Indians who had traveled with us came with his wife and two horses. We spent the night and the next day there, with sad thoughts running through my head. It was hard not to be always afraid with people like these, whom we couldn't look at without feeling horror. When I thought about the cruelty of what they had done and the danger we were in, I wanted to avenge the evil they had done us. It would have been easy to do while they were sleeping, but Monsieur Cavelier would not let us. He said he had more reason for vengeance than I did, having lost his brother and his nephew. Leave the vengeance to God, he said: vengeance was God's. The young Lord Cavelier, his other nephew, was just as eager as I to do to the murderers as they had done, there being such good opportunity. But Monsieur Cavelier persuaded us not to, and these thoughts passed.

The twenty-third we continued to the northeast, where we found the little path I mentioned, the one that led to the Ceni's village. We camped beside a river which was to give us much trouble getting across. It had overflowed its banks; there was not enough forest nearby for wood to make a raft; we did not have enough hides to make a canoe; and it would have taken too much time. The [Ceni] Indians saved us from our dilemma by offering to carry our clothes provided we gave them some knives. And they did. Earlier I described the cured hides that they use by folding them at the corners with thongs and reinforcing them with a few branches. They fill them with as much as they can hold and push them in front of them as they swim. Thus they transported all our equipage, and the ones of us who could swim swam across.

But several of our group did not know how to swim, and I was one of that number. We were puzzling over this new problem when one of the Indians beckoned to me to come get a seasoned log that he had seen nearby. When we had carried it to the river, he told me to put it into the water. Then he attached thongs to each end of it and made us understand that we should hold onto the log with one arm and try to swim with the other and with our feet. Monsieur Cavelier got into the water first and I followed. Father Anastase got in, too. The Indians swam, holding the log steady with one hand. But Father Anastase almost drowned us. He didn't try to do his part, but simply clung to the log. As I was trying to swim, stretching myself out and kicking with my feet, I caught him in the stomach. He immediately thought he was lost. I can assure you that he cried out invoking the patron of his order, Saint Francis, with all his heart. I couldn't keep from laughing, even though I realized I could drown. But the Indians on the bank saw what was happening, came to our rescue, and helped us across.

There were still others who had to cross: the young Lord Cavelier, the Tallon boy, and Tessier. We made hand signs to the Indians to go help them, but they had been upset during the previous trip across, and they did not want to go back. This grieved us greatly, but we had to be patient. What made matters worse was that there was a cold north wind blowing and the three on the other side had sent their clothes across and had nothing but their shirts on. It was hard for them not to shiver from the cold and for fear of the Indians, who were threatening to leave them there.

Then the Indians, after we begged them and offered more glass beads and other trifles, agreed to go back. This time they didn't want to take the log, remembering the trouble they had had with it. Instead they took one of those hides with which they had transported the clothes, and into it they put the young Lord Cavelier and little Tallon. Together they still were not too bulky, and the Indians kept them steady and pushed them across, just as they had the clothes. As for Tessier, he knew how to swim a little. He took his chances and did make it across. We rejoiced to find ourselves all together again, because we had not acted very wisely in trusting ourselves to the Indians, who, if they had meant to do us harm, could easily have finished us off for the sake of our goods once we were separated from one another.

[As supplies again ran short and violence threatened, Joutel, Father Anastase, Father Cavelier, Colin Cavelier, Lord de Marle, and Pierre Barthélemy sneaked away, along with Tessier, who had begged Father Cavelier's pardon. On June 24, they came upon the French Arkansas Post, from which Quapaw Indians guided them to the Mississippi River and French Illinois. When Spanish forces discovered the colony in Texas two years later, they found that almost all of the French colonists had died. One survivor, now living with local Indians, was Jean l'Archevesque, who told them of La Salle's murder but not his role in it. The boy Pierre Tallon lived for some time with the Cenis and was eventually found by the Spanish and taken back to France, then sent back to Louisiana on a subsequent French colonization attempt.]

Translated by John DuVal from Henri Joutel, "Relation," in *Découvertes et établissements des Français dans l'ouest et dans le sud de l'Amérique septentrionale (1614–1754)*, ed. Pierre Margry (Paris, 1878), 3: 319–32.

Discussion Questions

1. Why did the conspirators mutiny? What did they think would change by killing Morenger and La Salle?

2. Why didn't they kill Joutel and La Salle's remaining relatives (the Caveliers)? Why didn't Joutel and Father Cavelier kill Duhaut and Liotot?

3. What does Joutel mean when he writes, "It is hard to satisfy everybody, or to prevent there being a few malcontents"?

4. What does this account tell us about various Europeans and Indians and the relations between and among them?

Notes

1. Probably the ancestors of the Caddoan Hasinais.

2. The Shawnee was a man called Nika who met La Salle in Canada, traveled with him to France, and accompanied him on this mission.

3. Lord Crevel du Morenger was the son of La Salle's sister. "Monnier" was probably Pierre Meunier, who later testified about the events. The servant was La Salle's man Saget, mentioned earlier.

4. Tallon's little boy was a ten-year-old named Pierre. He, his parents, and five siblings, one of whom was born on board, had sailed from France to Texas with La Salle. The one whom Joutel calls not "worth much" was probably the young boy named Pierre Barthélemy. Father Jean Cavelier was La Salle's older brother, who was in his early fifties. Lord Colin Cavelier was their teenaged nephew, probably the son of their brother Nicolas.

5. On that mission, Duhaut had to stop and repair his pack and shoes, but Morenger had refused to wait for him, and Duhaut barely found his way back to camp.

6. Duhaut's brother had gotten lost during an earlier mission and never reappeared.

7. An Ottoman title.

Antonio de Otermín Describes the Pueblo Revolt, 1680

---

*S*IX DECADES AFTER CORONADO'S EXPEDITION, *Spanish adventurer Juan de Oñate led five hundred colonists and Franciscan friars from Mexico to settle New Mexico. The colonists established* encomiendas, *feudal estates worked by Indians. The Franciscans founded missions in more than fifty pueblos. By the 1670s, trouble was brewing. Prolonged drought had reduced the harvests, Apaches were regularly raiding Indians and Spaniards, and the priests seemed helpless to improve the situation. Some Indians began to revive their old religion publicly. In 1675 the priests reacted by killing several native religious leaders and whipping others, including Popé from Santa Clara Pueblo. Popé and others began to organize what has become known as the Pueblo Revolt of 1680. In the following letter, written as the Spanish were fleeing along the Rio Grande, New Mexico governor Antonio de Otermín recounts the revolt, his attempt to squelch it at Santa Fe, and the beginning of his flight south.*

Most Reverend Father, Lord, and Beloved Friend, Father Francisco Ayeta,

The time has come for me, with tears in my eyes and grief in my heart, to relate a portion of the lamentable tragedy, the like of which has never happened in the world before, but which has happened here in this miserable Colony and holy Dominion—happened with God's permission because of my manifold sins. Before beginning, it is my duty and pleasure to thank you, Reverend Father, for the love you have demonstrated and the favor you have shown me in enquiring so solicitously for news concerning my life and the lives of the other people in this Colony, even after hearing rumors of my certain death and the deaths of all of us, which had been spread abroad; and thank you for sparing no efforts on any account and no expense no matter how great. Only Heaven can sufficiently reward you, Reverend Father, although I have no doubt that His Majesty, may God protect him, will reward you, too.

After I wrote the last letter to you, by way of Colonel Pedro de Leyba, Reverend Father, asking for things the schools needed and for provisions to be brought as quickly as possible in carts and under escort—I grieve for what happened to the peace and tranquility of this miserable Colony, not only for the sake of the Spanish and the native Indians, but also for the heathen enemies!—several days had gone by without their doing any harm, as far as I knew, when news suddenly arrived of a general uprising among the Christian Indians.

It was my misfortune to learn about the uprising only the night before it happened. Although I immediately notified the Lieutenant General of Rio Abajo and the other Alcalde Majores[1] warning them to be on guard for whatever might happen and put all their efforts into guarding and protecting the priests and ministers and churches, the rebels were so cunning and crafty and daring that my measures had little effect; besides, there was some negligence in that no one really believed the uprising was going to happen, as evidenced by the ease with which the rebels seized and killed the escorts for the priests as well as other people in their houses. They made sure my messages did not reach the Lieutenant General, where the greatest forces in the Colony were concentrated and from where I had most reason to hope for help. Of the three messengers I sent, not one reached the Lieutenant General. They killed the first one I sent. The others didn't get any farther than Santo Domingo,[2] because they received confirmed reports of the deaths of the priests of that monastery, the Alcalde Major and other escorts, and six other Spaniards who were seized on the road. Another problem was that the Colony itself, as your Reverend Father knows, is composed of farms widely separated from one another and therefore ideally situated for insurgents to work their evil in.

On the eve of the feast of glorious San Lorenzo,[3] I received word of the uprising from the Indians who governed Pecos and Tanos, who informed me that it had started among the Tewas, specifically in the village of Tesuque, because two Indians had come from there to get them to join the uprising.[4] These governors came to warn me and tell me they had no intention of getting mixed up in such evil and treason and that they looked upon the Spanish as brothers. I thanked them for their kindness, told them to go back to their villages and not say anything, and sent the orders out that I have already mentioned, Reverend Father.

The next morning as I was on my way to mass, Lay Brother Pedro Idalgo, who had gone to the village of Tesuque with Father Juan Pío, who was supposed to celebrate mass there, brought news that the Tesuque Indians had killed Father Pío, that by a miracle he himself had escaped, and that the Indians, with all their horses and cattle and the monastery herds, too, had retreated into the Sierra.

We were all of course stunned by the news. I immediately sent out Colonel Francisco Gómez with a squadron of soldiers, as much to find out what was happening as to put out the flames of destruction which had already begun. He came back the same day and told me that Father Juan Pío was indeed dead, and that they had also killed Friar Thomas de Torres, Guardian of Nambe, and his brother and his brother's wife and a child and another resident, from Taos,[5] as well as Friar Luis de Morales, Guardian of San Ildefonso, and Francisco de Anaya's family; in Pojoaque, Don Joseph de Goita and Francisco Ximenes, his wife, and his family, and Doña Petronila de Salas with ten sons and daughters. They had also robbed and desecrated the monasteries, and the farms that belong to the victims and they had taken all the horses and cattle in the Colony.

[Otermín receives reports of deaths in many villages, particularly of priests, and orders the settlers living nearby to gather at Santa Fe in order to defend themselves together.]

On Tuesday the thirteenth of the month, at nine in the morning, there appeared before us in the Analco Barrio, in the cemetery of the San Miguel Hermitage, and across the river, all the Indians of the Tanos nation, the Pecos nation, and the Queres de San Marcos nation in arms and shouting war cries.

Because I recognized an Indian from the town leading them, one who had a little earlier gone to join up with them, I sent some soldiers out to call him and tell him for me that he could come in perfect safety and let me know what their purposes were in coming here. With this safeguard he came.

Since, as I say, I already knew him, I asked him how he could have gone so crazy—him, a clever Indian with so much common sense who had grown up and spent his life in this town among Spanish people, and after I had put so much trust in him—what was he doing, leading this Indian uprising.

He answered that they had elected him as their Captain and that he brought two flags with him, one white and the other red. If we chose the white, we must leave the land, and if the red, we would have to perish, because the Indians who had risen up against us were many, and we were few. There was no help for it now, seeing that they had already killed many priests and many Spaniards.

To this response, I urged that he was a Christian and a Catholic and so were most of his followers and how could they expect to live without priests, and that even after they had committed so many atrocities, there was still help and if they returned to obedience to His Majesty, they would still be pardoned; so he should go back to his people and tell them for me everything that I had said to him and urge them to pull back, and then he should let me know what they said.

After a while he did come back and told me that his people said we must hand over all of the Indians that were in our power, including those who served the Spanish and the Mexicans of the Analco Barrio,[6] and that we must hand over his wife and children to him, as well as all the Apache men and women that the Spanish held as prisoners of war, because some of the Apaches among them were asking for them. If we did not comply, they would declare war then and there. They would not go away, because they were waiting for the Taos, Picurís,[7] and Tewas nations, with whom they would finish us off.

I saw his determination and understood what he was asking of us, and particularly that what he was saying about the Apaches was a lie, because they are at war with all of them and these negotiations were only to get his wife and children out and gain time until the other insurgent nations arrived, when they would join forces and attack us. Meanwhile, they were robbing and pillaging the Hermitage and the houses of the Mexicans. So I told him, again appealing to him as a Christian and a Catholic, to go back to his people and tell them if they did not stop pillaging and go away, I would send out those who would chase them away. He went back to them, and they received him with a clamor of bells and a blowing of horns and loud cries of war.

After a while, when I saw that they had not only not stopped their pillaging but were coming against the town with shameless insolence, I ordered all our soldiers to sally forth and attack them and rout them. And so they rode forth and fought, killing some at the first clash. Realizing their disadvantage, the insurgents took refuge and fortified themselves in the Hermitage and the Mexicans' houses, from where they fired the guns that they had and shot their arrows, defending and attacking through the day.

We had set fire to some of the houses and had our enemies all hemmed in and about to perish when from the road to Tesuque a division of the people they had been waiting for appeared—all of the Tewas. Since the Governor's Palace was poorly defended, we had to use our strength to block their path to the town, so the Taos and Pecos got away to the mountains, where the new combatants joined them, and they slept that night in the Sierra above the town, though they left many dead and wounded behind. Of our own people, one was dead and Colonel Francisco Gómez and fourteen or fifteen soldiers were wounded. We withdrew to the Governor's Palace to tend to the wounded, dig in, and fortify ourselves as best we could.

The next morning, Wednesday, I saw the enemy coming down out of the Sierra where they had slept, all of them together, coming toward the town. I mounted my horse and led out the few troops I had to meet them uphill from the monastery.

As soon as they saw me and realized they had to withstand our charge, they stopped and took up better positions in the thick brush overlooking ravines. They let out war cries and taunted me, daring me to attack them. I halted for a moment, ready for battle, and the enemy cut back through the rugged hills to take the hill overlooking the back of Colonel Francisco Gómez's house. There they settled in, and the day passed without more encounters, because we had to guard against their sweeping down and burning the church and the houses in the town.

[The following day, Thursday, there are some skirmishes, but the insurgents avoid open battle because, Otermín explains, they are waiting for more reinforcements.]

The next day, Friday, having been reinforced the night before by the Taos, Picurís, Jémez,[8] and Queres nations, more than two thousand Indians threw themselves upon us, seizing the houses of the town, digging in at every street corner, cutting off the water that ran through the creek bed and the irrigation ditch from in front of the Governor's Palace, and burning the holy church and many houses in the town.

We fought many skirmishes over the water supply. With almost all of the soldiers wounded, I tried to hole up in the Palace and put up a defense by staying inside it. They were so insolent and bold they managed to set fire to the doors of the tower of Our Lady of the Governor's Palace. With this new act of audacity, realizing the great danger we were in, I resolved to ride out of the Palace with as strong a force of soldiers as I could muster to keep the enemy from feeding the fire.

And so we fought all afternoon. From the roofs of the houses and from trenches and from all around us, armed with plenty of harquebuses,[9] powder and ball, the enemy did us great damage.

Night fell upon us, and thanks be to God the arrows and the harquebus fire eased off. We spent that night like other nights, careworn and weary from thirst because of the lack of water.[10]

They began at dawn the next day, Friday, pressing us more relentlessly with arrows and stones, yelling that there was no escape from their hands because in addition to all of them, the Apaches, who were now their allies, would soon arrive. They wore us out that day. . . .

The insurgent Indians began singing songs of victory and screaming war cries and burning all the houses of the town, and so we spent the night in torment. I can assure you, Reverend Father, it was more horrible than you can imagine. The whole town was alight, screams and war songs everywhere, and what grieved us most, horrifying flames rising from the church, and the noise of those wretched insurgents, scoffing at and desecrating the holy things in the church, intoning and parodying the Introit[11] and other sacred prayers.

Seeing how things were—the church burned and the town burned; few horses; livestock and yard animals with nothing to eat or drink for days, many of them dead and all dying; so many people, almost all children and women, a thousand of us in all, dying of thirst with nothing to drink for two days other than from some jars and urns stored in the Palace; the screaming of women and children all around; conflict everywhere—I resolved to sally forth in the morning, charge the enemy, and conquer or die fighting.

Realizing that our best defense was prayers to appease the divine wrath, even though the poor women had already prayed fervently, that night I urged them to pray with even more fervor and told the rector and the two other priests to say mass for us at dawn, exhort all the people to repent their sins and conform their lives to the will of God, and absolve us of guilt and punishment.

With these preparations, those of us who could ride mounted our horses. The foot soldiers took their harquebuses, and some Indians in our service took their bows and arrows. We drew up with as best order as we could, facing Colonel Francisco Xabier's house, where most of the enemy thronged and shouted insults.

As soon as we issued out onto the street, we saw a large crowd of Indians. We charged them, and although at first they resisted bravely, at last they fled, and as many as we could reach, we killed. Then we turned on those who were in the streets leading to the monastery, and they too fled with little resistance. The houses that look out in the direction of Colonel Francisco Xavier's house were still heavily manned by Indians, so we headed toward them. When the Indians who had resisted the first and second charge saw that, they retreated to the hills with their wounded and dead, giving us a little room, and we set siege to the ones who were holed up in the houses. They tried to defend themselves, but how could they? Seeing the fires were already lit and that they were about to burn to death, those who were still alive surrendered, which made us glad, because the deaths here and on the streets in this battle and the other battles amounted to more than three hundred Indians.

Feeling some respite thanks to this miraculous success, even though I had lost much blood having survived two arrows in my face and, miraculously, a harquebus ball in my chest the day before, I set about getting the cattle to drink, and the horses, and the people.

By now our provisions were very low for so many people. We had no hope of reinforcements. For days we had not heard from the people at Rio Abajo, maybe because they had all been killed, as well as everyone else in the Colony, or at least because they themselves were under siege. Therefore, intending to go to their aid and combine with them for the best service we could do for His Majesty, the next morning, Thursday, I marched out on the road for Isleta, where I counted on finding the Rio Abajo companies,[12] trusting in Providence

and without a crust of biscuit, grain of wheat or corn, with no other equipment for transporting so many people than four hundred pack animals and
two carts that belonged to some residents, and for food, nothing but some
yard animals and a few cows.

With this excellent equipment, thanks to some ears of corn we found in the
fields, we reached the town of Alameda, where an old Indian (whom we found
in a cornfield) informed us that fourteen or fifteen days earlier the Lieutenant
General and all his people had set out for El Paso to meet the train of carts.[13]
This news disturbed me greatly because there was no way I could persuade
myself that he could have gone without hearing about me and what was happening to everyone in the whole Colony, and I can't help suspecting the destruction of this Colony will be the result of his absence.

I then dispatched four soldiers in pursuit of the Lieutenant General and his
forces with orders to halt wherever they caught up with them. The soldiers did
catch up with them in Fray Cristobal's parish; and the Lieutenant General
(Alonso García) met me at Las Nutrias.[14] A few days later I joined up with
Colonel Pedro de Leyba and all the people under his command, escorting the
carts and coming to find out for certain, as you, Reverend Father, had instructed them, whether we were dead.

Now I must see to the rescue, for what it's worth. What a lack of provisions!
All these people, and we need so much. I have a little corn to last for ten days.
With it, after God, who is our sole help and repair, we count on you, Reverend
Father—and on His good care by which and through which may you come to
us, Reverend Father. Because your presence is so important to the service of
God and King, I am dispatching Colonel Pedro de Leyba and his men to es-
cort you, Reverend Father, and the carts or pack animals that we are hoping
will bring the provisions we need. . . .

Little by little I am catching up with the other division,[15] which is still eighteen leagues off, intending to join with them and see if we can rescue this miserable Colony, for which purpose I will neglect no effort in service of God and
His Majesty, losing my life a thousand times if I had that many to lose, as I
have already lost my lands and some of my health, and spilt my blood. God
protect me and allow me to see you, Reverend Father, here, bringing rescue.

8 September 1680.
I kiss the hand of your Reverence.
Your servant, countryman, and friend,
Don Antonio de Otermín

Translated by John DuVal from Antonio de Otermín to Francisco de Ayeta, September 8, 1680, "Testimonio de Autos tocantes al alzamiento general de los Indios de
la Provincia de la Nueva Mexico," packet 2, folder 420, carton 29, part 1, MSS C-B 840,

Bancroft Library, Berkeley, California; original in Section V, Group A, Series 4, Audiencia de Guadalajara 138 (67-3-32), Archivo General de Indias, Seville, Spain.

Discussion Questions

1. Why did Governor Otermín blame his own "manifold sins" for the revolt?
2. Can you infer any motives of the Indians? What tactics did they use?
3. Do you think Otermín's superiors blamed him for abandoning New Mexico?
4. Why do you think that returning to "rescue this miserable Colony" was important to him?

Notes

1. The lieutenant general of Rio Abajo was Alonso García, second in command to Otermín and in charge of the settlements along the lower (southern) Rio Grande. The *alcalde majores* were the governors of particular settlements, subordinate to Otermín and García.

2. A Keresan pueblo, the closest on the Rio Grande to Santa Fe, but still far from García.

3. The Feast Day of San Lorenzo, or Saint Lawrence, is August 10.

4. The Indian leader from Pecos and others who warned Otermín came from Tano-speaking pueblos south of Santa Fe, which included Queres de San Marco, mentioned later in the letter. By August 13, they too had joined the rebellion. Tesuque is the Tewa-speaking pueblo just north of Santa Fe. The other Tewa-speaking pueblos around Tesuque include Nambe, Pojoaque, San Ildefonso, and Santa Clara.

5. A Tiwa pueblo, the northernmost of the New Mexico pueblos.

6. The neighborhood of the Tlaxcalan Indians, whose ancestors helped Hernán Cortés defeat the Aztecs. They are the "Mexicans" to whom Otermín refers, and they were on the Spanish side during the revolt. As you can see here, Indians from the pueblos worked as servants of the Tlaxcalans as well as of the Spaniards and probably resented them equally.

7. A Tiwa-speaking pueblo north of Santa Fe, near Taos.

8. A Towa-speaking pueblo west of Santa Fe.

9. A harquebus was an early matchlock gun invented in the fifteenth century.

10. The Indians were preventing the Spanish from getting to their water source.

11. The responsive chant sung as the priest enters the church to begin the mass.

12. Here, Otermín has decided to lead his people southwest from Santa Fe to the Rio Grande, then south along the Rio Grande to the pueblo of Isleta, where Lieutenant General García was stationed.

13. Alameda is a Tiwa-speaking pueblo just north of present-day Albuquerque. The news meant that García had headed for the Mexican border, at what is today El Paso,

Texas. The "train of carts" was the convoy of supplies from Mexico City being brought by Franciscan Father Francisco de Ayeta, to whom this letter is addressed.

14. Otermín has passed La Isleta and is somewhere south of Socorro. In his anger, he arrested García and charged him with desertion, but after García explained that none of the governor's messages had arrived and that his own messengers to the governor could not get through, Otermín dropped the charges.

15. The main part of García's forces.

Antoine Simon Le Page Du Pratz Describes French Conflict with the Natchez, 1729

<hr>

*I*N THE LATE *1600S, THE* N*ATCHEZ* I*NDIANS* A*GREED to allow French plantations on their extensive lands, believing that the French would serve as their tributaries. But as the plantations prospered, the French demanded more and better land. By the late 1720s, there were around four hundred French settlers and three hundred black slaves on Natchez lands, and tension was building. Du Pratz, the author of this account, grew up in France. In 1718, he arrived in Louisiana, determined to make his fortune with a tobacco plantation on Natchez land. In 1728, however, Du Pratz left to manage a larger plantation near New Orleans, so he was gone when the Natchez Indians attacked.*

At the beginning of December, 1729, people at the Capital learned to their great dismay of the massacre at the Natchez Post.[1] My Canoe Master, a very intelligent Black man who was very much attached to me, told me, with great sorrow, "Hurry to town, hurry! You'll learn some big news there. They say those Indian sons of bitches have killed the French people at Natchez."

I went right away, and the first person I saw when I got there was Monsieur de la Frênière (who was later a Council member). He embraced me and said, "You are so lucky, my dear friend. You foresaw exactly what has just happened in the Natchez territory. All the French people there—their throats are all cut. It's that idiot Commander's fault! You said you would love for him to prove you wrong and not bring disaster down on the Post." Then I went to the Government Building, where they told me all the rest, and I will report the whole event from the beginning. . . .

As soon as [Commander de Chépart] took possession of the Post, he made plans to build himself one of the most spectacular homes in the colony. With this in mind, he examined all the lands not yet occupied by French people but could not find one that was grand enough for his vision. Nothing but the White Apple village, which was at least a league square, could satisfy him. He made up his mind to settle there.

This land was almost two leagues from the Post, but a country house of any consequence should not be too close to a town, lest it lose its distinctive quality. Enraptured by the splendor of his own design, the Commander summoned the Sun Chief of the White Apple village to the Fort.[2] When the Sun Chief arrived, the Commander didn't waste time with compliments. He said he wanted to build right away in White Apple village, and all the Sun Chief had to do was find another place for his village, vacate the houses, and move there. . . .

The Commander must have thought he was talking to a slave that could be ordered around in a high and mighty tone. He did not realize that the natives of Louisiana hate slavery so fiercely they prefer death to it. The Sun Chiefs especially, accustomed to rule despotically, despise it even more.

The Sun Chief of the White Apple village thought that by speaking reasonably he could make the Commander see reason, and he would have been right if he had been dealing with a reasonable man. He replied that his ancestors had lived in the White Apple village for as many years as he had hairs on his white head and that it was therefore right for them to stay there still.

The interpreter had no sooner translated this answer than the Commander burst into anger and threatened the Sun Chief that by the end of a few days if he hadn't abandoned his village he would regret it.

The Sun Chief answered that when the French first came asking for land, his people had told them there were plenty of unoccupied lands for the French to settle on, the same sun would shine on all of them, and they would walk the same path. . . .[3]

He would have said a good deal more in support of his argument, but the Commander shouted that what he wanted was obedience, not replies.

Without anger the Sun Chief left, saying he would assemble the village Elders to hold Council about this business.

He did assemble them, and they concluded in Council that the Commander should be informed that the corn was already up on everybody's little plot in the village and that all the hens were setting and if they left their village now the grain and chicks would be wasted, because there weren't enough French people to weed all the corn in even their own fields.

As soon as they reached that decision, one of them went to inform the Commander, who rejected their proposal and threatened to punish them if they did not obey before a very short deadline, which he would determine.

The Sun Chief reported this response to his Council, who debated over it. It was a thorny question, but the Elders voted to propose to the Commander that he let them stay in the village until harvest and give them time to dry the corn and grind it, in return for which, within so many moons, which they would determine, each household would give him a basketful of corn, weighing one hundred fifty pounds, and a chicken—because this Commander struck them as greedy enough to accept the proposal, which would gain time for them; and they decided that during that time they would be taking measures to get themselves out from under the thumb of the French. . . .

The Commander's greed made him accept the proposal gladly, and he closed his eyes to the consequences his tyranny was leading to. Nevertheless, he pretended that he was only giving in out of kindness and because he wanted to satisfy a nation whom he cherished and who had always been a friend to the French.

The Sun Chief seemed content to have gotten a delay long enough to take precautions for the survival of the nation, but the Commander's claim to kindness did not fool him. When he got back, he assembled the Council and informed the Elders that the French Commander had agreed to their offer and had granted the delay they requested. Then he urged them to take good advantage of the time to shake free of their promise and of the tyranny of the French, who were becoming more dangerous in proportion to the speed with which they were multiplying. He reminded them how the French had waged war on them before, despite the peace treaty.[4] He told them that for this new war, declared against their one village, they must seek an appropriate and bloody vengeance, and that it would be an enterprise of the utmost importance which would require strict secrecy, careful planning, and adroit diplomacy. They must therefore display more friendship than ever toward the French chief. He also said they must think the business over for a few more days before deciding on this action and proposing it to the Great Sun Chief and his Council. . . .

After five or six days, he again called the Elders together. During the interval they had consulted with one another and were ready to give one voice to the same conclusion: that their only purpose, in order to achieve their goals, must be the annihilation of all the French in the province. When the Sun Chief saw that they were all assembled, he said, "You have had time to reflect on my proposal. I therefore believe that you are about to declare the best means of delivering ourselves, without risk, from our bad neighbors."

When the Sun Chief ceased speaking, the oldest of the Elders rose, greeted him in his fashion, and said, "For a long time we have perceived that having the French for neighbors does more harm than good. We see it, we old people, but the young don't. They like French merchandise. But what use is all that stuff? What use but to debauch our young women, make them vain and lazy, and corrupt the blood of the nation? It's the same with the young men, while the married men have to kill themselves working to feed their families and satisfy their children. Before the French came to this country we were men who were happy with what we had. It was enough. We walked bravely on all the paths because we were our own masters. But today we go groping along, afraid we'll step on a thorn. We walk like slaves, and it won't be long before we are slaves to the French. That's how they treat us already, as if we were their slaves. When they are strong enough, they won't bother with diplomacy anymore. For any little thing our young people do, the French will tie them to a stake and whip them the way they whip their black slaves. They already did it to one of our boys. Isn't death better than slavery?"

He paused briefly to catch his breath and continued, "What are we waiting for? Until we're in no position to oppose them? What will the other nations say? People see us as the cleverest of the Red Men. The other nations will say we're the stupidest. Why wait any longer? Let us take back our freedom and let it be known that we are men, men who make do with what we have. Let us begin from this day to get ready. Have our women prepare rations. But don't tell them why. Let us carry the calumet of peace[5] to all the nations of this country. Let us make known to them that since the French are strongest here where we live, we feel more than anyone how they mean to enslave us, and when they're strong enough, to enslave every nation in this land. Let them know it is in their interest to prevent this calamity; and to prevent it, all they have to do is join with us and destroy all the French at the same time on the same day. This will be the day of the deadline, the deadline that we persuaded the French Commander to put off when we agreed to bring the tribute; the time will be the quarter of the day (nine o'clock) when several warriors will take the corn as if beginning to pay the tribute; they will be carrying weapons, saying they are going hunting. Let them know that in every house there will be two or three Natchez for every Frenchman, and that they must ask for guns and powder for a great hunt for a huge festival and say they will bring back meat. Let them know that gunshots at the French Commander's house will be the signal for them to all fall upon the French at once and kill them, thus preventing any more people who intend to come up the Great Water from the Old French Village[6] from ever being able to settle here."

The Elder added that after persuading the other nations to take this violent course, they should leave a bundle of sticks with each nation, each bundle containing the same number of sticks as their own. These sticks would mark the number of days left until they were supposed to strike all at once. So as not to get the date wrong, they had to be sure every day to pull one of the sticks out of the bundle, break it, and throw it far away. A wise man should be put in charge of this responsibility. He stopped speaking and sat down.

All the Elders approved his advice and agreed with his feelings. The White Apple Sun Chief approved, too. But they still needed to get the Great Sun and the lesser Suns to join with them, because once all these princes agreed, the rest of the Nation would obey blindly. They took one more precaution. They decreed that the women, even the Sun Women, must not be told and must not have the least suspicion of what they were intending against the French.

The White Apple Sun Chief was very intelligent and was therefore easily able to persuade the Great Sun. The reigning Great Sun was young and inexperienced and all the more susceptible to persuasion because all the other Suns agreed that the White Apple Sun Chief was reasonable and wise.

[The White Apple Sun meets with the Great Sun and persuades him.]

The next morning, when the Suns came to greet him, the Great Sun told them all to go to the White Apple Sun's home without saying a word to anyone. They did go, and the White Apple Sun Chief's seductive intelligence drew the other Suns into his plans. They formed a Council of Suns and Noble Elders who all approved the plan. The Noble Elders were appointed delegates to visit the other nations, and warriors were appointed to accompany them. It was forbidden upon pain of death to speak to anyone about this. Once this resolution was passed, they went their separate ways, unknown to the French.

Although they kept their secret very close, the Council of Suns and Noble Elders made the people uneasy. It is by no means unheard of for subjects in any country of the world to try to penetrate the secrets of the court, but these subjects could not satisfy their curiosity. Only the Sun Princesses had the right to ask why secrets were being kept from them.

The Great Sun Princess was just eighteen years old. Only Tattooed Arm, who was very clever (and she knew it), took offence because nobody was telling them anything.[7] When she complained to her son, he explained that the delegations were being sent around to reaffirm the good relations with other nations, with whom they had not shared the calumet for a long time and who were beginning to suspect that their neglect was a sign of contempt. This bogus excuse seemed to appease the Sun Princess Tattooed Arm, but instead of relieving her anxieties, it redoubled them, especially when she saw the calumets (*Delegations*) return and all the Sun Chiefs, eager to learn how they had been received, gather with the Delegates in closed session instead of out in the open as was customary.

This Sun Princess was angry. "What?" she said to herself. "Are they hiding something from the Nation that the Nation ought to know? Hiding it from me?" She would have made a fuss if her prudence had not tempered her anger. It was lucky for the French that she thought she was being slighted, because I do believe that the Colony owes its survival more to the resentment of this woman than to any love she still had for the French.[8]

She was right to be afraid of making them close in even tighter around their secret if she made a fuss, and she adopted a much wiser tactic. She got her Sun Chief son to go with her, without telling anyone, to visit a sick relative in the Farine Village. She took him by the longer route on pretext that it was a lovelier walk but really because it was less frequented.

Being very perceptive, she had concluded that the only possible reason for all the secrecy had to be some sinister scheme against the French, and all the comings and goings of the White Apple Sun Chief supported this conclusion. She chose a solitary spot along the route and, trusting in the respect her son had always borne her, she said to him, "Let's sit down here. . . ."

[Tattooed Arm fails to persuade her son that he should save the French because he had a French father. However, she convinces him that she already knows about the plot, and he unwittingly confirms her suspicions and reveals crucial details, including the method of counting down by sticks.]

After telling her everything that I have set down here, he added that all of the nations had heard and approved the plan and promised to act in concert with the Natchez and that every village neighbor to the French would act on the same day at the same time.[9] The Choctaws were responsible for destroying all the French at the mouth of the Big River (Saint Louis River)[10] and upriver as far as the Tunica Nation. The Tunicas and Oumas had not been invited to join because they were too friendly with the French and it was better to destroy those nations along with the French living among them. Finally, he told her the sticks were inside the Temple on top of the Flat Wood.

When Tattooed Arm understood the whole plan, she pretended to approve of it. Her son was reassured, but from that moment on, all she thought about was how to make the whole barbaric plot fail. There wasn't much time. The deadline was almost upon them. Unable to bear the thought of all the French dying in one day because of the Indian conspiracy, she sought some means of saving most of them. She decided to warn a few young women who loved Frenchmen, and she did warn them, but she advised them never to tell that the warning came from her.

Hoping to open the Commander's eyes, Tattooed Arm stopped a soldier that she met on the path and told him to go at once and tell the Commander that the Natchez had lost their minds and he must be careful: all he had to do was make a few repairs to the fort in the presence of some of the Natchez to show them he suspected something, and all the resolutions and evil machinations would crumble.

The soldier did just as he was told, but the Commander, far from putting any stock in this advice, or making the least use of it, or checking to see if it had any basis, told the soldier he was a coward and a dreamer and had him put in chains. He said he would be careful not to make repairs on the fort or take any precautions, because if he did, any Natchez who observed him would think he lacked courage and was afraid of them. He probably thought that strutting and putting on a brave show would make his enemies more afraid of him than strengthening the fort.

When she heard about all the Commander's vain strutting, Tattooed Arm went to the Temple and pulled some sticks out of the fatal bundle of sticks to advance the deadline in the hopes that some French would survive the massacre and warn other French people.

[Tattooed Arm sends other messengers, but the commander ignores them all.]

Despite all the advice, the Commander took it into his head to go have fun with some other Frenchmen in the Great Natchez Village. They took enough whisky for the whole night and caroused until dawn, then went back to the Fort. He had no sooner returned than he received urgent warning to be on guard. This time he was not only contemptuous, but reckless, too. He ordered the Interpreter to go at once to the Great Village and demand of the Great Sun whether he really intended to come at the head of a war party to murder all the French. And he told the Interpreter to bring back an answer right away.

Day was breaking, and it took the Interpreter almost no time to perform his mission, but the readers can imagine, without having to read it, what the Great Sun's answer was. He was young, but he did know how to dissemble and speak to the Interpreter in a way that would satisfy the Commander and make him congratulate himself on spurning the advice he had been receiving. The Commander went back to his home at the foot of the Fort to rest from the fatigue of the night before.

The Natchez had laid their plans too well not to be successful. They set out on the Eve of St. Andrew [November 29], 1729, bringing a Stinkard armed with a club for clubbing the Commander to death, because they despised him so much no warrior wanted to be the one to kill him.[11] The French houses all filled with enemies of the French. Even the Fort was manned by Indians who had come in by the gate and through the breaches in the walls and deprived the soldiers, who had no officers or sergeants to direct them, or room to defend themselves. At this point the Great Sun arrived with some warriors bearing corn, which was supposed to look like the first load of the tribute.

The Commander, in his elation, immediately had all the advisers unchained so they could witness how wrong they had been. But as they came forth to watch the Indian tribute being delivered, several guns went off at once. Some were fired at the barge; others in the Commander's house: at the Interpreter, a servant, and some other Frenchmen.

Those shots are the signal. Then many shots. The Commander understands, too late, the wisdom of the advice he received. He runs into his yard.

He calls his guardsmen. Vain hope: they are no longer there. The Indians run at him with their guns charged, and they kill him. . . .

The massacre happened everywhere at the same time. The Frenchwomen who were taken were put into a house on a hill and guarded by warriors. From there they could look down on some of the tragic scene. They saw some women trying to save their husbands, others trying to avenge them. But these heroines were sacrificed to the vengeance of their enemies, who, according to their custom, spared only the young.

I draw the curtain on the rest of the scene. What has been shown is already too frightening. I will only say that of about seven hundred people, very few escaped to bear the horrible news to the Capital.

The Governor and the Council were shocked. Everywhere people were saying we had to get ready, we had to be on guard; but the bomb had already gone off, and there was nothing more to fear. The other Indian nations felt insulted by the way the Natchez had proceeded, thinking that they had advanced the agreed deadline to make them look foolish. They meant to get vengeance at the first opportunity, which was not long in coming.

While these other Indians were far from understanding why the Natchez acted too soon, we ourselves could not even guess how the plot began, or its details, or the immediate results of the horrible event. All that those who escaped the slaughter could tell us was that some women had foretold it, but that the Commander, whose greed had brought it on, had spurned all information about the plot developing against him and could have prevented it if he had prepared himself after such good warnings. None of those who were lucky enough to escape being murdered could tell any more about the day of the massacre than what I have just reported. With disasters like this one, each person is too busy saving himself. I learned these details, and a few others of which I make no mention, from those who escaped and from a woman who, after being enslaved, was my housekeeper. She was one of the first women captured, and she witnessed what was happening. As for the plans that the Natchez laid before the day of the massacre, I learned them from the Sun Princess Tattooed Arm when she was a prisoner in New Orleans.[12]

[In the following months, the Natchez's enemies went to war and expelled the Natchez from their homeland. By 1732, the surviving Natchez were French slaves in the West Indies or refugees among the Chickasaws, Creeks, and Cherokees. The war also had a profound effect on slavery in Louisiana. French administrators decided that large-scale plantation agriculture on Indian land was too dangerous, and they cut off nearly all African slave importation.]

Translated by John DuVal from Antoine Simon Le Page Du Pratz, *Histoire de la Louisiane* (Paris, 1758), 3: 230–60.

Discussion Questions

1. What was the disagreement between the Natchez and the French? How did the presence of black slaves affect Natchez-French relations?

2. The Natchez were a powerful nation, and their leaders were not accustomed to being told what to do by anyone. Why, then, did Commander de Chépart try to order them around? Do you think Du Pratz was right in placing most of the blame on him?

3. What do you think of the practice of including speeches in direct quotations in a work of history when the historian did not hear the speeches and has no recording of them?

4. Compare Du Pratz's account with Serra's account of the raid on San Diego and Otermín's account of the Pueblo Revolt. Does it make a difference that Du Pratz was a plantation owner, Serra was a priest, and Otermín was a military officer?

Notes

1. The "capital" was New Orleans. Natchez Post was on the Mississippi River, near present-day Natchez.

2. The village chiefs were called *Suns* (*Soleils* in French), and the chief of the entire Natchez nation was called the *Great Sun* (*Grand Soleil*). When the French translated these titles into their own language, they would have sounded familiar to French readers, for whom the most glorious king of recent memory was Louis XIV, who reigned from 1643 to 1715 and was known as the Sun King (*Roi-Soleil*).

3. The ellipses here are Du Pratz's, indicating that the commander (unwisely) interrupted the chief's speech.

4. In 1723, the White Apple village had negotiated peace with the French, yet Louisiana Lt. Gov. Jean-Baptiste Le Moyne, Sieur de Bienville, attacked the village the next year.

5. The calumet was a peace pipe, technically the feathered stem that attached to a pipe bowl, a symbol of peace and alliance between peoples.

6. That is, up the Mississippi River from New Orleans.

7. The Sun Princesses were female relatives of the Suns. The Great Sun Princess was the Great Sun's Wife or sister, and Tattooed Arm (Bras-Piqué) was the mother of a Sun Chief.

8. Du Pratz's note: "She was already very old, and her [French] lover had been dead for several years."

9. The Natchez had proposed the plan to the Yazoos, Koroas, Illinois, Chickasaws, and Choctaws. Only the Yazoos and Koroas killed their missionaries.

10. The mouth of the Mississippi, meaning New Orleans and its surrounding plantations.

11. The Natchez were highly stratified by class. The Suns were of the highest class, while the Stinkards were, obviously, the lowest. Du Pratz's note: "Others say he was shot to death with guns by warriors who ate his heart to appease their rage. In fact, who can affirm these things, since no French person present at that particular event escaped?"

12. She was captured and taken to New Orleans to tell what she knew.

George Washington Recalls His Defeats at Fort Duquesne, 1754–1755

*B*Y THE 1740S, THE FRENCH WERE WORRIED THAT BRITISH SETTLERS *would soon overwhelm the French colonies, which covered a vast region but had relatively few settlers. For protection, the French built a string of forts from Lake Erie to the Ohio River. In the meantime, Virginia land speculators, including Lawrence and Augustin Washington and Governor Robert Dinwiddie, formed the Ohio Land Company, to which the British king granted a vast tract in the contested Ohio Valley. To advance the company's claim, Dinwiddie ordered twenty-one-year-old George Washington, the half-brother of Lawrence and Augustin, to march Virginia provincial troops to the Ohio Valley. Three decades later, Washington wrote the following notes for a biographer.*

By the indefatigable industry of the Lt. Colonel [George Washington] and the Officers who seconded his measures the Regiment was in great forwardness at Alexandria (the place of general rendezvous) early in the spring of 1754. And without waiting till the whole should be completed, or for a detachment from the Independent Companies of regulars in the Southern Provinces (which had been requested by the Executive of Virginia for this service) or for troops which were raising in North Carolina[1] and destined in conjunction to oppose the encroachment of the French on our Western frontiers, he [Washington] began his march in the month of May in order to open the roads (and this he had to do almost the whole distance from Winchester in the County of Frederick, not more than 80 miles from Alexandria to the Ohio)[2] . . . and for the especial purpose of seizing, if possible, before the French should arrive at it, the important post at the conflux of the Allegany and Monongahela[3]; with the advantages of which he was forcibly struck the preceding year; and earnestly advised the securing of, with militia, or some other temporary force. But notwithstanding all his exertions, the new, and uncommon difficulties he had to encounter (made more intolerable by incessant rains and swelled waters of which he had many to cross) he had but just ascended the Laurel Hill 50 miles short of his object: after a march of 230 miles from Alexandria when he received information from his scouts that the French had, in force, seized the post he was pushing to obtain; having descended from Presque Isle by the Rivers Lebeauf and Allegany to this place by water with artillery etc. etc.[4] The object of his precipitate advance being thus defeated, the detachment of Regulars, which had arrived at Alexandria (by water) and under his orders being far in his rear, and no account of the troops from North Carolina, it was thought advisable to fall back a few miles, to a place known by the name of the Great Meadows, abounding in forage more convenient for the purpose of forming a magazine and bringing up the rear, and to advance from (if we should ever be in force to do it) to the attack of the post which the enemy now occupied, and had called Du Quesne. At this place, some days after we were joined by the above detachment of Regulars, consisting (before they were reduced on the march by desertion, sickness, etc.) of a Captain (McKay[5] a brave and worthy Officer), three Subalterns, and 100 Rank and file.

But previous to this junction the French sent a detachment to reconnoitre our camp and obtain intelligence of our strength and position; notice of which being given by the scouts, GW marched at the head of a party, attacked, killed 9 or 10; and captured 20 odd.[6] This, as soon as the enemy had assembled their Indian allies,[7] brought their whole force upon him; consisting according to their own compared with the best accounts that could be obtained from others of about 1500 men. His force consisted of the detachment above mentioned, and between two and 300 Virginians[8]; for the few Indians[9] which till now had attended him; and who by reconnoitering the enemy in their march had got terrified at their numbers and resolved to retreat as they advised us to do also but which was impracticable without abandoning our stores, baggage, etc. as the horses which had brought them to this place and returned for provision had left us previous to the attack.

About 9 o'clock on the 3rd of July the enemy advanced with shouts, and dismal Indian yells to our entrenchments,[10] but was opposed by so warm, spirited, and constant a fire, that to force the works in that way was abandoned by them; they then, from every little rising, tree, stump, stone, and bush kept up a constant galding fire upon us; which was returned in the best manner we could till late in the afternoon when there fell the most tremendous rain that can be conceived, filled our trenches with water, wet, not only the ammunition in the cartouche boxes and firelocks, but that which was in a small temporary stockade in the middle of the entrenchment called Fort Necessity erected for the sole purpose of its security, and that of the few stores we had; and left us nothing but a few (for all were not provided with them) bayonets for defense. In this situation and no prospect of bettering it, terms of capitulation were offered to us by the enemy which with some alterations that were insisted upon were the more readily acceded to, as we had no salt provisions, and but indifferently supplied with fresh [provisions]; which, from the heat of the weather, would not keep; and because a full third of our numbers Officers as well as privates were, by this time, killed or wounded.[11]

[Washington returns to Alexandria to report his defeat to Dinwiddie. To their surprise, the British crown supports war and sends two Irish regiments of the Regular Army, under Gen. Edward Braddock. They arrive in Virginia to raise more provincial troops and try again to dislodge the French from the Ohio Valley. In the meantime, the French reinforce Ft. Duquesne. Washington's narrative resumes as he awaits orders in Alexandria in early 1755.]

[News spreads of] some new arrangement of rank by which no Officer who did not immediately derive his commission from the King could command one who did.[12] This was too degrading for GW to submit to; accordingly, he resigned his military employment; determining to serve the next campaign as a volunteer; but upon the arrival of General Braddock he was very particularly noticed by that General; taken into his family as an extra-aid; offered a Captain's commission by *brevet* (which was the highest grade he had it in his power to bestow) and had the compliment of several blank ensigncies given him to dispose of to the young gentlemen of his acquaintance to supply the vacancies in the 44 and 48 Regiments which had arrived from Ireland.

In this capacity he commenced his second campaign; and used every proper occasion . . . to impress the General, and the principal Officers around him, with the necessity of [designing] the nature of his [Braddock's] defense to the mode of attack which, more than probably, he would experience from the *Canadian* French, and their Indians on the march through the mountains and covered country, but so prepossessed were they in favor of *regularity* and *discipline* and in such absolute contempt were these people[13] held, that the admonition was suggested in vain.

About the middle of June, this armament consisting of the two Regiments from Ireland, some Independent Companies and the Provincial troops of Virginia Maryland and North Carolina, began to move from Fort Cumberland whither they had assembled.[14] After several days march; and difficulties to which they had never been accustomed in regular service, in campaign countries; and of which they seemed to have had very little idea, the General resolved to divide his force, and at the head of the first division which was composed of the flower of his Army, to advance; and leave Colonel Dunbar with the second division and the heavy baggage and stores, to follow after. By so doing, the first division approached the Monongahela 10 miles short of Fort Duquesne the 8th of July; and which time and place [Washington] having so far recovered from a severe fever and delirium from which he had been rescued by James's powder, administered by the positive order of the General as to travel in a covered wagon, he joined him and the next day though much reduced and very weak mounted his horse on cushions, and attended as one of his aides.

About 10 o'clock on the 9th, after the van had crossed the Monongahela the second time, to avoid an ugly defile (the season being very dry and waters low) and the rear yet in the River the front was attacked and by the unusual hallooing and whooping of the enemy,[15] whom they could not see, were so disconcerted and confused as soon to fall into irretrievable disorder. The rear was forced forward to support them, but seeing no enemy, and themselves falling every moment from the fire, a general panic took place among the troops from which no exertions of the Officers could recover them. In the early part of the action some of the Irregulars (as they were called) without directions, advanced to the right, in loose order, to attack; but this, unhappily from the unusual appearance of the movement being mistaken for cowardice and a running away was discountenanced, and before it was too late, and the confusion became general an offer was made by GW to head the Provincials and engage the enemy in their own way; but the propriety of it was not seen into until it was too late for execution. After this, many attempts were made to dislodge the enemy from an eminence on the right but they all proved ineffectual, and fatal to the Officers, who by great exertions and good examples endeavored to accomplish it. In one of these the General received the wound of which he died; but previous to it, had several horses killed and disabled under him. . . . [Washington] also had one horse killed, and two wounded under him, a ball through his hat, and several through his clothes, but escaped unhurt. Sir Peter Halket (second in command) being early killed, Lt. Colonel Burton and Sir Jno. St. Clair (who had the rank of Lt. Colonel in the Army) being badly wounded, Lt. Colonel Gage (afterwards General Gage)[16] having received a contusion.

No person knowing in the disordered state things were, who the surviving Senior Officer was, and the troops by degrees going off in confusion, without a ray of hope left of further opposition from those that remained, GW placed the General in a small covered cart, which carried some of his most essential equipage, and in the best order he could, with the best troops (who only continued to be fired at) brought him over the first ford of the Monongahela;

where they were formed in the best order circumstances would admit on a piece of rising ground; after which, by the General's order, he rode forward to halt those which had been earlier in the retreat: Accordingly, after crossing the Monongahela the second time and ascending the heights, he found Lt. Colonel Gage engaged in this business to whom he delivered the General's order. . . . The shocking scenes which presented themselves in this night's march are not to be described. The dead, the dying, the groans, lamentation, and cries along the road of the wounded for help (for those under the latter descriptions endeavored from the first commencement of the action, or rather confusion, to escape to the 2nd division) were enough to pierce a heart of adamant. The gloom and horror of which was not a little increased by the impervious darkness occasioned by the close shade of thick woods which in places rendered it impossible for the two guides which attended to know when they were in, or out of the track but by groping on the ground with their hands.

Happy was it for him, and the remains of the first division, that they left such a quantity of valuable and enticing baggage on the field as to occasion a scramble and contention in the seizure and distribution of it among the enemy, for had a pursuit taken place, by passing the defile which we had avoided, and they had got into our rear, the whole, except a few woodsmen, would have fallen victims to the merciless savages. Of about 12 or 13 hundred which were in this action eight or 9 hundred were either killed or wounded; among whom a large proportion of brave and valuable Officers were included.[17] The folly and consequence of opposing compact bodies to the sparse manner of Indian fighting, in woods, which had in a manner been predicted, was not so clearly verified that from hence forward another mode obtained in all future operations.

As soon as the two divisions united, the whole retreated towards Fort Cumberland; and at an encampment near the Great Meadows the brave, but unfortunate General Braddock breathed his last. He was interred with the honors of war, and as it was left to GW to see this performed, and to mark out the spot for the reception of his remains, to guard against a savage triumph, if the place should be discovered, they were deposited in the road over which the Army, wagons etc. passed to hide every trace by which the entombment could be discovered. Thus died a man, whose good and bad qualities were intimately blended. He was brave even to a fault and in regular service would have done honor to his profession.

From George Washington, "Biographical Memoranda," in *The Writings of George Washington from the Original Manuscript Sources, 1745–1799*, ed. John C. Fitzpatrick (Washington, DC, 1939), 29: 36–45.

Discussion Questions

1. How did Washington explain his defeat at the hands of the French and Indians in 1754?

2. Braddock's 1755 defeat was the most thorough trouncing of the British army in the mid-eighteenth century. How did Washington explain it?

3. What lessons might Washington have learned in these experiences that he could apply to his command of the American troops in the American Revolution?

4. This is Washington's version of his most embarrassing moments—what can you tell about him from this account?

Notes

1. Washington was able to gather only about 150 men, by promising them land in the Ohio Valley.

2. This road-widening trek included crossing the Allegheny Mountains.

3. A post that the Ohio Company had built that February.

4. On April 17, French troops had forced the Ohio Company representatives to surrender and had built French Ft. Duquesne, named for the governor of New France.

5. James Mackay, an officer from Georgia.

6. Washington's brief description is of a much-disputed incident in which French ensign Joseph Coulon de Villiers de Jumonville was sent out to observe the strength of Washington's party and to offer to talk. Hearing of their approach, Washington set off with a group of his soldiers and the Seneca Indian Tanaghrisson and some of his followers. Apparently not understanding Jumonville's offer, Washington's men fired, killing Jumonville and several others.

7. The Indian allies of the French included Ottawas, Hurons (Wyandots), Potawatomis, Shawnees, Delawares, and some Iroquois.

8. More Virginians had arrived, in addition to MacKay's company of regulars.

9. Tanaghrisson's men, who had been unable to attract more Indians to the British side.

10. The French had approximately six hundred French troops and one hundred Indians.

11. The British suffered over one hundred casualties, while the French and Indian forces had only a handful.

12. As an officer in the Virginia regiment, rather than the regular army, Washington had received his commission from Governor Dinwiddie.

13. The French Canadian troops and their Indian allies.

14. After Washington's retreat, provincial troops from North Carolina and Maryland had built this fort on the Potomac River in western Maryland near the current border with Virginia and Pennsylvania, about halfway between Alexandria and Ft. Duquesne.

15. Fighting against the British were some 250 French and over 600 Indians. Braddock had missed his chance to attract Indian allies when, in negotiations with representatives at Ft. Cumberland, he refused to promise British protection of their land rights in the Ohio Valley.

16. In 1763, Thomas Gage became commander of the British forces in America, a post he held during Pontiac's War and through the first year of the American Revolution. Along with Washington, two other survivors of Braddock's defeat became generals in the American Revolution on the American side: Horatio Gates and Charles Lee.

17. British casualties included the women hired to serve the camp, of whom half were killed and half were taken captive. The French suffered only a few dozen casualties.

Louis-Antoine de Bougainville's Journal of the Seven Years' War, 1756

---

*I*N 1756, DECLARATIONS OF WAR BY BRITAIN AND FRANCE *officially began the Seven Years' War, and twenty-six-year-old Louis-Antoine de Bougainville was appointed aide-de-camp to Louis-Joseph, Marquis de Montcalm, the command-ing general for New France. The previous fall, the British had defeated French forces at the Battle of Lake George (which the French called Lake St. Sacrament) in present-day upstate New York and established their presence at the south end of the lake. In response, the French fortified Ft. Carillon (which the British called Ticonderoga) to the north, recruited Indian allies, and began reconnaissance to see how difficult an attack on the British position would be. The following ac-count comes from the journal that Bougainville kept, which was not published until 1924.*

September 6. With the enemy so well positioned and strong, and so few of us—no boats or barges, no forts on Lake St. Sacrament[1]—I think it will be impos-sible for us to undertake any considerable action against troops three times more numerous than us, solidly entrenched everywhere, and with good forts. We make do with harassing them constantly, and so have recently been taking prisoners from as far away as Boston and have readied ourselves to resist them if they should attack us. Our battle plan is laid out in advance, the orders are given for the movement and dispositions of the various units, and the signals are agreed on; I do believe the enemy could fail if he attacks, and we all want him to come on, but it doesn't look as if he will.

We have about 180 Indians, all of them camped along the portage path and at Monsieur de Contrecoeur's outpost.[2]

September 11. At six in the morning we went out to visit the positions at the falls and the portage[3] and the outposts of Monsieur de St. Martain and Monsieur de Contrecoeur. At Monsieur de Contrecoeur's, the Indians held council. . . . Every bit of land we've covered, taking the road to the right and coming back by the one to the left, is mountains and precipices, ideal for ambushes and slipping away. Back at Ft. Carillon at 2:00.

At 6:00 the Iroquois who had gone out to follow some trails they had discovered brought back two prisoners, a cadet from the Scottish regiment and a militia captain. I questioned the cadet, and he was from the same group as the soldier brought to Ft. St. Jean[4] on the ninth.

About 300 Indians, Iroquois, Saulteaux, Ottawas, &c., came into camp tonight. As usual: big Indian council. . . .

September 12 & 13. Nothing new. A few Indians reconnoitering on the lake. . . .

We have 600 Indians now. We're holding council with them to send a detachment of them out, but getting them to make up their minds is a whole long operation, costing brandy, supplies, food, &c. A constant, bothersome detail.

September 14. Workers and soldiers as usual in the fort. Agreement finally concluded with the Indians that one detachment should go along the bay[5] and another along Lake St. Sacrament, striking at Ft. Lydius,[6] Ft. George, and the road between the two forts. Some Iroquois who had been out scouting for two days came in with 7 deer they had killed and invited their brothers to a party. So much for a departure tonight.

They leave tomorrow. Two picket detachments from the Béarn regiment arrived at Ft. St. Jean.

September 15. Along with Messieurs Desandrouins and Mercier, I've been assigned to the escort of a large detachment of Indians to reconnoiter the English positions on the Lake St. Sacrament islands and get as close as we can to their forts. Orders: return if the Indians disband and the spying becomes too risky.

At six o'clock we reached Monsieur de Contrecoeur's advance post.

The Indians who were going to leave this evening are no longer going to leave. Even the detachment's destination is changed. No more talk of going along the bay. Now they want to go all in one party along Lake St. Sacrament. The detachment, French and Indian all together, adds up to 700 men. If some mission presents itself where we can all act together, we will. If not, the detachment will break up into little platoons to make separate strikes. They say departure time is fixed for tonight, but that's just a "They say," and of all caprices the caprice of Indians is the most capricious.

September 16. Indians finally made up their mind to set out. Left from Monsieur de Contrecoeur's post about 6:00 this evening. 100 Canadians and 400 Indians under the command of Monsieur de la Perrière, Captain of the Colonial Militia.[7] 34 canoes, sheltered behind a point of land, waiting for sunset.

Indians decide when we move, when we halt, where we spy; and in this kind of warfare, we have to go along with them.[8]

Set out above Barque Island on the north shore.[9] Spent the night bivouacking by the boats. A canoe was sent out reconnoitering. The canoe caught sight of an English boat crossing the channel that runs through the islands. Full moon. Our canoe darted under the shade of some trees and observed the movements of the enemy canoe, which almost immediately started back in the other direction without observing us. As soon as our canoe came back to where we were camped, another went out, and it returned at daybreak.

September 17. At daybreak the nations' war chiefs held a council, and when they broke up, twenty-five Indians were sent out with three Frenchmen. Their orders were to separate into two parties after a certain distance, one going along the shore, the other through the mountains. The Indians can see a long way for spying out the islands where the enemy is said to be entrenched.

[The scouts find little to report.]

After they came back, a herald walked along the beach summoning the nations' chiefs to a council. All went to the campground of the Iroquois, who, being the most numerous in this detachment, took charge without even asking advice from the French commander.

Their bodies covered with blankets and their spears in their hands, the chiefs advanced gravely, took their seats, and smoked the council pipe. The orator reviewed the detachment's mission and repeated the reports of the scouts. They deliberated at great length over what the orator said, always in the presence of a French interpreter.

The result is that two canoes of scouts are being dispatched to search the islands. They leave at nightfall and will camp two leagues up-lake on the south shore.

This they have now done.

Anyway, the Indians act imperially toward us. They make laws for us that they don't follow. People are suspecting the Iroquois of double dealings.[10]

September 18. Nothing new from the night expedition. All they found was some old tracks and some fires still going. Halted around two in the morning about 4 leagues from Ft. George. Most of the men spent the night in the canoes.

At dawn the scouts went out as usual and a council took place and it was decided we would stay here another day. The orders were repeated: no fires; no noise. The Indians make both.

At 10:00 I went with Messieurs Mercier and Desandrouins and an escort to the top of a mountain near our camp. From there we could see to the end of Lake St. Sacrament and the placement of Ft. George. From what we saw, it could be almost impossible for the enemy to keep us from crossing among the islands scattered throughout the lake, even if they set up little forts. But the fort and the outer defenses were too far off for us to be certain.

The Iroquois seem to want to spend another night here and consequently all day tomorrow. Discontent and grumbling from the other nations. Discord in the camp now. Scouts came back and reported they saw a canoe putting in at a point of land on the north shore, where they had seen tents or huts.

Decision to send two canoes out at nightfall to reconnoiter the point. They returned at eleven in the evening and confirmed the first report. We set out at once and crossed the lake in absolute silence. Halted behind one point of land a league and a half down-lake from the point where we believed the enemy was camped.

September 19. An hour before daybreak we set out across the woods to attack, leaving people in the canoes to paddle out onto the lake and move in to meet us at first sound of shots. We moved through the woods in several files, the Indians almost naked and painted black and red. We overran the point, but all we found were some old fires burned down low among the roots and some abandoned huts.

We returned right away, suspecting that the Iroquois had tricked us, especially since, if they had wanted to cut off the enemy's retreat—if there was one—we should have landed up-lake rather than down-lake from the enemy.

More grumbling among the other nations, and the Iroquois have been relieved of their command. By common consent, 110 Indians have been chosen, the fleetest of foot in the detachment, to leave with thirty of the most able-bodied Canadians, head straight for the fort, and not come back without striking.

The canoes have been dragged into the woods and the rest of the detachment is to guard them. It is agreed that if the warriors are not back in two days, they would have decided, being hotly pursued, to return to Ft. Carillon by way of the mountains, and so the canoes would be able to return, too. They leave at 11:00.

2:00. About a league and a half from Ft. George, they chanced upon a detachment of 53 English. They attacked them immediately and captured and killed all the English except for one who must have gone back with the news. The Iroquois suffered two deaths and two wounded. The Indians did things on the battlefield that were so cruel that even talking about them is horrible.

At noon Messieurs Mercier, Desandrouins, and I left in a canoe. We arrived at Ft. Carillon at 7:00 in the evening. Lake St. Sacrament runs almost straight northeast-southwest. With chains of mountains enclosing either side, there's hardly a wave or a ripple. Navigation is good, with clear beaches for coming in to shore. The mountain chain on the south runs almost to the end of the lake. On the north side it stops about three leagues from the fort. From there on the land is flat and the woods clear. The English have opened up a good path through them that continues beyond the mountains.

September 20. The Indians came back by lake to Monsieur de Contrecoeur's post, with constant firing of rifles. Just above the post, some of them held back and burst into loud lamentations. A canoe ahead of them turned and asked what was wrong.

"Marin is dead!" they cried—because if they lose any men, it's as if their chief were dead.[11] A few words of consolation, and they continued their death laments, shooting off rifles, and came to shore.

At 7:00 Monsieur de Montcalm reviewed the troops at Monsieur de la Corne's post[12] and Monsieur de Contrecoeur's post. The Indians had 17 prisoners. They had already clubbed some to death. A detachment of one lieutenant and 30 men was ordered to bury the two dead men. The cruelty and insolence of these savages appall and darken the soul. It's an abominable kind of warfare. The reprisals are frightful, and the air a person breathes infects him with the habit of not caring.

[The British forces built Ft. William Henry at the south end of Lake St. Sacrament, and Montcalm seized it the following August. After France eventually lost the war, Bougainville became the first Frenchman to circle the globe, the namesake of the tropical plant bougainvillea, and a rear admiral in the French navy who again fought the British in the Revolution.]

Translated by John DuVal from Louis-Antoine de Bougainville, *Écrits sur le Canada: Mémoires, journal, lettres* (Québec, 2003), 132–37.

Discussion Questions

1. What were French goals here on the border with the British colonies?
2. What do you think Indians' goals were?

3. What did Bougainville think of France's Indian allies? If he had a copy of the Great Law of the Iroquois League, might it have influenced his attitude toward the frequent councils he witnessed, usually dominated by Iroquois?

4. How might the Iroquois have answered Bougainville's accusation that their battlefield actions were cruel and abominable?

Notes

1. The French named this lake in honor of the Catholic sacrament of the Holy Eucharist. The British victory in the Seven Years' War determined that the Protestant English name—Lake George, for King George II—would stick.

2. The outpost of Capt. Claude-Pierre Pécaudy, Seigneur de Contrecoeur, was the regiment's advanced post, where the Indians were. The French Indian allies included Abenakis (of whom you can read in Johnson's account), Ottawas, Shawnees, Delawares, Hurons, Saulteaux, and some Iroquois.

3. The portage was on Lake St. Sacrament, and the falls were on Lake Champlain, north of Lake St. Sacrament. Indians carried their canoes between the two.

4. Ft. St. Jean was on the Richelieu River, north of Lake Champlain.

5. The south bay of Lake Champlain.

6. Ft. Lydius was founded by Dutch trader John Henry Lydius in the 1730s on the Hudson River, south of Lake George. Its location was the southern end of what Indians in the region called the "Great Carrying Place," where they carried canoes from the Hudson to Lake George and Lake Champlain. The French destroyed the fort in the 1740s, and the British rebuilt it as Ft. Lyman (and subsequently Ft. Edward), but the French and Indians still called it Ft. Lydius.

7. Bougainville was one of only three representatives of Montcalm's French army assigned to accompany this crucial detachment of colonial French troops and Indians of various nations.

8. You can see from the Indians' large numbers and role in directing the war why British colonists called it the "French and Indian War."

9. An island in Lake George.

10. There were Iroquois on the British side, and many Iroquois hoped to stay out of the war entirely.

11. Paul Marin was the French colonial officer with the Indians. He was not dead, but, as Bougainville notes, the other deaths made them sorrowful as if one of their leaders had died. According to Bougainville, Indians who had worked with Marin held him in high regard.

12. At the upper end of Lake George.

Ohio Indians Talk to the British, 1764

---

*I*N JULY 1763, PONTIAC AND THE OHIO VALLEY INDIAN CONFEDERACY *(including Ottawas, Delawares, Shawnees, Ojibwas, and Senecas) seized ten British forts and commenced sieges at Ft. Detroit, Ft. Niagara, and Ft. Pitt. Needing to hunt to feed their families, they let the British reoccupy the forts that winter, but they had shown their strength. In October 1764, Delaware, Shawnee, and Seneca representatives conducted peace negotiations with British colonel Henry Bouquet. This engraving depicts those negotiations on the Muskingum River (present-day Coshocton, Ohio). The Indians promised to return prisoners, and the British promised to recognize Indian land rights. Here, Seneca chief Kiyashuta is making a speech and holding up a string of wampum.*

Discussion Questions

1. Look at the body language of the Indians and the British in this picture—who do you think is winning Pontiac's War?
2. How has each side dressed to impress the other?
3. What do you think Chief Kiyashuta is saying?
4. British officials agreed to prevent their colonists from settling on most of the lands west of the Appalachians. How do you think the colonists took this news?

Engraving by Charles Grignion after a sketch by Benjamin West, in William Smith, An Historical Account of the Expedition against the Ohio Indians in the Year 1764, under the Command of Henry Bouquet, Esq. *(London, 1766), plate 14. Courtesy the Library Company of Philadelphia.*

Further Reading

Primary Sources

In addition to the works cited at the end of each document, see these books to read the full English versions of excerpted documents or additional related documents.

Adorno, Rolena, and Patrick Charles Pautz, eds. and trans. *Alvar Núñez Cabeza de Vaca: His Account, His Life, and the Expedition of Pánfilo de Narváez.* 3 vols. Lincoln: University of Nebraska Press, 1999.

Barbour, Philip L. *The Complete Works of Captain John Smith (1580–1631).* 3 vols. Chapel Hill: University of North Carolina Press, 1986.

Biggar, H. P., ed. and trans. *The Works of Samuel de Champlain.* Toronto: Champlain Society, 1922–36.

Burns, Louis F. *Osage Indian Customs and Myths.* Tuscaloosa: University of Alabama Press, 2005.

Calloway, Colin G., ed. *Our Hearts Fell to the Ground: Plains Indian Views of How the West Was Lost.* Boston: Bedford Books, 1996.

Cook, Ramsey, ed. *The Voyages of Jacques Cartier.* Toronto: University of Toronto Press, 1993.

Dunn, Richard S., and Mary Maples Dunn, eds. *The Papers of William Penn.* Philadelphia: University of Pennsylvania Press, 1981–87.

Dunn, Richard S., James Savage, and Laetitia Yeandle, eds. *The Journal of John Winthrop, 1630–1649.* Cambridge, MA: Harvard University Press, 1996.

Foster, William C., ed., and Johanna S. Warren, trans. *The La Salle Expedition to Texas: The Journal of Henri Joutel, 1684–1687.* Austin: Texas State Historical Association, 1998.

Gathorne-Hardy, Geoffrey M., ed. and trans. *The Norse Discoverers of America: The Wineland Sagas.* Oxford, UK: Clarendon Press, 1921.

Hamilton, Edward P., ed. and trans. *Adventure in the Wilderness: The American Journals of Louis Antoine de Bougainville, 1756–1760.* Norman: University of Oklahoma Press, 1964.

Lemay, J. A. Leo, and P. M. Zall, eds. *Benjamin Franklin's Autobiography.* New York: Norton, 1986.

Marshall, Joyce, ed. and trans. *Word from New France: The Selected Letters of Marie de L'Incarnation.* Toronto: Oxford University Press, 1967.

Mason, Julian D., Jr., ed. *The Poems of Phillis Wheatley.* Chapel Hill: University of North Carolina Press, 1989.

McElrath, Joseph R., Jr., and Allan R. Robb, eds. *The Complete Works of Anne Bradstreet.* Boston: Twayne, 1981.

Mora, Carmen de, ed., *Las Siete ciudades de Cíbola: textos y testimonios sobre la expedición de Vázquez Coronado.* Sevilla, Spain: Alfar, 1992.

Pascarella, Cesare. *The Discovery of America.* Trans. John DuVal. Fayetteville: University of Arkansas Press, 1991.

Pinckney, Elise, ed. *The Letterbook of Eliza Lucas Pinckney, 1739–1762.* Chapel Hill: University of North Carolina Press, 1972.

Secondary Sources

See these for more information on the events covered by the documents.

Anderson, Fred. *Crucible of War: The Seven Years' War and the Fate of Empire in British North America, 1754–1766.* New York: Alfred A. Knopf, 2000.

Axtell, James. *After Columbus: Essays in the Ethnohistory of Colonial North America.* New York: Oxford University Press, 1988.

Bailyn, Bernard. *Atlantic History: Concept and Contours.* Cambridge, MA: Harvard University Press, 2005.

Barr, Juliana. *Peace Came in the Form of a Woman: Indians and Spaniards in the Texas Borderlands.* Chapel Hill: University of North Carolina Press, 2007.

Berlin, Ira. *Many Thousands Gone: The First Two Centuries of Slavery in North America.* Cambridge, MA: Belknap Press, 1998.

Brooks, James F. *Captives and Cousins: Slavery, Kinship, and Community in the Southwest Borderlands.* Chapel Hill: University of North Carolina Press, 2002.

Calloway, Colin G. *One Vast Winter Count: The Native American West before Lewis and Clark.* Lincoln: University of Nebraska Press, 2003.

Carretta, Vincent. *Equiano, the African: Biography of a Self-Made Man.* Athens: University of Georgia Press, 2005.

Dowd, Gregory Evans. *War under Heaven: Pontiac, the Indian Nations, and the British Empire.* Baltimore: The Johns Hopkins University Press, 2002.

DuVal, Kathleen. *The Native Ground: Indians and Colonists in the Heart of the Continent.* Philadelphia: University of Pennsylvania Press, 2006.

Fenn, Elizabeth. *Pox Americana: The Great Smallpox Epidemic of 1775–82.* New York: Hill and Wang Publishers, 2001.

Foote, Thelma. *Black and White Manhattan: The History of Racial Formation in Colonial New York City.* New York: Oxford University Press, 2004.

Gleach, Frederic. *Powhatan's World and Colonial Virginia: A Conflict of Cultures.* Lincoln: University of Nebraska Press, 1997.

Gray, Edward G. *New World Babel: Languages and Nations in Early America.* Princeton, NJ: Princeton University Press, 1999.

Greer, Allan. *Mohawk Saint: Catherine Tekakwitha and the Jesuits.* New York: Oxford University Press, 2005.

Gutiérrez, Ramón A., and Richard J. Orsi, eds. *Contested Eden: California before the Gold Rush.* Berkeley: University of California Press, 1988.

Hackel, Steven W. *Children of Coyote, Missionaries of St. Francis: Indian-Spanish Relations in Colonial California, 1769–1850.* Chapel Hill: University of North Carolina Press, 2005.

Hanke, Lewis. *The Spanish Struggle for Justice in the Conquest of America.* Dallas: Southern Methodist University Press, 2002.

Hatfield, April Lee. *Atlantic Virginia: Intercolonial Relations in the Seventeenth Century.* Philadelphia: University of Pennsylvania Press, 2004.

Higginbotham, Don. *George Washington and the American Military Tradition.* Athens: University of Georgia Press, 1985.

John, Elizabeth A. H. *Storms Brewed in Other Men's Worlds: The Confrontation of Indians, Spanish, and French in the Southwest, 1540–1795.* College Station: Texas A&M University Press, 1975.

Knaut, Andrew L. *The Pueblo Revolt of 1680: Conquest and Resistance in Seventeenth-Century New Mexico.* Norman: University of Oklahoma Press, 1995.

Landers, Jane. *Black Society in Spanish Florida.* Urbana: University of Illinois Press, 1999.

Longmore, Paul. *The Invention of George Washington.* Berkeley: University of California Press, 1988.

Lovejoy, Paul E. "Autobiography and Memory: Gustavus Vassa, Alias Olaudah Equiano, the African." *Slavery and Abolition* 27 Issue 3 (2006): 317–47.

Merwick, Donna. *The Shame and the Sorrow: Dutch-Amerindian Encounters in New Netherland.* Philadelphia: University of Pennsylvania Press, 2006.

O'Brien, Jean M. *Dispossession by Degrees: Indian Land and Identity in Natick, Massachusetts, 1650–1790.* New York: Cambridge University Press, 1997.

Pfleger, Birte. *Ethnicity Matters: The History of the German Society of Pennsylvania since 1764.* Washington, DC: German Historical Institute, 2007.

Richter, Daniel K. *Facing East from Indian Country.* Cambridge, MA: Harvard University Press, 2001.

———. *The Ordeal of the Longhouse: The Peoples of the Iroquois League in the Era of European Colonization.* Chapel Hill: University of North Carolina Press, 1992.

Sandos, James A. *Converting California: Indians and Franciscans in the Missions.* New Haven, CT: Yale University Press, 2004.

Schwartz, Stuart B. *Implicit Understandings: Observing, Reporting, and Reflecting on the Encounters between Europeans and Other Peoples in the Early Modern Era.* New York: Cambridge University Press, 1994.

Seed, Patricia. *Ceremonies of Possession in Europe's Conquest of the New World, 1492–1640.* New York: Cambridge University Press, 1995.

Sensbach, Jon F. *Rebecca's Revival: Creating Black Christianity in the Atlantic World.* Cambridge, MA: Harvard University Press, 2005.

Shoemaker, Nancy. *Strange Likeness: Becoming Red and White in Eighteenth-Century North America.* New York: Oxford University Press, 2004.

Sleeper-Smith, Susan. *Indian Women and French Men: Rethinking Cultural Encounter in the Western Great Lakes.* Amherst: University of Massachusetts Press, 2001.

Taylor, Alan. *American Colonies.* New York: Viking Penguin, 2001.

Thomas, David Hurst. *Columbian Consequences.* 3 vols. Washington, DC: Smithsonian Institution Press, 1989–91.

Thomas, Nicholas. *Cook: The Extraordinary Voyages of Captain James Cook.* New York: Walker and Company, 2003.

Weber, David J. *The Spanish Frontier in North America.* New Haven, CT: Yale University Press, 1992.

Weddle, Robert S. *The Wreck of the Belle, the Ruin of La Salle.* College Station: Texas A&M University Press, 2001.

Wheeler, Mary Elizabeth. "The Origins and Formation of the Russian-American Company." PhD diss., University of North Carolina at Chapel Hill, 1965.

White, Richard. *The Middle Ground: Indians, Empires, and Republics in the Great Lakes Region, 1650–1815.* New York: Cambridge University Press, 1991.

Wood, Peter H. *Black Majority: Negroes in Colonial South Carolina from 1670 through the Stono Rebellion.* New York: Alfred A. Knopf, 1974.

Wood, Peter H., Gregory A. Waselkov, and M. Thomas Hatley, eds. *Powhatan's Mantle: Indians in the Colonial Southeast.* 2nd ed. Lincoln: University of Nebraska Press, 2006.

Index

About the Editors

Kathleen DuVal is assistant professor of history at the University of North Carolina, Chapel Hill. She is the author of *The Native Ground: Indians and Colonists in the Heart of the Continent* (2006).

John DuVal is professor of English and Literary Translation at the University of Arkansas. His books of translations include *Cuckolds, Clerics, and Country-men* (*Choice* "Best Academic Book of 1982"), *Tales of Trilussa* (Raissiz/de Palchi Award from the Academy of American Poets), Cesare Pascarella's *The Discovery of America* (Harold Morton Landon Award from the Academy of American Poets), *Fabliaux Fair and Foul*, and *From Adam to Adam: Seven Old French Plays* (NEA Award and D.C. Commission on Arts and Humanities Grant).